Jim Crace

⊙ Contemporary British Novelists

Series editor Daniel Lea

already published

J.G. Ballard Andrzej Gasiorek
Pat Barker John Brannigan
Graham Swift Daniel Lea
Irvine Welsh Aaron Kelly
Jeanette Winterson Susana Onega

Jim Crace

Philip Tew

Manchester University Press

Copyright © Philip Tew 2006

The right of Philip Tew to be identified as the author of this work has been asserted by him in accordance with the Copyright, Designs and Patents Act 1988.

Published by Manchester University Press
Altrincham Street, Manchester M1 7JA, UK
www.manchesteruniversitypress.co.uk

British Library Cataloguing-in-Publication Data is available

Library of Congress Cataloging-in-Publication Data is available

ISBN 978 0 7190 6913 0 paperback

First published by Manchester University Press 2006

This edition first published 2016

The publisher has no responsibility for the persistence or accuracy of URLs for any external or third-party internet websites referred to in this book, and does not guarantee that any content on such websites is, or will remain, accurate or appropriate.

Printed by Lightning Source

Contents

	Series editor's foreword	*page* vii
	Acknowledgements	ix
	Prologue	xi
1	Exploring Craceland	1
2	Communities and change: *Continent* (1986) and *The Gift of Stones* (1988)	35
3	Parables of distress: *Arcadia* (1992) and *Signals of Distress* (1994)	75
4	Death, belief and nature: *Quarantine* (1997) and *Being Dead* (1999)	115
5	Excess, passion and the uncanny: *The Devil's Larder* (2001) and *Six [Genesis]* (2003)	155
	Addendum: *The Pesthouse* (2007)	193
	Bibliography	205
	Index	216

Series editor's foreword

Contemporary British Novelists offers readers critical introductions to some of the most exciting and challenging writing of recent years. Through detailed analysis of their work, volumes in the series present lucid interpretations of authors who have sought to capture the sensibilities of the late twentieth and twenty-first centuries. Informed, but not dominated, by critical theory, *Contemporary British Novelists* explores the influence of diverse traditions, histories and cultures on prose fiction, and situates key figures within their relevant social, political, artistic and historical contexts.

The title of the series is deliberately provocative, recognising each of the three defining elements as contentious identifications of a cultural framework that must be continuously remade and renamed. The contemporary British novel defies easy categorisation and rather than offering bland guarantees as to the current trajectories of literary production, volumes in this series contest the very terms that are employed to unify them. How does one conceptualise, isolate and define the mutability of the contemporary? What legitimacy can be claimed for a singular Britishness given the multivocality implicit in the redefinition of national identities? Can the novel form adequately represent reading communities increasingly dependent upon digitalised communication? These polemical considerations are the theoretical backbone of the series, and attest to the difficulties of formulating a coherent analytical approach to the discontinuities and incoherencies of the present.

Contemporary British Novelists does not seek to appropriate its subjects for prescriptive formal or generic categories; rather it aims to explore the ways in which aesthetics are reproduced, refined and repositioned through recent prose writing. If the overarching architecture of the contemporary always eludes description, then the grandest ambition of this series must be to plot at least some of its dimensions.

Daniel Lea

Acknowledgements

Jonathan Coe suggested my methodology, offering a 'eureka' moment. I thank him for his friendship and general support. I am indebted to Jim Crace for allowing generous access to both his archive and himself. Our series of MP3 interviews recorded over the telephone helped shape both my thoughts and my critique and supplied vital quotations. Transcribed from the interviews, they were edited further by Jim Crace, and these amended versions are included in this book.

For listening to my ruminations, and for their concrete suggestions, I am grateful to Nicola Allen, Gavin Budge, George Tew, Zsuzsanna Varga, and particularly Steve Barfield for inspired suggestions, specifically the notions of repetition and the uncanny, which were so crucial in allowing me to shape and develop my fifth chapter.

I commend the staff of the Humanities Two reading room at the British Library for their quiet efficiency. UCE provided a semester's sabbatical in 2004 for the initial research, early interviews with Crace, and draft versions of the first three chapters. I discussed ideas and delivered sections as short papers at variously my MA classes at the University of Szeged and UCE in 2001–2004, at the staff–postgraduate seminar series at the University of Northampton in spring 2005, and at the 'Near and Dear' conference at the University of Hull in May 2005 organized by Dr Katharine Cockin. I must acknowledge Amanda Martin of the Isles of Scilly Museum for her prompt despatch of Luke Over's pamphlet on the kelp industry used in preparing Chapter 3. Finally, thanks once again to my parents.

Professor Philip Tew, Humanities Two, British Library

Prologue

This study of Jim Crace's fiction represents a change of direction, not in terms of subject matter, as all my work is very much concerned with the novel, but regarding its theoretical emphasis. My previous critical work has been regarded as heavily theoretical. Certainly it has been informed by a conscious attempt to engage in a meta-realist understanding of literary texts, critiquing the poststructuralist-postmodern axis that has until recently so dominated literary studies in the Anglo-American world. Fortunately that tide has turned, and consequently my critical predispositions can remain largely implicit, where possible, especially given that my ambition is to facilitate reading of Crace. However, I do not imagine I can claim any mythical 'neutrality' or 'disinterestedness.' No such states exist, because all interpretation is an intervention. Like every critic, I am engaged in the 'takings of positions,' to paraphrase Pierre Bourdieu. One must admit that such critical discrimination is unavoidable. Consequently, certain of my readers may well disagree with both my assumptions and conclusions, but hopefully the following exposition of Crace's texts will prove sufficiently informative.

My methodological readjustment also responds to the recent public pronouncement of certain academics avowing a notion of honouring the text, which position-taking initially suggested to me a covert intention of dismantling theory as an explicit exegetical tool, and thereby encouraging a return to naturalizing a liberal-humanist avowal of an Arnoldian–Leavisite axis of aesthetic judgment. While I could never accede to such a manoeuvre, I was inspired to rise to this challenge from a critically informed perspective, appropriately enough for the first study of an author about whom there has been limited academic response. This dictates an introductory, accessible and yet critically instructive combination of materials. While pondering the problems peculiar to this synthesis, a strategy was suggested, that of allowing Crace and Crace's work to speak for themselves, reserving my exegesis for demonstrating both wider issues and something of the author's opinion of his creative process.

This recommendation satisfied the aforementioned shifts in the academic zeitgeist, thus offering me a 'eureka moment.' I have tried to use certain selected critical and theoretical works to supplement descriptions of Crace's texts and their major inclinations and themes, including: the narrative neo-Darwinian impulse in humankind; mythic and parabolic understandings and symbols that persist despite modernity; belief and the self; death and love; the problematic dialectic of the individual within communities; urban realities countering bucolic or pastoral myths; and humankind's place within the greater evolutionary scheme of nature. Once I had my method, a framework and methodology emerged since it seemed logical to consider Crace's work chronologically, which itself suggested certain phases and groupings of the texts; this scheme is introduced below. The major published works consist of *Continent* (1986), *The Gift of Stones* (1988), *Arcadia* (1992), *Signals of Distress* (1994), *The Slow Digestions of the Night* (1995),[1] *Quarantine* (1997), *Being Dead* (1999), *The Devil's Larder* (2001),[2] *Six* (2003) and forthcoming *The Pesthouse* (2007).

My first chapter, 'Exploring Craceland,' initially outlines a biographical sketch of Crace and considers its relationship to his fictional world, focusing upon the pastoral impulse which shaped his Arcadian visions and their origin in the area in which he lived until he left school at eighteen. Adam Begley, in his punning reference to Elvis Presley's fantasy domain, coined an influential term in his essay-interview in the *Southwest Review*, 'A Pilgrim in Craceland' (2002). According to Begley's preface, 'Jim Crace: The Art of Fiction,' (2003) "Craceland, [is] *a place both strange and familiar, historically specific and timeless.*" (184) This chapter analyses Craceland's dynamics and characteristics, considering it as a world apart from our own, often but not always found in an additional sixth (inhabited) continent. Much derives from Crace's earlier travels, especially his understanding of Third World communities where the narrative impulse and the propensity for symbolic forms persist strongly, where one senses something beyond the literal. It also considers the development of Crace's writing, from his early attempts, his career as a journalist and finally the emergence of the rhythmic prose that has come to typify

Crace, with its preciseness of observed detail. Also considered are the traditional mythopoeic, storytelling and pastoral traditions that Crace incorporates so as to reinvigorate the novel, and as Eleazar M. Meletinsky explains in *The Poetics of Myth* (2000), "Twentieth-century mythification is unthinkable without humor and irony, which inevitably result when the modern is wedded to the archaic." (303) This combination creates the energy of Crace's comedy and yet sustains his serious themes.

Chapter 2, 'Communities and change,' outlines the sense of historical and personal transition for two communities in *Continent* and *The Gift of Stones*, one a Third World seventh continent and the other a Stone Age village. In both, traditional cultures are challenged. Crace's commentary is embedded in the parabolic and allegorical structures of his fictions, and his worlds are not fantastical ones. *Continent* has a loose form, with varied characters and settings. Modernity consistently threatens local traditions with various interwoven tales featuring the electrification of a small town, the race of an American runner competing with a local rider on a horse, a son whose rational modern education conflicts with the superstitions of his father, the tale of a political prisoner, the recollection of a long-forgotten scientific expedition into an unexplored forest, the work of an aged calligrapher, and the madness of a company agent in a distant mining camp. Despite the dynamics of modernity, individuals retain a sense of the past and certain mythopoeic possibilities reassert themselves almost uncannily. Invented elements recur, such as the manac beans dropped by the prisoner on his arrest in 'The World with One Eye Shut,' which are sold to prevent erotic desire in *The Devil's Larder*. Crace's storytelling strategies depend on the innate, if partial, failure of more rational and familiar methods of explication.

In *The Gift of Stones* the community is prosaic and familiar, its emphases dehistoricized. The technological transformations threatening this community have clear parallels in late modernity, change demanding a process of adaptation. The bronze brought by a band of marauding horsemen supersedes the flint that has sustained this community. They fear cultural and technological redundancy, one outcome of the immovable logic of trade and the marketplace. By appealing to the imaginative dimension of narrative a disabled storyteller inspires the group first as a quixotic and comic visionary, and then literally in leading them through the environment he has described, beyond to a wider world.

The third chapter, 'Parables of distress,' considers *Arcadia* and *Signals of Distress* and the relationship of the individual to the larger community, in particular the sense of marginality. In both novels, published in the early 1990s, new arrivals and existing inhabitants face uncertainty in periods of great transition. The two settings are contrasting. The first novel is decidedly urban, and as Crace says to Begley in *The Paris Review*, echoing the central impulse of the work of Jane Jacobs discussed in Chapter 3, "I'm addicted to the imperfections of city life." (198) However, key characters are drawn from the countryside. Victor, the protagonist of *Arcadia*, first encounters the city as a baby carried by his mother, a beggar. By the end he is an ancient plutocrat developer, reshaping the market that once nurtured him, but unable to connect with the present or the past, essentially an isolated, rich old man. Crace draws upon the mythic and fairytale to sustain symbolic archetypes.

A sense of arrival is a strong element in both *Arcadia* and *Signals of Distress*, and in the latter a mix of outsiders is drawn to a small fishing town by fate. Its narrative works towards a series of departures that have unexpected consequences. In both novels certain individuals seem periodically at odds with both the landscape and the trajectory of history. All of them explore the rituals of everyday existence, especially those of trade and desire, in a series of crises of identity and social conflicts. In the imaginary settings, the first unnamed and the second a rendition of an obscure backwater in the early nineteenth century, Crace creates what might be termed an 'imaginary realism,' distinguished by a feel for social nuances and the detail of objective reality woven into a decontextualized environment where archetypes and archetypical events can be readily identified, with an emphasis on the symbolic synthesized with emotional verisimilitude. The internal coherence of the environments militates against the fabulist or magic realist dimensions, which are subtexts. *Arcadia* rather than reinventing the bucolic retrieves its persistent and recurrent ambivalence, the sense of fractured idyll that means even within the classical pastoral, as Renato Poggioli explains in *The Oaten Flute: Essays on Pastoral Poetry and the Pastoral Ideal* (1975), "the few men who earnestly heeded the pastoral call found in no time that country life is at best purgatory, and that real shepherds are even less innocent and happy than citydwellers and courtiers," (2) which explains Crace's creation of Joseph to offset Victor's pastoral fantasies.

Prologue

Chapter 4 considers two books published at the end of the 1990s, *Quarantine* and *Being Dead*, which together represent perhaps Crace's most lauded fiction. Each seems very different from the other, but both correlate human responses, emotional and physical, to hostile environments at the edge of civilization, away from the rhythm of people's habitual lives. Both are concerned with transformation. The first is set in the Judean desert at the time of Christ and describes five unconnected travellers who arrive in the desert for a ritual fasting. One is Crace's version of Jesus, a young boy from Galilee hesitantly seeking to test himself and his spiritual endurance and seeking a connection with God.

Being Dead is concerned with events surrounding the murder and decomposition of a middle-aged couple, with a retrospective account of their meeting, marriage and the events of the fateful day that will lead to them being bludgeoned to death on a cliff-top, their decomposition explored as part of a quasi-Darwinian metaphysical theme. Crace uses overlapping themes and episodes arranged in a complex structure which allows the intersection of different time sequences and the integration of his overarching themes. The novel opens with their bodies, and immediately diverges from this fact, most notably in a strand of the narrative that reverses the couple's activities on their last day so that the events occur as if spiralling away from the trauma of their murder. Further intercalated strands simultaneously focus on the natural world and its decomposition of their bodies, a series of memories of their first youthful meeting as students, and the search for them by their daughter, Syl.

Begley in 'Jim Crace: The Art of Fiction,' says of the two novels, they "can be read as a matched pair ... In both, he [Crace] zigzags between the secular and the sacred." (184) More particularly, both novels present a recurrent pattern into which other recognizably Cracean elements are interwoven; the landscape itself and its place in nature subsumes and dwarfs various individuals who are faced with the issues of human belief, human identity and the universal presence of death in life and its metaphysical meaning, or lack of it. Death is immanent in life. In both texts a sense of the mundanity of the quotidian intersects with descriptions that evoke the symbolic power of nature.

The fifth chapter, 'Excess, passion and the uncanny,' considers the two books that were published at the beginning of the new millennium. Crace particularizes issues of love, family and other intimate or domestic interpersonal relations in *The Devil's Larder*, and *Six* (2003), or *Genesis* as it was entitled in North America. Of *The Devil's Larder*, some of whose stories had appeared previously in *Slow Digestions of the Night*, Crace admits the project was long planned, and represents "an attempt at a piecemeal, patchwork novel," something inspired by Italo Calvino's *Invisible Cities* and Primo Levy's *The Periodic Table*.³ In Crace the short pieces at times feel like narrative equivalents of philosophic aphorisms, particularly with their broadly common gastronomic themes and the implicit architectonic of an overriding cumulative intention. Generally, the recurrent contexts and themes are overt and therefore easy to identify, they include: relationships, sexuality and desire; families and their patterns of behaviour and t raditions; sociability, jollity and its absence; and forms of poisoning or allergies. The protagonist of *Six* is a famous stage actor, Felix Dern, or Lix, and his performativity in life is one of the themes of the novel. The other is his serial procreative successes, despite his failing in relationships and lovemaking. The novel both begins and ends with Lix in his middle age, when Mouetta, Lix's second wife, announces an unexpected pregnancy. "Every woman he dares to sleep with bears his child. So now it is Mouetta's turn. Whispering and smudging his ear with her lipstick, her breath a little sour from the garlic in her lunch, she confirms her first, his sixth pregnancy. His sixth at least." (1) The slight concluding provisionality echoes throughout the text.

The novel has seven chapters, the first preliminary one is unnumbered and focuses largely on the conception of Mouetta's child; of the following six numbered chapters, the first five are concerned with the different phases of his life that bring about the conceptions of the first five children. The final chapter returns to Lix's middle age and in almost Woolfian manner depicts a simultaneous moment in the overlapping and yet disconnected lives of all of his children, implying an overarching intersection. The only commonality is genealogical and biological, something larger than the self.

Finally there is a short, critical addendum on Crace's work-in-progress, *The Pesthouse*, which will be published in 2007. I have been privileged to read and discuss with Crace several drafts of his as yet incomplete electronic manuscript. I attempt to explore its major themes, deriving largely from its setting in a post-industrial America where society has regressed to the kind of superstition and ignorance associated with the medieval. Planned some years before its commencement, Crace says in a short note, 'THE PEST HOUSE (working title only) – to be delivered summer 2004 (?):' "The theme is *The Gift of Stones* in reverse. It is not about a prehistoric community adapting itself to progress, but a modern, slightly futuristic community adapting itself to a world without science, political institutions or social coherence."

There are consistent features throughout Crace's work, many of which I will identify subsequently. The notion and significance of storytelling recurs, largely because the figure of the storyteller illuminates and helps explore the curious and persistent interdependence of people even in modernity. Narrative may be manipulated, but it is finally concerned with the coming together of subjects, a fusion of imaginations. As Georges Bataille comments in *The Accursed Share: An Essay on General Economy; Vol. II The History of Eroticism* (1976): "That man who assumes in the eyes of each participant of a community the value of the *others* can do so ... insofar as he signifies the *subjectivity* of the others. That presupposes the communication from *subject* to *subject* of which I speak, in which *objects* are intermediaries, but only if they are, in the operation, reduced to insignificance, *if they are destroyed as objects.*" (243) Crace reinforces a sense that just as each person cannot absent himself from the living stream other than through death, neither can the story nor its narrative eye sever itself from the material detail and its constant perceptual intersection with the world of humanity.

In conclusion, I hope this study engages in what might be described as 'plain criticism.' If there is an emergent critical shift in literary studies it needs close reading techniques (a method that survived in many seminars, tutorials and classrooms) informed by appropriate secondary material, preferable to my mind than the aggressively theoretically deconstructive approach. As readers will see below, each book by Crace is dissected, its features explained as I draw upon Crace's own statements of his intentions and his retrospective interpretations of his *oeuvre*, in very large part drawn from a series of interviews undertaken over a period of eight months, a protracted engagement specifically aimed at supporting and augmenting my critical efforts. Other supplementary critical and theoretical materials are deployed where appropriate and illuminating.

Notes

1 This pamphlet contains stories that were already scheduled to be published in *The Devil's Larder*, which will be considered with the full collection and not separately.
2 *Six* was published under the title of *Genesis* in North America at the suggestion of his publishers, the original alluding to the six children of its protagonist.
3 Telephone conversation between Jim Crace and Prof. Philip Tew, 21 March 2005, part A 14:30–15:10; hereafter referred to as 'Crace–Tew: Telephone Interview 6A.'

For my son
George Alister Tew

1

Exploring Craceland

Jim Crace insists "I don't have any theories of literature." However, his careful attention to structure, rhythm, motifs and the architectonics of the text suggest otherwise.[1] I hope to persuade readers that, at the very least, he does have an acute and conscious sense of narrative. Certainly, he insists fiction is a form of equivocation, claiming "Ambiguity is the soul of fiction; fiction is all about ambiguity."[2] Crace himself appears enigmatic. As Begley writes in 'A Pilgrim in Craceland,' (2002) "Though he claims to be very private, even secretive, Jim Crace doesn't avoid contact with journalists and critics." (227) Sally Vincent writes of interviewing Crace in 'Death and the Optimist,' (2001) "He smiles his pretending, see-how-open-I-am smile and assures me he has the kind of voice that slides off tape recorders. He says I will find nothing about him through biographical details, and that there is a space between what he does and who he is, an inscape, that he has no wish to explore. He is secretive, he says, a mystery to himself." (39) And yet there are certainties to be perceived in Crace. He is most definite concerning his own identity, commenting, "I would say I'm extremely clear about who I am as a person. I'm very dogmatic politically, but when I'm a writer I become something different . . . When you read me it's hard to work out who I am and what I believe."[3] Crace emphasizes this separation of his life and work; Boyd Tonkin comments in 'Jim Crace: Reasons to Be Cheerful,' (2003) "Every profile of Crace labours the contrast between the mesmerising strangeness of his books and the suburban serenity of his life," adding that "The gulf between man and work intrigues, and exercises, Crace." (32) Begley's notion of the impenetrability of the work derives from this public persona created by Crace, one that has assumed a certain critical orthodoxy, one that this chapter will challenge.

Another certainty is that Crace accepts that he dissembles in private and public, constructing an unreliable narrative from the details of both his books and his life. This problematizes the repeated protestation that fictionally there is no autobiographical influence. Despite his equivocations, he is far more definite about the happiness of his childhood, and its familial certainties, a context he returns to repeatedly in numerous interviews and accounts of himself. His sense of a harmonious private self has been supplemented and reinforced subsequently by a happy family life as an adult. He says, "There was no distress in my childhood at all. I had really great parents whom I loved. Anyone who had to write a biography of me would have nothing to say."[4] Without over-determining such personal contexts I intend to illustrate that a number of biographical details influence Crace's texts, beginning with his childhood, upbringing and education, all relatively fixed points even in his accounts of himself. On 1 March 1946 Jim Crace was born at Brocket Hall, a stately home near Welwyn in Hertfordshire, which had been turned into a maternity hospital during the Second World War. Vincent reduplicates a Cracean attempt to use the location as a veil of modesty, "The only interesting thing about him, biographically, is that he was born in von Ribbentrop's bedroom . . . So there you have it. He came into the world where Hitler's foreign minister had laid his head, just down the hall from where Lord Melbourne breathed his last and Maggie Thatcher wrote her memoirs." (39–40) At six-weeks old, Crace's family moved to Forty Hill in Enfield, a borough to the north of London. Its centre is the former market town where John Keats attended John Clarke's radical Enfield Academy from 1803 to 1811, an institution contributing to a dissenting tradition that persisted in the local Co-operative movement and Labour Party, which were central to the life and political commitment of Crace's father, Charley Crace. Vincent reports that he was, "A stalwart, a trade unionist, a socialist, a member of the Labour party, a paragon. An old fashioned atheist, the sort who just doesn't believe in God and who provides an environment for his progeny in which the tenets of religious observation have no cachet." (40) Although Forty Hill was on the edge of a growing conurbation, it retained even in the 1950s and 1960s a certain quasi-pastoral charm, set in what Crace describes in 'Hearts of Oak' (1993) as "The Essex, Middlesex, Hertfordshire borders," (75) where his father planted a thousand oak trees. As Crace has often commented, he recognizes in this area a kind of liminality, a site of various paradoxical juxtapositions including class conflicts, and the proximity of the urban and the pastoral, dominant themes in *Arcadia* and *Being Dead*. The pastoral recurs more than simply as a setting, but as a generic precursor offering archetypes and well-developed themes of spatial dislocation and ambiguity. As Begley says in 'A Pilgrim in Craceland,' "Crace's talent is hard to pin down because he seems to be straddling a divide." (228) This in part derives from his melange of fable, myth and parable set in a multiplicity of landscapes and cityscapes. The allegorical features, common to classical pastoral, extend these environments inferentially to those of the world, as do the details of interactions and immediate environment. 'Talking Skull' is the first story of his first collection, *Continent*, which opens as the narrator, Young Lowdo, addresses his classmates, reminding them of both their privilege and admitting his rural origins:

> You are the sons and daughters of rich men. Who else but rich fathers could spare the money for tuition fees, for examination bribes, for graduation robes? Calculate the value of those family businesses – the import/export companies, the trucks and bus firms, the riverside farming enterprises, the chickens and egg franchises, the Rest House chains, the strings of market booths. Include, also, the lands in town and country, the houses in the New Extension, the investments in foreign banks. (3–4)

The conjectural, suppositional tone and style, the implicit or explicit addressing of an internal and external reader or listener all recur in Crace's later fiction. Lowdo offers his peers and ourselves a world of inheritance, of implied rivalry, and of profit and privilege all derived from the banalities of trade and commerce. The setting is a less-developed seventh continent, a non-existent, imaginary realm, offering Arcadian and nostalgic possibilities. Among the exotic or unfamiliar elements, specificity suggests other universal, realist characteristics rooted in the familiar and the mundane. This represents a paradoxical legacy of classical pastoral. As E. Kegel-Brinkgreve explains in *The Echoing Woods: Bucolic and Pastoral from Theocritus to Wordsworth* (1990), Theocritus' style and form involve a synthesis of realistic elements that appears to have "combined the ways and means of literary realism with various stylizing and un-realistic elements in a subtle and at times disconcerting manner," (10) and hence his style echoes with the liveliness of the iambic but without its actual form. Crace's prose shares both an apparently iambic or rhythmic quality (without iambic metre), and the realism, dislocation, and energy that Kegel-Brinkgreve had identified in the pastoral form typified by Theocritus and Vergil. In *Theocritus' Pastoral Analogies: The Formation of a Genre* (1991) Kathryn J. Gutzwiller, in surveying major critics of the genre, explains how despite its "surface simplicity" (15) pastoral deviates from the epic (10) by shifting its focus upon urban–rural contradictions (13), which may help situate Crace's grandiloquence, the residue of epic vision that subtends pastoral allegory. In accounting for pastoral's underlying dynamics, Gutzwiller crucially cites first Heather Dubrow (13), whose earlier study comments "pastoral has a predilection for binary oppositions so fundamental that if the genre did not exist the structuralists would have invented it," (117) and additionally Gutzwiller cites William Empson, who in his classic study *Some Versions of Pastoral* (1935) identifies "the ways in which the pastoral process of putting the complex into the simple . . . have been used." (23) The first predilection informs Crace's style and the latter the emphasis or mood of his whole *oeuvre*. Gutzwiller adds that "the nature of analogy that underlies pastoral is not just comparison or similitude but proportion, the parallelism of relationships within systems." (13–14) Similarly constituted are the essential co-ordinates of Craceland, a world proportionate to reality, and yet largely a system within itself. As with the archaic pastoral world, Craceland is neither vague nor unrealizable, sharing a comparable relation with reality to Gutzwiller's description of that of traditional Arcadian literature:

> Expression there is almost always concrete, in the sense that it refers to tangible reality. The principal literary subject is myth, in which meaning is inseparable from narrative. Thought takes the form of images that represent both part of the world and the whole of it . . . The interrelationship of these images constitutes a holistic mental structure, the thought system of the archaic mind; it is made manifest in literature by the juxtaposition of objects and activities that have common traits. (23)

Additionally as Andrew V. Ettin makes clear in *Literature and the Pastoral* (1984) a strictly pastoral environment is not essential to the genre even in its earliest manifestation (2) and it remains often allegorical and cryptic (4), all decidedly Cracean characteristics. Doris Teske in 'Jim Crace's *Arcadia*: Public Culture in the Postmodern City' (2002) identifies the Arcadian as avowing a "non-urban alternative way of life," but recognizes that in Crace, "This dream, however, has to be placed in the context of the novel's real subject: the question of what urbanity and urban community are about, and the problem of coming to terms with the political city which is losing its traditional structures and its fixed symbolic language in a post-urban and postmodern revolution." (166) Nevertheless her reading assumes an almost post-historical cultural transition and emphasizes the mythical, escapist and paradisiacal aspects of the traditional concept of Arcadia, both of which exegetical accounts perhaps exaggerate Crace's rupture with pastoral dynamics as outlined above, rather identifying what Teske describes as his "rejection of various aspects of the Arcadian vision." (169) Importantly there remains in Crace a seriousness, what Ian Sansom describes in 'Smorgasbits' (2004) as "Kurt Vonnegut without the jokes: a voice assuming a certain comic wisdom." (13)

Both a complex sense of the pastoral, and that of paradox and ambiguity referred to by Begley, result in part from Crace's direct experience, the social aspects and literal location of his origins and their incongruities. His family's ground-floor flat on the Pilgrim Estate was part of a working-class area, a site of under-privilege within a privileged culture, but positioned almost magically, according to Crace's account, as the last buildings of London. Facing north Crace overlooked fields and woods, adjacent to the grounds of Forty Hall, a Jacobean manor house set in gardens and parkland. He lived close to the remainder of the Tudor monarchy's hunting grounds. It is an unusual conjunction, and affected the clarity of Crace's bioscopic capacity, expressed in the descriptions of both cityscapes and landscapes, as Crace says:

> Existing literature is not the only way to new literature. You cannot be in any doubt that I love landscape. My novels are full of it. Landscape is almost a character in them all. But I don't write about landscape because I read landscape books. If I write about landscape it's because at every opportunity I go out, I walk the coast, or I go up hills, or I go caving or whatever. That's where I obtain my raw materials.[5]

In "The Reluctant Storyteller" (2000) Crace comments to Nicolas Wroe, "That combination of urban politics and country walks has always been with me. The flat where we grew up was on the very edge of north London. Out of the front windows it was houses all the way to Croydon. But out of the back it was fields all the way to Cambridge." (13) Crace repeats this observation to Vincent, adding, "'It's a bit like this,' he says, 'a bit like my life. A bit like my books. The conflict between town and country, nature and civilization, the way we associate the countryside with all that is virtuous and dull, and the city with all that is sinful and exciting.'" (39) This juxtaposition combines the elements of an essentially Arcadian or bucolic view, which are reflected fictionally, particularly in the suggestively titled *Arcadia*. A young mother with a suckling child escapes the poverty of the countryside for an unnamed city's market: "They left the fields behind. They reached metalled roads, and rows of houses with lawns and carriage drives. They came through high woods and found a measured townscape spreading out in greys and reds and browns, with a shimmering mirage of smoke which made it seem as if the hills beyond were chimney products of the city mills and that the sky was spread with liquid slate." (78) When asked about the pastoral tradition, Crace responds, "The urban/rural quandary is always relevant. It's always contemporary. I see myself as a landscape writer. There are interesting landscapes to be explored both in and out of the city, in books and in life."[6] This is evident towards the end of *Arcadia* when Victor stands paying homage to a makeshift shrine to a man killed as a result of a riot on the site of the old Soap Market, the mob protesting against Victor's plans to replace it with a contemporary steel and glass mall:

> The weather worsened. They could hear it growing sullen. The candle flames curtseyed in the damp, cold air which pierced the fabric chapel. Water made its way beneath the cobblestones and crept into a puddle beneath their feet. They might have been upon some Afghan plain, three hundred years ago, pinned in by space and sky and frost. The office blocks and tenements which circled them, though distantly, invisibly, were ancient cliffs, shrinking in the cold and wind and rain. (320)

The rhythmic insistence of Crace's style often prioritizes the strong presence of landscape as a characterized presence, rather than a sense of internal subjectivity. Images serve to mediate between people and the objective world. Crace aesthetically interfuses perception and the objective, most dramatically in *Being Dead*. As Mikel Dufrenne says in *In the Presence of the Sensuous: Essays in Aesthetics* (1987), "Intentionality . . . always expresses the solidarity of the subject and object, but without either of them being subordinated to a superior agency or absorbed into the relation uniting them. The externality of the object is irreducible, even though the object is only an object of the subject." (4) What might be called this noetic tension persists as a generative force in Crace; he perceives such relations concretely, certainly in his life, expressing them experientially and as a matter of psychogeography. The underlying sense of a primeval, natural quality of the environment recurs throughout Crace's fiction, permeating his symbolic sense of the objective world, as with the weather and the rocking stone in *Signals of Distress*. This repeated trope counters the anthropomorphic view of the human world, as do the decaying corpses in *Being Dead*.

In *The Happy Ant-Heap and Other Pieces* (1998) Norman Lewis describes a historical, pastoral sense of his childhood home, capturing something of the location that survived in Crace's childhood and adolescent forty years later. "Forty Hill was . . . on the borders of Enfield Chase, a landscape covered with ancient oaks, many of them hollow, cleared, in the far past, of human habitation by terrible kings, and designated for hunting stags." (1) He comments in *Jackdaw Cake* (1985) upon its "strangely unfinished look." (44)[7] Crace reflects upon the impulse to contribute continually to the survival of this pastoral setting when reflecting upon his father's life and his relationship with him in "Hearts of Oak," recalling his last walk with the dying man:

> One afternoon in early March we walked to his allotment overlooking the grounds of Forty Hall in north London and then into Gough Woods to see what birds were there. He was slow already. His scalp was patchy with alopecia. His abdomen was bloated and tender. His pockets as usual were full of acorns. We heeled them into the ground in hedgerows where elm disease had destroyed the trees. We were oaking the landscape. Dad had always planted acorns, even before elm disease. It was not a mission. He heeled them in without any introspection. The sports club where he had been groundsman had – still has – a stockade of oaks, some more than thirty years old by then, from acorns which dad had dropped or thrown. The Essex, Middlesex, Hertfordshire borders where he had walked for years can thank him for a thousand trees. (74-5)

Crace offsets the suffering by synthesizing the landscape and the man, creating an elegy. Crace's father continues to be a major influence. Crace inherits from him an ecological sense, a shared love for landscape, a passion for tennis, as well as a shared set of deeply held radical political views. He records his father's support during his final illness for the Liverpool grave-diggers striking in the so-called Winter of Discontent. "Dad was not a sentimentalist. He wouldn't want his corpse to cross a picket line." (75) Crace demonstrates a similar lifelong affiliation to radicality and the Labour Party, articulating a committed sense of social justice and equality. He is imbued with a scepticism concerning authority, of a kind that historically characterized these borderlands derived from a local religious dissent and republican agnosticism, and which was so prominent in the education received by Keats.

Crace passed the eleven-plus examination. From 1957 until early 1965, he left behind the working-class children of his home to attend daily Enfield Grammar School, founded in 1558. This selective establishment is situated in Enfield Town, a mile from his home, with extensive playing fields through which loops the New River, offering another almost idyllic, pastoral image.[8] Crace admits feeling dislocated both in his local community and at school, where he was alienated by the better quality clothes and seemingly effortless social graces of the more affluent boys. He feared being bullied by the local children who were hostile to his perceived privilege. This had a tangible effect. Crace is clear about his origins and their part in shaping his life, remembering potential pressures on him while alluding to some of the early literary influences in adolescence:

> I come from an intelligent North London working class background. I was the only boy from the flats who went to the grammar school, and felt a little bit of a fraud there. When I returned home I couldn't say, 'Hey! Guess what? Walt Whitman!' and 'Hey! Jack Kerouac!' People wouldn't have appreciated that. It would be too fancy. I'd have had the shit kicked out of me. So I learnt very early on to hide that part of myself. Instead I became the comedian among those kids who went to the secondary modern. It sounds snobbish, but that's what you had to do. And in a way I was comfortable with that. I would have been less comfortable if I'd come back and said 'I'm into literary fiction, I'm writing poetry and here's my notebook,' which is what some of the boys at the grammar school were doing. So I learnt the trick of keeping my interest in literature separate from public myself, so it's hardly a surprise when I write literature that secretiveness continues.[9]

From this point Crace's life was split as he moved between classes, although he retains well-developed political and class loyalties. Many of his characters like Victor similarly leave the lower classes, often abandoning a pastoral context, but in contrast to Crace such characters reject their humble origins. Like Lowdo some are embarrassed by their roots. In contrast, rising to affluence Victor sentimentalizes his rural origins, but he remains firmly allied to a neo-utilitarian, harsh view of progress.

Begley comments in 'A Pilgrim in Craceland' that Crace feels his first four books are about communities in transition (230), reaffirming a perspective reflected in my previous interview. Earlier Crace agrees key individual characters are defined by transition: the storyteller/father in *The Gift of Stones*, Victor, Rook and Joseph in *Arcadia*, and Aymer Smith, escaped slave Otto, Miggy Bowes, Robert and Katie Norris in *The Signals of Distress*.[10] Often they are out of sympathy with those around them. Consider the father in *The Gift of Stones*, who is central to his daughter's account but initially is a subsidiary voice in the community. He escapes to discover himself. Equally in *Signals of Distress* Aymer Smith faces the hostility of the fishing community and his own family. Such a sense of brooding isolation is familiar to Crace, saying of his schooldays, "I felt rebuffed by my education. The very first day I was told I shouldn't do P.E. I had to have elocution lessons. The cheeky chappie, that I was in those days, was not appreciated."[11] In schooldays, like so many other boys in such a hybrid cultural position, partly inspired by his auto-didactic father who served on the local authority's library committee, Crace absorbed high-brow literary and musical culture. He combined these with his putative political radicalism, and developed a facility for narrative, often comic, deflective and whimsical, thus deflating aggression from his working-class peers. This humorous and laconic world-view disguises a sharp and penetrative interpretative mind, which pervades Crace's work and lurks beneath the surface of many recorded comments. The importance of his father is mirrored fictionally in *The Gift of Stones*, where the unnamed narrator pays homage to her storytelling guardian, whom by implication she emulates since she narrates his life, which homage provides Crace with his narrative voice. The father's right arm, severed because of the need to remove an arrow, later oozes its "brackish pus. The arm was rarely dry or free from pain." (1)[12] This suppuration is biographically suggestive, as it echoes the medical condition of Crace's father, who contracted osteomylitis aged eleven in 1922, effectively ending his education. He suffered muscle wastage in his left arm, thereafter stiff and with periodically weeping wounds left by the boils and lesions. He remained nevertheless an active man, cycling, playing tennis, gardening, walking in the countryside, and generally energetic. Crace recalls, "My dad was very interesting, a bizarre and an odd character, a curmudgeon, and yet interested in a multitude of things. I owe my attitude and my politics to him, my interest in the arts, and my love of wildlife and natural history, whereas I owe more social things to my mum."¹³ In his quest for knowledge and culture, Crace's father took his son to concerts, exhibitions and the theatre. Crace recalls numerous key moments shared with his father: shaking Paul Robeson's hand at the Enfield Co-Operative Hall at a concert held during the singer's exile in East Germany after the McCarthy witch-hunt, attending plays including Arnold Wesker's at Joan Littlewood's theatre workshop in Stratford East, seeing the first Jackson Pollock event in Britain in 1958 at the Whitechapel Gallery, a Picasso exhibition at the Tate Gallery, and Mark Rothko's first exhibition in 1961. These are radical cultural co-ordinates, and they indicate that Crace's vision lay beyond both his origins and the petit bourgeois aspirations of his school. A sense of the outsider, of sharing a different cultural perspective, which recurs in the fiction, permeates much of his own life.

After his brief return to school to sit examinations, Crace began to travel in 1965, and while in the south of France he saw an advertisement in *The Observer* for external University of London degrees offered by the Birmingham College of Commerce. For three years from autumn 1965, Crace studied for a degree in English Literature. He recalls being more interested in running a student newspaper, engaging in political activity and making a short film rather than focusing upon literary studies. His contemporaries included the novelists Gordon Burn and Patrick McGrath, and Abbas, the renowned Iranian-born photographer and founding former president of Magnum Photos who remains a close friend. Crace acknowledges him as a great influence. Crace was editor of the *Birmingham Sun*, a city-wide student newspaper, while Gordon Burn acted as features editor. Also, it was at college that he lived with four others in shared lodgings costing them a total of £5 weekly above a haberdasher's shop in Handsworth Wood, including the step-brother of his future wife, Pam Turton. She was later to train as a teacher in Birmingham, which explains his later return to the city. As a student Crace was very much part of the creative, radicalizing surge of the 1960s with its broad interest on the part of the young in the arts and performance. He recalls:

> We even had a pop performance group, before pop performance groups were thought of. We ran a small club called the Fourth Dimension in a pub near Aston, and performed in a musical and comedy band called the Nose Flutes. We actually travelled a couple of times for performances. So maybe my ability to read in public was fed by the cheap laughter that I got in those days.¹⁴

Crace graduated with honours in 1968, although he now admits he spent most of his time on various extra-curricular interests and projects.

During his early years Crace was a member of the Young Socialists, and campaigned actively for nuclear disarmament and colonial freedom. His radical conscience in part inspired another epiphany. Along with two other roommates, he applied to work for the Voluntary Service Overseas in Africa. Two were sent to the Sudan and the other to Botswana. From 1968 to 1969 Crace worked for Educational Television in Khartoum and Omdurman. Retrospectively Crace recognizes these rites of passage as inspirational:

> The whole business of being in Africa was essential, of living in the Sudan, and in Botswana, of travelling around, especially being that age, and simultaneously discovering drugs and sex and all of that stuff during that time. It did mean that I missed out on the Swinging Sixties, because they were basically '68 and '69, and I was away, but nevertheless I had this massive travel stimulation, which I think really has coloured my whole attitude since then.[15]

Subsequently, he travelled overland to visit his former student housemate, Paul, in Molepolole in Botswana, working briefly at a secondary school. This experience forms the basis of 'Cross-Country,' a story originally set in Africa.[16] Crace then took a trip around the Indian Ocean on a commercial freighter that took passengers, visiting Mauritius, Madagascar and L'Ile de la Réunion. Finally he returned to Africa visiting Tanzania, Kenya and Ethiopia. These experiences influenced the sympathetic and local viewpoints adopted by Crace's narrative voices in *Continent*, portraying a sense of the Third World both as nuanced and complex. Importantly Crace evokes a sense of the pervasive poverty and inequalities, while reflecting the exuberant human spirit exhibited in such areas. He was inspired to several early attempts at creativity, including poetry. In the corrected typescript of one poem, 'Nile Marshes/Green Moon,' appended with the note "The Koit-Juba ferry (The Sudan, May 1969)," there is a vision of the familiarity and strangeness of the landscape encountered by the twenty-three year old Crace, which is suffused with images of the colonial past and an underlying sense of the guilt of slavery and the despoliation of this continent. The poem also alludes structurally to Ginsberg's neo-Whitmanesque vision in 'Howl,' as the poet physically encompasses and surveys the world.

As I turn on my heels at dusk
The arc of my vision
Is a complete circle
Perfect and undisturbed,
As if we were rounding
A tiny green moon
Returning again and again
To the same spot,
Each glimpse indistinguishable
From the next
And each curve of the river
The same curve
Which is the roundness of the globe.
Across the tops of the fraying grass,
Like a Confederate mansion
Rising white and wooden
From [a] the pine [wood]
The Kosti paddle steamer passes
Reminding us of lawns.

Something of this perspective persists in the co-ordinates of Crace's fictional world, for as Sansom comments in 'Smorgasbits,' "Crace has been describing the same landscape since *Continent*: a somewhere familiar, but not quite here. It's an Afro-Euro-Hiberno-Yankee-Asian kind of place. A fusion." (13) In his retrospective view of his African period, Crace undercuts his own presence because of its ideological implications, aware of his relative privilege and the dangers inherent in his use of such experiences as cultural capital. With hindsight he admits to Wroe: "'I had the arrogance only a white Englishman on an overseas aid programme could get away with.'" (13) In the original version of 'Cross-Country', first published in the *New Review* before the revised version that appeared in *Continent*, Crace's protagonist is an Englishman, John Channon (note the initials), who has been in Africa, clearly a self-portrait. At Channon's English school his excitable pupils are unable to exercise because of the rain and he tells them of the 'Special Punishment' of Christopher Mathe digging a hole six foot square during his time in Africa three years previously, later recollecting for himself how his running inspired a race with Israel on horseback. This middle section is the basis of the revised story. At the end of the original, in the afternoon Channon shows his boys "the map of Africa – an old one with the red of Empire zagging its way across and down from Bathurst to Cape Town." (52) Their ignorance of the country's name further fuels his nostalgia and the story concludes, "He wrote the name on the board. 'And that's where I'd rather be, lads. Instead of nursing you lot through the rain.'" (52)

Transformed by such experiences, taken beyond his curiously urban-rural English origins, Crace returned to London in 1970, living in Southfields. After teaching briefly, he contacted the BBC concerning the possibility of writing educational programmes. He was commissioned on the basis of his African stay to write a play about the Arab world, his first paid commission, 'Peter's First Ramadan.' He continued with commissions:

> I spent a great deal of time in Paris because I had a French girlfriend. I was doing mostly stuff for radio programmes that could be recorded in Europe, and it just gradually grew in the way that these things do. Fairly soon I was asked to do more for LBC, the London Broadcasting Company, which was then a news channel, doing reports. In the mid-seventies I started writing my first fiction. The first story called 'Refugees,' set in Botswana, won a short story competition with Socialist Challenge. The judges were John Fowles, Terry Eagleton and Fay Weldon.[17]

At this time staying with friends in Liversedge in Yorkshire, he was reintroduced to another weekend guest, his future his wife, Pam. Thus their relationship began. In August 1974 he would return to Birmingham to live with Pam who was studying to be a teacher.

Crace next moved into Fleet Street, participating in what he perceives very much as journalism's factual register, a contrast to the ambiguity of fiction with its "journalistic clarity."[18] Although occasionally inspired to write fiction, it took time to establish himself. An initial flourish in the mid-1970s proved to be a false start. The story, 'Annie, California Plates,' appeared in the June 1974 edition of the *New Review*, an influential literary journal edited by Ian Hamilton, and later was included as the first story of two from Crace in a Faber and Faber anthology *Introduction 6: Stories by New Writers* (1977). The original version is prefaced, alongside the title, by a photograph of Crace, looking post-hippyish with long hair, Zapata moustache and faded denim shirt. Crace says of its acceptance by Hamilton, "It was really quite a coup to be picked up by them, because it was early days and this represented significant attention from a big, subsidized, high profile magazine which had high quality stuff. The story was published and became famous in a way, because I think its tone of voice was so unusual for that kind of magazine and people were very impressed. I received invitations to write a novel, to meet with publishers and agents. Everybody thought that the story promised a certain kind of novel that they were excited about."[19]

The story pays homage both to the influence of American popular culture and an iconic generation of American writers, such as J. D. Salinger and Jack Kerouac, and opens with a litany of popular songs. The narrator comments archly, "It seems that all the bad places have people *leaving* all the time, writing nostalgic songs sure, but never actually *living* there. They're always Good-bye on-the-road songs." (30) The journey is based on Crace's own travels with a French girlfriend in America. The hippy protagonist conjures a lost freedom with this last attempt to retrieve a sense of the open road "before I got into Health foods and settled down, more or less, with my old lady in Columbus, Ohio." (30) He must return to his partner who has stipulated a deadline of "seven days to get from San Francisco, California, to New York City," (30) reversing the escapism of the westward search for the frontier. A huge old Chevy station-wagon, "a kind of bean-can gold, California plates, and with her name Annie, printed in white on the front fender," (31) rescues him from a threatening backwater: "Roadside Nevada's no place to be with hair and a beard, specially when you're carrying half a K of best Mexican dope like I was." (30) A "black cat," Gerald, has stolen the vehicle, but run out of "gas" money; the hitchhiking hippy's answer is to pick up every hitchhiker for a fee, first Mel, then a guy from Indianapolis, and then two "chicks." Crace's story is very much a product of its time, mixing realism and the argot of the period, and a post-1960s ethos when rebellious youth was maturing, often reluctantly. The hippy has been forced by his "old lady" to stop spinning tales to other women, "especially the sort that the Indianapolis cat was laying down on these chicks." (33) On its appearance in the anthology it was well reviewed by Susan Hill, who comments, "An exciting talent . . . Jim Crace, to judge by 'Annie, California Plates,' a gem of a story about a hitch-hiker trying to get from Nevada to New York. Annie, the heroine, is the car which takes him. Within a few pages, Mr Crace builds up a world beyond the immediate story, several characters and some suspense, as well as conveying the wonderful open freeways, the joy of riding, and the ending is neat and richly comic." (12) Certainly, there is an element beyond the literal in the quasi-personification of the car:

> She was a real hitch-hikers' car. Never ending. She'd go go go, back and forth across the States picking up and dropping every highway rider

with a thumb to wave and some cents for her tank. People'd get out and people'd get in and nobody'd be too sure whose she was or where she'd come from. Some little black cat called Gerald had ripped her off in uptown San Francisco and set her free to see the land. I was thinking all that, *humming* it to tell you the truth, till my last ride picked me up at the side of the road and ran me into New York City. (33)

In such non-realist moments one can see a glimmering of his later perspective. Finally, the car represents eternal transcendence and youth, and by the end first Gerald and then the hippy traveller abandon her to others. Two years later hitchhiking with his old lady he sees Annie. "There were the California plates, and, fainter but still there, those five white letters on the fender. I just kept my thumb out but she didn't stop to give us a ride. She was full of people." (33) Despite Hill's approval, Crace fictional progress was slow. His second story for the *New Review*, 'Helter Skelter, Hang Sorrow, Care'll Kill a Cat,' was published in December 1975. It reappeared in *Cosmopolitan* and was also included in *Introduction 6: Stories by New Writers*. The first person narrator, Joe Revie (a comic reference to arguably the most famous British football manager of the period, ironically deployed since Crace establishes his protagonist as a 'Spurs' supporter),[20] complains of the loss of his wife, June, and baby daughter, Kate, to squash-playing Brian, a quantity surveyor in Tottenham, a very prosaic north London environment similar to Crace's own origins. The couple has argued initially over her cat, Jerome, even though June abandons the animal because of her new lover Brian's antipathy to cats. When she visits Joe, the two reconcile by making love, and that night she telephones offering to return. One senses it is the loss of both independence and youth that make his wife's betrayal harder for Joe to accept, since he sentimentalizes about a very unspecific youthful rebellion, evoking a similar sense of lost youth to the one that pervades 'Annie, California Plates.' Joe reflects unconvincingly, "I used to be wild once, for a year or two. But I've lost the habit. I didn't use to care what people did because, being young and wild, not angry-wild but *natural*, no one could *hurt* me. I was on my own then. None of this bits-and-pieces and anger. But I lost the habit, going after love. I got tame. I can't go back again, God damn her. I'm too old. I'm too house-'old! I can't manage on my own." (46–7) The tone is comic, the feelings somewhat bathetic, and the setting firmly realist. Domesticity is a recurrent motif, the irony being that the cat has become wilder than Joe's domesticated self. Crace extends Joe's account of himself both by this touch of ironic unreliability and by the further irony that as they broker a potential reconciliation, he secretively rids himself of the cat, cycling off to some woods to abandon the creature. "It's not revenge. It's not cruelty. It's just the settling of scores, a closing of wounds." (49) The story is pervaded by his sense of emotional trauma offset by his self-pity. And finally as his wife is about to return, Joe reflects, "Cat's get lost all the time, marriages break up. We can't manage on our own, we domestics, we've been spoilt. Married people, kids, dogs, cats, pigeons, peacocks, ducks. It's all the same. We can't get away from it. Clipped wings." (49)

Paradoxically Crace's *New Review* connection served to further delay his attempts at a novel, specifically by providing him with contacts that allowed him to increase his freelance journalism and earn a more sustainable income than the small advance for his first novel. As Crace explains:

> I had published three stories in the *New Review*, my first taste of literary life, which included hanging out in the Pillars of Hercules pub in Greek Street, a very remunerative experience because first of all Ian Hamilton was always there – basically it served as his office – and one day I complained about having trouble coping financially. He said, "We'll get you a grant." Moments later Melvyn Bragg came in and he had read my stories and evidently liked them. So Bragg nominated me for an Arts Council grant, which I received. On another occasion I was chatting to Jonathan Raban at the bar and I mentioned having always wanted to get into journalism, but I had been rebuffed. He said he knew the woman who I had written to just months previously and who had refused me, an editor at the *Radio Times* which at that time was using known writers for all their articles. Within a few days I had a phone call and I was commissioned. My writing career started to mushroom because of whom I knew and where I was hanging out. In a weird way the contact with the *New Review* gave me an inroad into writing fiction, but that option was never taken up because those contacts enabled further contacts in journalism, and it was the writing of the journalism that prevented me getting on with the fiction.[21]

After publishing his first stories, between 1976 and 1987 he began working as an increasingly successful freelance features journalist, first on 'retainer' for *The Telegraph*, the *Sunday Telegraph Magazine* and occasionally other less right-wing newspapers. Writing longer fiction remained an unfulfilled, often unconscious desire. As Crace comments to Wroe, "I got loads of phone calls from editors and agents wanting to work with me. Most of my friends were walking around with finished fiction but no publisher or agents. I had publishers and agents but no fiction. It wasn't until 1986 that I could be arsed to actually write a novel." (13) Part of this reluctance resulted from his political awareness, a commitment to his assignments and a sense of truth that kept him from storytelling, a Platonic reluctance of a kind. "'I spent half of my working life, up to the age of 40, as a journalist because I thought fiction was a bourgeois indulgence. If you wanted to be involved in politics and writing it had to be through journalism. Of course it turned out to be slightly difficult to raise the clarion call to the barricades because most of the time I worked for the *Sunday Telegraph*.'"[22] Nonetheless even for this paper Crace's journalistic career offered positive attractions. It was finally the departure of John Anstey, his editor at *The Telegraph*, which changed Crace's trajectory:

> He was a reactionary human being, but very open to trusting his journalists and keen to have fine writing. This suited me – but when he left that situation sort of folded. The new editor said her idea of the perfect *Telegraph* article was The Rise and Fall of the Shoulder Pad. We all thought that this was deeply witty, but lo and behold that was in her first edition. I'd been writing quite serious stuff up to that point, so I left. I moved to a looser relationship with *The Sunday Times*, and they gave me some fantastic things to do. In fact, the piece of journalism I've always been most proud of is about the effect of the Chernobyl disaster on Welsh hill farmers. It contains many of my flourishes and traits. I think you can see that; I think you can hear my tone of voice, because it's landscape writing more than anything, that piece.[23]

Crace seeks to explain his relationship with two such right-wing newspapers, given his own leftist leanings. "The facts were eloquent on their own behalf. The facts would always argue left is what I always thought."[24] In view of later repeated claims about the uneventfulness of his middle age, ironically this phase of life was neither mundane nor uneventful. As he records in 'Hearts of Oak' he was sent on assignment to interview George Martin at his new recording studios in Montserrat in the Leewards, to Skye to interview Ian Anderson of the rock group Jethro Tull, to New York for an interview (that failed to transpire) with Debbie Harry, iconic lead singer of Blondie, and to California to drive Pacific Highway One for a travel piece. He visited an oil platform in Piper and Forties to report on disaster control in the North Sea oilfields and was 'rescued' from the sea off the Lizard in

Cornwall by a Wessex 5 helicopter for a piece called 'High Wire Hero' which depicted him "swinging from a 300-foot winch-line above a stroppy sea . . . courageous for a fee, reckless on expenses." (73) As Helen Brown reveals in 'A Writer's Life: Jim Crace' (2003) the earlier stories failed to convince Crace that he had yet discovered the right kind of voice for a full collection or a novel. Early attempts to fulfil his contract for the first book were disillusioning. "While maintaining his journalistic career, he tried to write a realist political novel set in Birmingham. 'It was terrible,' he nods emphatically. 'Then I reviewed a novel by Gabriel García Márquez and I thought: this guy is just making things up! I can do that. And I wrote *Continent* without any trouble at all. My voice wasn't what I hoped it would be, but I had found it.'" (2)

Crace recalls at this time rereading Samuel Johnson's *Rasselas*, which helped by demonstrating how he might adopt a different style and tone from the realist, influencing his decision to adopt a dislocated setting.[25] Another key moment came with his father's death in 1979. Crace records the preceding period and his loss in 'Hearts of Oak:' "Instead of tears I shed my first piece of fiction for many years: a monologue by a woman whose father is dying called 'Seven Ages'. It was published by Craig Raine in *Quarto* and then broadcast on Radio 3, and marked the start of my migration from journalism to fiction . . . That was the year we swapped Thatcher for my Dad." (77–8) The understated, laconic political dismissal of Thatcher typifies Crace's strong ideological awareness, a position that subtends much of his fiction, often obliquely or tangentially. *The Gift of Stones* is an allegory of the decimation of industries and working communities by Margaret Thatcher. The poverty in *Arcadia* similarly reflects such upheavals. Crace considers the reasons why Em, the mother, becomes a beggar in the city, and why she might need to abandon her rural home. Crace refuses simply to individualize her plight, contrasting her fate to the underlying cultural myths, choosing a series of polemical, rhetorical questions. "What of the free food of the countryside. The mushrooms and the nuts? The stubble grain left over by the thresher and harvesters? The berries and the birds? The honey and the fish? Life's not like that, except in children's books. The free food of the countryside is high and maggoty before it's ripe; or else it's faster than the human hand and can't be caught." (76) This is not simply a pastoral voice, but varies the interrogative of the fairytale, caustic and moralizing at times. Despite Crace's elusive elements, and his fabulist tendency, he creates a coherent set of recognizable human relations offsetting the ambiguity. Sean Matthews writes in 'Jim Crace' (2005): "Crace's work has consistently evoked imaginary, self-sufficient fictional worlds which are in teasing or troubling parallel relations to the 'real' one(s) we inhabit. This is not, however, a matter of fantasy or fable for its own sake. Crace is, crucially, addressing the vital and essential themes of contemporary life, and is in this sense a powerful political writer."

After his first story it took Crace another eleven years to finish *Continent*. He relates the difficulty of moving from an essentially naturalistic mode, and shaking off the influence of the Beat Generation. The inclinations of the British scene militated against him. "We're used – in the twentieth and twenty-first centuries – to novels being basically autobiographical, that's the convention these days."[26] Some early efforts are contained in a manila wallet folder dated 1965 and originally labelled in capitals, "CHRISTOPHER MARLOWE: PLAYS AND DRAMATIC BACKGROUND." This description of student notes has been overwritten, by a revealing and self-critical inscription in blue: "OLD UNPROMISING FICTION PIECES – plus." Here lies a different putative Cracean world, in many ways the obverse of Craceland. One unfinished manuscript adopts a naturalistic, autobiographical mode. 'The Theory and Practice of Non-Violent Resistance' attempts a personal reflection upon the community and hippy politics of the 1970s in a north London setting. The narrator is a hippy living in a squat. He has been beaten up by yobs, and his girlfriend, Terry, consoles him by reading Shelley, her favourite poet after Sylvia Plath, both poetic passions very indicative of the tastes of this era. The narrator's first person account bemoans his life, reflecting the disillusion of the late 1970s. The story presents in detail a social mood and a setting about which Crace seems less than sympathetic, a world of squatting, travellers, run-down post-war inner-city housing, and despair. The latter is stated explicitly as his central theme:

> There's much despair in London, particularly in Archway where me and Terry squat. We've got one three-tiered derelict just off the Archway Road. We're in a row of eight and, though ours is pretty settled, some of the others are just doss pads. The Irish have got one but they're families mostly so don't really count as part of the scene. There's a Black Liberation squat which is usually full of white South Africans doing the Grand Tour. They sit around all day and drink Uhuru coffee. Then there's the Women's Centre which the Feminists have got – but nobody sleeps

> there because every drunk in the neighbourhood would be round giving them a hard time. Then there's the dosser's place which is really an overflow for tramps who can't get into the Sally or are too stoned to try. Then there's our place and after us the three other traditional squats. We're the settled end of the street, and in some respects the most despairing. Some of us are too young and too hysterical. And the rest of us are too old and have been here too long. Our hysterias have been de-energised. That's despair. In the early days it was fine. I was younger and tougher. I had bounce.

Once again a male character bemoans the loss of youth, symbolizing the end of an age. The narrator's hidden secret is that he harbours ambitions to return to paid employment, away from the community centres and the claimant's union. Curiously Crace was on the verge of moving in the opposite direction in a sense, risking a full-time writer's life, away from regularly paid employment.

Finally Crace learnt to blend the perception of difference which had informed his observations of Africa with a non-realist mode of writing, responding to the examples in Márquez and Samuel Johnson. Throughout he maintains his eye for detail, for the interactions between individuals and within communities that were evident in his early writing, but had been burdened with superfluous or biographical detail. In 1976 'Cross-Country' appeared in the *New Review*, which after substantial revision evolved into the first material that was to become *Continent*. He completed this while serving as Writer in Residence at the Midlands Arts Centre in Birmingham in 1983, at which time he also directed the city's inaugural Festival of Readers and Writers.

Wroe records Crace's reluctance to switch full time to fiction away from journalism. The final decision was out of his hands, half-formed intention both superseded by circumstances and aided by Crace's ideological sense of the world. He found the *Sunday Times* under the editorship of Andrew Neill increasingly difficult and the style of management unpalatable. There came a final confrontation, one which allowed Crace to clarify his feelings about his future. This episode, which transforms him by allowing the novelist within to replace the journalist, reveals the underlying ethical and political sympathies of the author:

> I had a particular problem writing a piece about the Broadwater Farm Estate in Tottenham a year after Blakelock was murdered. I put this long piece into the *Sunday Times Magazine*, about 6,000 words.

> The section editor liked it, so it would be published, no problem. And then, evidently, Andrew Neill – for what was reported in the gossip columns as *quasi*-political reasons (I don't know what that 'quasi' represents), ever the hands-on journo it was said (another quote from one of the other gossip columnists) – pulled the article because he was appalled by what he saw as its anti-police position. It wasn't anti-police at all. But nor was it anti-community. The *Sunday Times* had instructed me to report on this 'hell hole.' But Broadwater Farm wasn't a hell hole at all. It was just a complicated, challenged community where things had gone wrong, and part of those things that had gone wrong was that some of the policing methods were inappropriate, as was evidenced by the death of Mrs. Cynthia Jarrett. This is not to make any excuse about what happened to P.C. Blakelock. And the article argued, of course, that they had convicted the wrong people, and I was right about that as it turned out. About that time, *Continent* was sold for a great deal of money in the States, for $40,000, which gave me the opportunity to take a principled stand over writing for the *Sunday Times*. I wonder whether without a pocketful of dollars I would have had the courage of my principles. Perhaps I probably wouldn't, but the truth is that there's no excuse not to stick by your principles if you have got the comfort of those American dollars in your pocket.[27]

The final self-deprecation perhaps typifies Crace's self-questioning view. Turning away from attempts at a realist novel about his generation in a midlands town much like the Moseley area of Birmingham, Crace attempts to create a made-up world, a larger territory of experience through imagination, its parameters dislocated and free-ranging. This literally served as a creative revelation, an epiphany.[28] He had to write the book that had been contracted for those liberating dollars, and so he completed the sections that constituted *Continent*, finding the work relatively easy after years of hesitations, delays and obstacles.

Despite its very different mode or style of writing from his earlier successes, *Continent* continued the critical recognition achieved by his earlier stories. Gillian Greenwood in 'The Geography of Bleak New Worlds' (1986) says:

> The stories are all concerned with the impingement of the newer culture on the older. The corruption from without and within the old communities is a familiar theme, but seems concentrated in a clear, fresh, poetic style. The best pieces are 'Sins and Virtues' and 'On Heat'. The first is the story of an unworldly calligrapher who has the last word on an absurd community of art collectors; the second is a beautifully

constructed 'lost tribe' mystery about an ethnic group that enjoys a specific mating season. Although each piece stands on its own, the seven create a new world that is strangely familiar. (19)

Certainly the book's publication marked a further transition; within three weeks it was awarded three major prizes, the Whitbread First Novel of the Year Award, the David Higham Prize for Fiction, and the *Guardian* Fiction prize. Given the unexpectedly significant profile, Heinemann, excited about its prospects, halved its price to just under five pounds; hence the cover sticker on most copies that announces: "You can afford to make the journey!" Not everything was smooth, as Michele Field relates: "In the States something extraordinary happened – about which, Crace confesses, he may not know the whole story. 'Harper & Row by mistake pulped the hardback of *Continent* soon after delivering the subscribed copies. It was a case of getting a computer number wrong. So they rushed the paperback out, and it came out too soon. So though the reviews were transcendental, sales of that book were a bit of a disaster.'" (49) Nevertheless, Crace's subsequent journey as a writer and novelist had truly begun. This career suited him, as he confesses to Peter Wild in *Bookmunch* (2004):

> It's not a bad life, after all, earning a good living from telling lies in the comfort of your own home. There are harder jobs and lower wages. Besides, as a non-autobiographical writer, I don't have to carry my subject matter around with me. I can close the study door and lock the goblins up for the night. That's why I seem saner and duller in the flesh than many of my colleagues.

Yet despite Crace's attempts to convey his life as seamlessly mundane and dull, it is significant he reached this point of intellectual and artistic development; for as Tonkin comments, "He is deeply interesting, of course. Enfield estates are still far more likely to breed world-class footballers than world-class literary fabulists." (32)

Other recognition soon followed. By 1987 *Continent* had been translated widely and the consequent financial success allowed Crace confidently to continue writing fiction full time for the foreseeable future.[29] Greenwood notes early examples of what will become the characteristics of Craceland: "Jim Crace's form, to which he has clearly given some thought, is tinged with fantasy: and there are some borrowings from that specific genre, including a slightly pretentious tone which occasionally slips into his style. But for the most part he fuses folklore and political parable, moral fable and myth, into something rather original and also very modern in its fragmentation." She also notes the concentration of the major theme, corruption, expressed "in a clear, fresh, poetic style." (19)

Given Crace's high-profile journalistic career, being in the public eye and being read widely were neither new nor significant experiences in themselves. And yet, the first book became particularly meaningful for him because, as he describes retrospectively, the project allowed him to explore writing by responding simultaneously to his own experiences and those of a different ethical and social view of the world. It freed his imagination from a narrow ideological engagement that had constrained his factual work. He achieved this by consciously releasing himself from previous constraints. Crace evokes a sense freedom that had been alien to him in the journalistic mode:

> Emotionally I was completely without tension. I was young and I was not beset by having any pre-existing reputation that mattered. And I'd just found a new toy which was writing as a fabulist, that is making things up and feeling licensed to do it, and being startled by how convincing were my versions of the world. I startled myself and so it was absolutely a joyful experience and there were few expectations when the book came out. It was certainly a relief after writing non-fiction, after writing journalism, because I was an extremely straight-laced journalist; I did not tell a fib, nor change a quotation. Surprisingly, for someone who later has made a reputation for lying for a living and also is known for lying socially, as a journalist I didn't do that. I was far too po-faced and monastic in my approach. I always tried to get things exactly right. And also if I tried any fine writing – I mentioned that John Anstey liked fine writing – which always comes second to the subject matter, I really couldn't come up with any of my best flourishes when I was doing the journalism. I found in writing *Continent*, that's exactly what I could do, coming up with great musical sentences and writing that had meaning in it, but was also full of percussion and full of rhythms, and that was great fun.[30]

His percussive, rhythmic quality would develop and mutate in subsequent books. After the first, Crace's methods and progress become both more workmanlike and aesthetically diverse, producing ten prose books (six of them novels), with another in draft.

Critical acceptance has been limited, although reviewers have identified Crace's originality, but the diversity of his work may have inhibited widespread recognition, since it is difficult to situate. As Matthews concludes, "The peculiarity of Crace's position is that this place has been secured with writing which bears no obvious relation to the prevailing currents and concerns of his peers. His career as a writer has been marked by a set of formal, ethical and aesthetic interests which set him apart from the mainstream of writing in English." Although neither fully an experimentalist nor a postmodernist in the manner of B. S. Johnson, J. G. Ballard or Salman Rushdie, Crace mirrors movements in the novel form from the late-1970s, away from middle-class post-war realism in its apparent rejection of modernism, but not towards the naturalistic, rather exploring other possibilities. Crace engages in an interfusion of traditional narrative and forms with certain modes – in Crace's case folktale storytelling structures, fabulism, mythopoeic possibilities and a rehistoricizing of the past – that link him to his peers. Frank Kermode identifies in 'Into the Wilderness' (1998) certain central qualities among the heterogeneity that is Crace's fictions:

> Each of his disparate worlds is rendered with unshakable assurance and in impressive detail. The description of a great produce market in *Arcadia* is a fine example; you would think the author had spent his life studying fruit and vegetables. Then, in *Signals of Distress*, we meet him as an expert on matters nautical and on life in an early Victorian seaport. This intense focusing on, or inhabitation of, a particular milieu means that there is little obvious thematic continuity from one book to the next. What they share is this imaginative power, these variously obsessed landscapes and cultures. (8)

Crace's major aesthetic and thematic dynamics are familiar: a crisis of faith and meaning, the elusive quality of love, an interrogation of the essentials of identity within a broader social context, a consideration of the crises of modernity in terms of its mercantile/capitalist instincts, and an awareness of the human narrative impulse. However, as Kermode notes, Crace is not explicitly politicized: "If this is politics, it is very abstract politics." (8) Although his fiction is not conventionally realistic or naturalistic, intercalated within various interwoven narrative traditions – fairytale, parable, allegory, myth, magic realism and historical narrative – mimetic and observational verisimilitude persist strongly.

Crace was perhaps finally endorsed as a noteworthy contemporary British author by two public events: his nomination for the 1997 Booker Prize (which he did not win) and the award by the US National Book Critics Circle of its twenty-sixth annual book prize for *Being Dead* in 2000. On the television discussion programme that accompanied the broadcast of the Booker Prize's award ceremony, A. S. Byatt's described Crace as the most significant writer in English fiction of the previous ten years.[31]

Charting precise biographical coordinates or sources for Crace's work is problematic, especially given Crace insistently proselytises the dogma that his life is uneventful, his origins without particular distinction and that neither can help in situating the fiction. This may partly further explain his being marginal in academic criticism, especially as such claims are disingenuous; his fiction is permeated by specific lived experiences that provide the subtext to his work. The tendency towards adopting a journalist as narrative *personae* is both intriguing and suggestive. That Crace appears almost too eager to dismiss any biographical relevance, insisting on a total separation of his life and work, may derive from the secular Puritanism that characterizes the area in which Crace grew up, where that tradition is suspicious of notions of superiority, excellence and egotism. Begley in 'A Pilgrim in Craceland' follows the authorized Cracean view concerning the uneventful south Birmingham suburban life:

> Crace's biographer will have a hell of a time. It's not just that he leads a quiet life, that the most fascinating thing he does is to sit alone in a room and write . . . No – the real problem for the would-be biographer is that on the pages of Jim Crace's novels there are very few clues as to what he himself, the man outside that lonely room, is like; and only an especially gymnastic critic could show how the life accounts for the work. This pleases Crace, he's proud of it: he likes to be invisible, a writer who erases himself. 'I am not my own subject matter,' he says. (227)

Crace's life and identity are not extraneous to his writing. As Brown discovered, Crace exhibits both an analytical quality and often very established opinions that inform his world-view. She says only half-playfully, "I have spent only a few minutes with Jim Crace, but it is clear that his world is fraught with fine moral distinctions. Visitors must tread carefully, and I have made one wrong choice already: 'Tea is unpretentious and working-class, coffee is bourgeois and American.' Oops." (2) One technical error of mine became part of the self-effacing narrative with which Crace deflects interest in his personal life, and is so familiar in his many public pronouncements. As Brown demonstrates, Crace indulges the narrative urge or impulse that he commonly refers to as intrinsic to human adaptation, moulding the events to create narrative coherence:

'A couple of weeks ago I had a guy come here and announce that he is my biographer,' he groans. 'I gritted my teeth and tried to be cooperative while he recorded the whole story: I never heard my parents argue; I have only married once and I'm happy with my children; I have no addictions and I'm an optimist. Two hours later he phoned from the train – and the tapes were blank!' He trills his fingers on the tabletop in satisfaction. 'It was as if the goblin of justice recognised that the story of my life is so dull that the electronics of the machine refused to record it. Perfect!' (2)[32]

However conventional the trappings of Crace's middle-class home, he is celebrated, recognized particularly in the United States as a significant literary figure, and his opinions are sought. Admittedly he preserves his urbanity and ordinariness, but he travels the world extensively to promote his books. He has received numerous prizes, public tributes, and academic awards and scholarships.[33] His ordinariness is rooted in his level-headedness and exemplifies his radical, egalitarian commitments rather than simply reflecting the conditions off his life which might be considered by many to be extraordinary. As Paul Thewlis reports in 'Death Warmed Up,' (2000) "Unlike so many successful writers, whose heads swell exponentially after a flurry of good press, Jim is the epitome of humility. One of the first things that strikes you about this award-winning author is what a nice guy he is – friendly, down to earth, easy to talk to." (20) Clearly his journalism seems to have taught him the transience and fragility of both success and fame.

Admitting the variability of his settings, Crace sees consistency in the style which patterns his prose, saying, "The subject matters change, but I do think my books have an indelible imprint on them. If you know anything about my writing, I think you can read any paragraph of mine and recognize who wrote it. The books are very changeable, but stylistically they're not. I think stylistically, they've got an unchanging imprint."[34] In identifying the importance of Crace's style Richard J. Lane in 'The Fiction of Jim Crace' (2003) draws upon Kermode's review of *Quarantine* where the latter cites Iris Murdoch's category of 'crystalline' construction in order to situate Crace at one end of a fictional spectrum, "where the novel is most like a poem, most turned in on itself, most closely wrought for the sake of art and internal cohesion," (8) as opposed to the journalistic mode.[35] Admittedly there is an aesthetic sense of internality, although mediated by a pastoral realism, but surely Crace's prose remains largely domestic, mostly robust, and mixes the lyrical potential of landscape and of events with their earthy presence. Given the plurality of Crace's work in terms of the quotidian settings, characters and plot, nevertheless his stylistic attributes remain insistently masculine and knowing. Adam Mars-Jones in 'Hurrying Back to Nature' (1992) indicates as much, commenting: "The strangest aspect of *Arcadia* is undoubtedly its reliance on verse rhythms. Not since *Moby-Dick* has blank verse thrummed so relentlessly beneath the prose. In passage after passage, Crace's style is as iambic as a migraine." (22) In 'Write and Proper,' an interview in the same year, Sophia Sackville-West refers to the "abbreviated lyricism and visual impact of Crace's style." (30) Crace's short sentences, grammatical inversions and pattern of connective detail provide a proverbial sense of structure, a verbal topology proportionate to variabilities of content and setting. The style acts as a matrix, or substrate. Repetitive both visually and in its tonal qualities, the prose offers more than a residual lyricism. Through grammatical and auditory iterations Crace implies a familiarity and multiplicity in each series of images, consciously interconnecting or interlinking them with larger themes. Mars-Jones adds of *Arcadia*'s protagonist whose business is the novel's axis: "If Victor is almost fetishist in his attachment to vegetables and to fruit, so too is his author. When he isn't describing greengrocery – and the book is full of hymns to produce – then he is comparing other things to it." (22) A sense of textual enclosure and self-referentiality permeate the narrative and its auditory chain of images. Anna, a secretary in Victor's corporation, encounters the Soap Market and the passage is literally a cornucopia of visual motifs, reflecting several underlying themes such as epiphany and death, and its stylistic insistence creates a rhythmic effect. Iteratively each passage reduplicates a portion of the intended overall effect:

> Anna burrowed deep into the Soap Market. She passed the ranks of orange, the monsoon fruit, the chicory, the sea kale, the Valentino pears, the commonwealth of apples, and came into the cooler kingdom of the leaf. She wanted just one lettuce, but she was teased by the choice and colour. She rummaged at a stall for a garden lettuce with a tight rosette. She'd never noticed how they smelled before. The salads at the produce counter of her local delicatessen were odourless. But here, banked up in such profusion, the leaves were acrid almost, funereal. Their odour was precisely that of damp clay newly turned to take a coffin. (222)

The lilt and pace suggest iambic regularity, the prosaic poeticism like that of blank verse, intersecting the profusion and regularity of the images, and underlying the final phase of alliteration are the motifs of death and desire as a sexual union, Thanatos and Eros. Thus two major themes are reinforced. Other effects are subtle. The implied allusion to a warren in the use of the term 'burrow' implicitly allows at least an unconscious reading of profusion as referring or alluding to issues of both multiplicity, and sexuality and availability. Such textual implications and movements are implicit, each object as a thing in itself suggestive. The profusion of object words and sensual images are painterly, extending the explicit meaning, using visual symbolism alongside structural iteration. Crace creates more than a residual, contracted poeticism; he supersedes prose's contracted rationality, allowing the object to cohere with the subjective, a correlation of the kind described by Bataille in *The Accursed Share, Vol. II* (1991):

> We escape this empty and sterile movement, this sum of objects and abstract functions that is the world of the intellect, only by entering a very different world where objects are on the same plane as the subject, where they form, together with the subject, a sovereign totality which is not divided by any abstraction and is commensurate with the entire universe. (112)

Craceland amplifies both the meaning of the objective and its ability to mirror the subject's experience of events, and does so through successive momentary movements articulating subjective-objective empathy. This recurs in small details, but is most evident in certain motifs expressing the relationship of characters to certain physical objects such as the arrowheads at the beginning and end of *The Gift of Stones*, the rocking stone in *Signals of Distress*, and the curled staff in *Quarantine*. Craceland rejects the reductively rational view of objective forms of naturalism, incorporating the mythopoeic possibilities of objects. As Milton Scarborough in *Myth and Modernity* (1994) makes evident in rejecting the mythological as unscientific, modernity separates the within from the without, removes the mythic penetration of the self by the objective and affirms the act of consciousness where: "modern theories interpret myths as referring, when properly understood, to some aspect of mind (the inside) or, in a primitive and mistaken fashion, to some feature of the objective world (the outside)." (9–10) In such concretion as Scarborough concludes, "the result is that myths understood as allegories of nature could no longer be squared with science. The cosomological function of myth, the telling of the story of the whole of the universe, was discredited." (12) Crace is conciliatory and although he operates on the very margins of both myth and reality, he effects a displacement and destabilization of their diametric duality, attempting a mediation of their opposition. He interfuses the mythic and modernity, a reconciliation where the objective remains suggestive, meaningful and allegorical.

Contrary to Kermode's impression of Crace's style, which they note in their commentary, John Constable and Hideaki Aoyama in 'Testing for Mathematical Lineation in Jim Crace's *Quarantine* and T. S. Eliot's *Four Quartets*' (2001) conclude that the lyrical quality of Crace's fiction's is not strictly poetic in form or cadence, but exists as a potentially rhythmic and poetic extension of the prose register. They comment that "Crace uses slightly more disyllables than would be predicted from the geometric distribution, whereas the prose corpus texts employ slightly less." (42) Finally the exact form is elusive, although as they comment, "It is tempting to suppose that *Quarantine* must lie closer to the prose end of the continuum, on account of its lack of concentrated order." (51) Crace's work eludes easy definition and one cannot reduce it to any totalizing uniformity of his style. His persuasive heterogeneity spans settings and periodizations that range from a Third World additional continent in the present, a Stone Age landscape in an archetypal seashore setting, a nineteenth-century west coast fishing village, the banality of a market in the present transformed from traditional to monolithic steel and glass, to another contemporary setting in a coastal vista in a westernized unnamed region, and medieval, post-apocalyptic America. Sub-textually he maintains the oppositional dynamics familiar in the classical pastoral perspective.

As Lane points out, Craceland is a world constituted by ongoing, cumulative change rather than simply reflecting major moments of transitions:

> Not only does narrative continue, it continues reinvigorated by the various protagonists' pratfalls, their lurching and leaping from the sublime to the ridiculous. Somewhat controversially in *Quarantine*, one of these protagonists is portrayed as Christ; in *The Gift of Stones*, the protagonist is a storyteller; in *Signals of Distress*, the protagonist is a humanist, someone who thinks he cares, but is revealed to be a pompous prig out of touch with the world he wants to save. Why save a world which has already moved on? These protagonists all suffer in a sense an

> ontological and epistemological displacement from the world; they are in the world, but do not live according to its rules; they think they understand the world, but they are using the wrong interpretative parameters. They see through a glass, darkly. The world has always moved on, and in the fracturing between character and world, there is much laughter: huge, stomach churning bursts of laughter countered by a redemptive/narrative force that may, or may not, be a result of that laughter. Who laughs? Is it Crace? Is it the reader? Is the laughter nihilistic? Any hint of nihilism in Crace appears to undergo transformation; nihilism becomes affirmation. (27–8)

Given his ideological predilections, Crace's affirmation reflects and derives from his life experience and his own positive instincts, affirming his personal history, the core of his familial being rather than transforming nihilistic laughter. His sardonic humour represents the irreverence of the radical. Like Crace, his protagonists are optimistic against the odds. As he says to Wild, "I'm also a very lucky person and an optimist. There have been few dark corners in my life so far. Rather, I have enjoyed more everyday love and peace and health and good fortune than most people on our planet. That's a very 'ordinary' boast, I know, but not something to be undervalued." Hence his redemptive appeal to the quotidian, the joy or munificence of the moment, and thus nature potentially offering transcendence of the nihilistic and the laughable. Anna's vegetables reflect symbolically such a possibility, found even in the simplest intervention into the world of things.

Crace illustrates the immediacy of the everyday, with its mundane detail enveloping his reader, surrounding the characters, suggesting a rhythmic and performative externality, exemplified in the opening of *Signals of Distress*. "Both men were *en voyage* and sleeping in their berths. Hard winds swept in and put their ships ashore." (1) Two fates are balanced. The predicament of Aymer, the anti-heroic protagonist, represents the domain of the past, but historicized largely beyond the grand narrative of public events (apart from the minutiae of the moral dilemmas of the early nineteenth-century slave trade):

> The *Tar* was only fifty yards from shore. Two sailors had to land a line by rowboat and secure the ship to capstans on the quay. And then they had to coax the *Tar* to dock. Aymer lay awake. He wasn't any use on deck. His shoulder hurt from where he'd fallen from his bunk. The muscles in his throat and stomach ached from vomiting. His breath was foul. His temper, too. He should have travelled overland with the

company carts, he decided. He should have stayed at home instead of meddling abroad. (1-2)

The use of *abroad* for anywhere beyond one's immediate locality even in England establishes a sense of period, and contributes to the impression of a puritanical young trader found in a state of flux and transition, confronting the world beyond his ideological and comforting certainties. Both Aymer's bruising and sickness in crisis confirm a typical humanistic commonality, a vulnerability of existence and embodiment, but are symbolically suggestive. In terms of details or co-ordinates each of Crace's narratives remains familiar and relevant territorially for the contemporary reader because of a sense of shared emotional and material references concerning everyday living. Crace's characters inhabit a world that seems adjacent to the sociohistorical world shared by the readers because the behavioural co-ordinates and parameters of human motivations and activities are comprehensible and familiar. Crace's recentring is a displacement, a mythological edging, rather than any comprehensive fantasy or imaginary zone. The tales are conceptually and geographically taut, the scope of consciousness localized and implicitly framed by its familiarity of perceptual range. Thereby the unfamiliar is transformed. A verbal repetition patterns the texts in the manner of Biblical and evangelical narrative, although like such accounts they deal with quotidian and largely common human occurrences. The perceptual schema is of common sense mediated by a sceptical questioning; he admits to Peter Wild, "I'm an old fashioned moralist, so the big topics are my natural hunting ground." Nevertheless, the focus remains the minutiae of interactions and the symbolic possibilities of environment and landscape. Even with the imaginary sixth continent in *Continent* the narrative's horizon and its images are expected ones, defined within the individual's visual referent, offering a perceptual immediacy. Any expansiveness is provided by the parabolic or moralistic aspects of the tales. Various almost archetypal figures – the student, the teacher-storyteller, the scientist and the engineer – find their lives disturbed. Hence Crace replicates or incorporates in terms of both structure and content the twin features of parable: the inclusion of the familiar and mundane and yet reworking these elements in a fashion that Bernard Harrison suggests in *Inconvenient Fictions: Literature and the Limits of Theory* (1991) typifies parable since: "parabolic narrative has as one of its functions the subversion of the conceptual scheme in terms of which its hearers construe the world and their lives in it." (226) In

Crace this is doubled since this effect applies both to the listeners within the tale and the readers of the novel, implying some parallels within both the narrative and the external world. And yet, the storytelling device and the unfamiliarity of emerging new conflicts all stress "the *riddling* character of parables," (239) noted by Harrison. Such aspects permeate Craceland as we shall see in detail in subsequent chapters. My second chapter is concerned primarily with how Crace's first two books foreground the narrative act itself, exemplifying the storytelling urge, which is required by the various communities or members within them to make sense of the clash between traditional values and lifestyles, and change. In both books individuals are ambivalent, identifying their dilemmas in the phenomenological symbols of their world. In this sense the very settings allow Crace to create a marginal hinterland, a territory not fully absorbed by the modern where its cultural problems and dynamics are played out both literally and allegorically.

Notes

1 Crace's insistent comment is taken from a recording of an unpublished interview of Jim Crace by Dr Philip Tew at the UCE Birmingham on 12 February 2003, referred to hereafter as the 'UCE 2003 Interview.' However, Crace propounds what might be taken as a theory of literature, albeit a pragmatic one.
2 This is transcribed from a recording of an unpublished interview of Jim Crace by Dr Philip Tew at the University of Westminster on 2 June 1998, referred to hereafter as the 'Westminster 1998 Interview.'
3 Ibid.
4 Ibid.
5 'UCE 2003 Interview.'
6 See www.jim-crace.com. This is taken from an e-mail interview conducted on 27 January 2000 for publication on a website dedicated to Crace.
7 Curiously 'Namek and the Smoked Ancestor,' by Norman Lewis is published in *21: 21 Picador Authors Celebrate 21 Years of International Writing* (1993), which also includes Crace's 'Hearts of Oak.'
8 This school was attended by: Walter Pater (for coaching); Boris Karloff (then Eric Pratt); Norman Lewis; Bob Cobbing, and later myself; hence my knowledge of its qualities and characteristics. My experience as a working-class entrant broadly mirrored Crace's own. Until the 1970s the school remained a prestigious and conservative establishment, with close links to various colleges of Cambridge University. Until the Second

World War it had catered for both fee-paying borders, often from Imperial families, and local pupils.
9. 'Westminster 1998 Interview.'
10. Ibid.
11. Ibid. He adds that "I put a lot of effort into being a member of societies, and a cross-country runner, but when it came to it I was never taken seriously in the sixth form. I was one of three boys who weren't made a prefect. It was a snub. The other two were both working-class boys. There were other working-class boys who were made prefects, but they were good at being 'prefecty' types. What I had wasn't appreciated."
12. Charley Crace's arm can be seen in the photograph prefacing 'Hearts of Oak' where he is holding his son at the seaside (72).
13. Dr Philip Tew, an unpublished telephone interview with Jim Crace recorded on an MP3 file, conducted from approx. 15:30 on Wednesday 13 October 2004. Hereafter referred to as 'Crace–Tew: Telephone Interview 1.'
14. Ibid.
15. Ibid.
16. In the first version Channon runs around the playing fields of the English school remembering "the prefabricated tin rondavels of a school in Africa, three years ago," (47) and his classroom is decorated with maps and clichéd mementoes of his "African flirtation," (52) which constitute something of an ironic cultural iconography.
17. 'Crace–Tew: Telephone Interview 1.'
18. 'Westminster 1998 Interview.'
19. 'Crace–Tew: Telephone Interview 1.'
20. 'Spurs' is Crace's family's team, popular in his home area; it refers to Tottenham Hotspur Football Club.
21. 'Crace–Tew: Telephone Interview 1.'
22. Ibid.
23. Ibid.
24. Ibid.
25. Ibid.
26. 'UCE 2003 Interview.'
27. 'Crace–Tew: Telephone Interview 1.' Michele Field reports in 'Jim Crace: Moral Activist, Conservative Romantic' (1995): "Ted Solotaroff at Harper & Row paid $40,000 for Crace's first novel" (49) supplementing £10,000 in advance. The riots occurred on the Broadwater Farm Estate, Tottenham on 6 October 1985. Separated from colleagues, policeman Keith Blakelock was surrounded by masked rioters in balaclavas armed with sticks, knives and a machete and hacked to death. The subsequent conviction of a violent petty criminal, Winston Silcott, became a *cause célèbre* among many radical groups. In 1991 the convictions of Silcott and

two others, Mark Braithwaite and Engin Raghip, were quashed by the Court of Appeal. In 1999 Silcott was awarded a £50,000 out-of-court settlement for malicious arrest and false imprisonment.
28 Crace's term in the 'Crace–Tew: Telephone Interview 1.'
29 To date Crace's work has been translated into nineteen languages: Brazilian, Croatian, Danish, Dutch, French, German, Greek, Hebrew, Hungarian, Italian, Japanese, Korean, Lithuanian, Norwegian, Polish, Portuguese, Spanish, Swedish and Turkish.
30 'Crace–Tew: Telephone Interview 1.'
31 My source here is some hastily scribbled notes made while viewing the television transmission.
32 I rang from an intercity train on its way back to London. It was after this incident that we devised the method of recording interviews electronically over the telephone, a method familiar to Crace after so undertaking many media interviews.
33 See bibliography section, 'Literary Awards Including Nominations'. Crace used the E. M. Forster Award (given to enable a writer from the United Kingdom or Ireland to stay in the United States) to travel down the Outer Banks and the barrier islands of the US eastern seaboard, the landscapes suggesting the setting for *Being Dead*. In 1998 Crace was elected a member of the Management Committee of the Society of Authors and in 1999 he was elected as Fellow of the Royal Society of Literature. On 3 March 2000 he received an honorary doctorate (D.Univ.) from the University of Central England for Distinguished Literary Achievements.
34 'Westminster 1998 Interview.'
35 Lane refers here to Frank Kermode, 'Into the Wilderness: Review of *Quarantine*.' (1998)

2

Communities and change: *Continent* (1986) and *The Gift of Stones* (1988)

Continent

The unnamed locations of *Continent* reflect the permeation of traditional Third World civilizations by late modernity and its transformations. Each tale combines the exotic with reassuring familiarities of human response, an early Cracean device. Crace describes it as an "un-English book." Many reviewers and critics cannot resist situating Crace. For Brian Stonehill, in the *Los Angeles Times Book Review*, "The stories take place, for one thing, in an exotic locale that seems to be Latin American, although the fanciful names suggest some generic Third World." (4) Lowry Pei in the *Boston Review* (1987) suggests the setting, "lies at the world's outskirts . . . The stories could take place in Africa, or South America, or the Caribbean." (30) Crace's microcosms are interwoven with incursions from the larger known world, which threaten to supersede the local conditions. George Kearns, in 'Post-Colonial Fiction: Our Custom is Different' (1987) in the *Hudson Review*, wonders sceptically whether *Continent* constitutes a novel, but concludes that "The best of these seven stories are about the passing of ancient ways as they become 'inconveniences' in the neocolonialized eyes of natives on the make." (487) In 'A Pilgrim in Craceland' Begley reports Crace's view: "He calls [it] a 'patchwork novel' (seven separate stories all cut from the same cloth), he invented a part of the world pressured by progress – the where and the when are hazy, but the place and its emergent crises are unforgettable. This is pure Craceland: the geography just out of reach, like a buried memory or a troubled dream, the moment in time at once specific and curiously elastic." (230–1) Despite the certainty of detail and emphasis, the recurrent and identifiable themes, mythopoeic undertones create a dreamlike quality, suggesting a collective unconscious.

Crace reflects upon the book's provenance in his own earlier experience:

> If you've only encountered different cultures through fiction before, then when you finally make actual contact with an unfamiliar culture, at close hand, it can seem as if you simply inhabit another book. The culture and its everyday behaviour patterns seem so bizarre that they could be invented, and yet you know they're not. This encourages your imagination to invent alternatives to your own familiar Western world. Take the Sudan and the Islamic uneasiness towards images of any living thing, which encouraged calligraphy and made it a much more important form of expression than it has ever been in the non-Islamic world. That very much comes across with the piece in *Continent*. And – another direct influence from my time in the Sudan – there is the issue of a different set of moral imperatives, such as the importance of not losing face, the importance of honour, and the way in which both are bound up with the whole business of hospitality. All of these things interested and stimulated me, making me think I could invent versions of alternative moralities myself. To some extent *Continent*, even though it was influenced by my subsequent travels as a journalist and even though it owes much to places other than Africa, owes its biggest impulse to my time in the Sudan and in Botswana.[1]

This collection's partially closed world centres upon aspects outlined in the previous chapter: the mythopoeic, the power of storytelling and the agency of ideas themselves as conceits. The unfamiliarity of the setting helps Crace's synthesis of universal possibilities and ethical interpretations. In 'Electricity' the teacher warns the local community about electricity, thereby cautioning them not only about civilization's incursions into undisturbed realms of nature, but of humankind's very dependency on energy in subsequently defining its relationships with the world. Crace explains that as a political modernist he favoured such a march towards progress in the Sudan, but also revelled in a slightly more romanticized notion of their environment. Emotionally, perhaps, and certainly fictionally he responds differently than his ideological view of progress, the story considering many of the contending impulses within himself:

> My political self always takes the side of modernity, and progress and the young view of things, and slightly despises the old traditional view. However, in storytelling it's usually the older wise person who gets the better of the young guy and so it was in *Continent*. This is the chief reason I say that the book is much more reactionary than I am myself,

because in *Continent* old, traditional ways of humankind better the modern ways of humankind. So it is in 'Electricity.' My political self would very much want anyone in any small African village to have electricity. In fact, when I was living in Botswana in 1969 in a big village called Molepolole, there was no electricity. My political self very much wanted that community to have electricity, but the traditional, reactionary part of myself knew that when electricity came certain things would be lost. Big romantic night skies with bright stars, for example. You know the way in which street-lamping blocks them out. But nevertheless there was this contention in my mind between the old ways of humankind and the new ways, and of course the most intimate form of that contention is between a father and a child.[2]

The generational conflict in 'Talking Skull' involves the growing loss of belief of the new generation, among those influenced by the rational, as opposed to a traditional order where the phenomenological is regarded as capable of representing something more magical and thereby offering a more meaningful world. The father is entrenched in traditional values, the son in scientific, enlightenment ones. As Paul Ricoeur says in *Figuring the Sacred: Religion, Narrative and Imagination* (1995):

> One fact of our culture is that we live in a desacralized world. Our modernity is constituted as modern precisely by having moved beyond the sacred cosmos. Nature, for modern persons, is no longer a store of signs. Its great correspondences have become indecipherable to them. The cosmos is mute. Human beings no longer receive the meaning of their existence from their belonging to a cosmos itself saturated with meaning. Modern persons no longer have a sacred space, a *templum*, a holy mountain, or an *axis mundi*. Their existence is decentered, eccentric, a-centered. They lack festivals, their time is homogeneous like their space. This is why we only speak of the sacred world today as *something archaic*. The sacred is archaic. (61)

In 'Talking Skull' Crace recuperates the possibilities of the past, recovers its sedimentary beliefs, and ironically for a supposed rationalist he evokes the sacral origins of culture, by appealing to an intuitive faith in the world of things. In such imaginary, essentially un-locatable settings mythic and parabolic storytelling may transform reality.

This transformative potential persists both as theme and possibility throughout *Continent*, but explicitly so in 'Electricity,' with its interplay of internal and external features. The environment undergoes change as it is illuminated by the forces of modernity; nevertheless traditional, mythic forms persist. The story opens: "'Neglect,' says Awni, the Rest House warden. For one hundred years we have been neglected. Now we are remembered!' and who claims credit? Warden Awni does. 'My petitions worked the trick,' he says. He displays carbon copies. Anyone is welcome to read his fawning paragraphs, to Ministers and Civil Servants. Now the town's supplicant has turned braggart." (117) Although Crace humanizes this process, revealing Awni as a serial petitioner, nonetheless the town's connection by a series of pylons to the grid results from self-interest and corruption on the part of the Minister's personal secretary who plans to build a hotel on land acquired from his neighbour, the landowner Nepruolo, who will also benefit. Ironically Awni is likely to suffer. The imagery conveying the literal process of electrification is anthropomorphic.

> More strange are the electricians, clean workers with hard fingers, who have come from the city in neat trucks and taken up noisy residence in Awni's best rooms. Hear these men sing and argue as they work! They bury flayed mechanical limbs of wire deep into wall plaster. They handle the tendons and sinews, the long red arteries, the blue veins, with the intimacy of surgeons. The children stand close to dive and wrestle for snips of wire and plastic which falls to the ground. How will it be, they ask, when the Minister and the President of the Company arrive to switch on the current? Will the electricity flow like water . . .?" (119–20)

The incredulity of the children and their eager anticipation mirror that of the whole community as it prepares to be transformed. They perceive magical possibilities in electricity, indicating their preservation of quasi-mythical possibilities, a traditional sacral view of the world.

Crace interrupts this plot, contrasting the teasing electricians – who liken electricity to messages to the body from the brain, confident of their profession and electricity's positive instantaneity – with the schoolteacher's story-within-a-story, which is suggestive of other possibilities. He draws on an incident in Denmark from the time he trained as a teacher. "'Beware of electricity,' says the schoolteacher. 'You will become addicts.'" (121) He describes to his audience a day reading in the Jorgensen's conservatory, of entertaining their children, Christoffer and Kirsten. Although earlier he was "being economical at the request of the Minister of Power who complained daily in the newspapers and on the television that Danes had become reckless with electricity," (121) as an experiment they turn on as many appliances as possible which, like the garden mower, take on a life of their own until this disc moves too fast to be perceptible:

> How did the spinning disc survive this onslaught? The teacher lowers his voice and leans forward to tell. 'It had disappeared,' he said. 'It was moving so fast that we could no longer see it. I climbed on the chair and tried to view it from above. But no, nothing. Only the faint smell of scorched metal and a cloudy smoking of the glass.' This is the point – with the teacher high on the chair, the twins holding their ears and laughing, the Jorgensen home clamouring like a nightmare – where Jens and Lotte returned. 'We screamed our explanations. We retraced our routes and unplugged. We picked the fibres from the shaver; we unpicked the keys of the typewriter; we replaced the scorched towelling on the ironing board; we rewired the lawn-mower; we patched up the burns on Lotte's hand (she had leaned on the toaster); we apologised to neighbours; we blushed. But, now, here is a mystery. Once the house had cooled and quietened, still the energy disc was missing. The Jorgensens said it must have disintegrated at speed, like a meteorite, and its flaming pieces had fallen into the workings of the meter. Certainly the digits on the ampage counter never budged again. But I can't accept so prosaic an explanation.'
> We look to the teacher for *his* explanation. But he is being playful. He has none. He is teasing us, that is all. 'Soon,' he says, 'thanks to Awni's obsequious petitions, this town, with its oil lamps, its hand pumps, its long nights, its stillness, will be a powered cauldron of heat and light and sound. It will spin with electricity. And it will disappear.' (124)

This is the clash of the rational and the imaginary. His electricity disc symbolizes electricity's voracious appetite for permeating all aspects of one's life. The narrative voice merges with that of the teacher and then re-emerges, but, despite the final third-person undercutting of the storytelling act, here in this mixture of the exaggerated, the anthropomorphic and the unbelievable Crace indicates a moral to be derived from the tale, implying too that the village will be subsumed culturally, transformed into something different.

In *Continent* Crace maintains a realistic strand, a mimetic quality that becomes fractured, and is often relegated as an undercurrent. In *On Realism* (1973) J. P. Stern summarizes fiction's appeal to the everyday, commenting that "The riches of the represented world; its weightiness and resistance to ideals; its consequential logic and circumstantiality – these I take to be among the attributes one would expect to find in realistic literature . . . they amount to an inventory of the qualities relevant to realism," (28) and yet he adds that within textual disjunction and incongruity one can allow "patently non-realistic or fantastic elements [to] combine with one or two kinds of realism: the one that has to do with the detailed description of fictional elements, the other that has to do with an evaluation of these elements." (130) Crace inverts this and allows realistic impulses to permeate his sense of dislocation. Crace's combination is more complex than Stern's model, where in Crace a residual commonsensical understanding fluctuates, and the mythic, the parabolic, the exaggerated tale and the intuitive all contend with the coherent and expected. And yet he returns to a "consequential logic and circumstantiality" repeatedly, only to subvert this effect and the overall mood of calling attention to detail and event. In the Rest House the customers have to dine on the veranda as the inner room is closed. Closer to nature, they revert to superstitious and archaic beliefs quite contrary to modernity, such as reading the signs on a bat-moth they have caught. "All eyes trace a line along the bat-moth's body and down its red-tipped spike. The spike is pointing at the policeman's wife. The moth is telling her fortune. She counts the grey smudges along the moth's still back: seven children! She measures its wing-latch: long life!" (125) The town's curiosity forces Awni to reveal in advance a huge fan as wide as the room in which it is installed, an absurd centrepiece he claims is a gift to the town. The details cohere in an unexpected fashion later at the party when the invited guests gather beneath the fan in expectant mood and the townspeople mimic the electricians' actions explaining the electrical messages from the brain, shaking their backsides and twitching their noses. This perplexes the Minister's secretary, who responds by ordering soldiers to suppress what he sees as ludicrous and parodic behaviour. This emphasizes a feature that Kegel-Brinkgreve identifies in the pastoral, and very specifically in Virgilian Eclogues, which is an "Awareness of the town-dweller's disdain for the simple life of the rustic mingles with praise of its attractions." (85) The comic and an underlying seriousness collide in this offhand suppression, the detail of which behaviour is also explored in 'The World with One Eye Shut.' 'Electricity' has recurring motifs and detail, of a type already hinted at in Crace's earlier published and unpublished stories. The story achieves a manner of estrangement that emphasizes the ironic meaning of its interrelated phases, which as can be seen are comparable to pastoral elements found in folktales. As Kegel-Brinkgreve says of the pastoral, its trivial incidents offer a kind of "artful symmetry." (15) Crace reflects the essentials of the pastoral tradition of Theocritan realism, which according to Kegel-Brinkgreve's model is situated in geographically determined settings, and social contexts using several time periods which are elaborated upon formally in terms of a life-likeness accentuated by the *in media res* technique. "These add to the *tranche de vie* effect, the impression that we, the readers, overhear the conversation of individuals who did already exist before we started to listen to them, and whose life will continue afterwards, like our own. Interaction with the environment, people or incidents intruding upon character's consciousness and reflected in his utterance, may be added under this heading." (26) After the Minister's speech, the moment of the ceremonial pulling of the power-switch transforms literally the perspective and scale, presaging other transformations.

> It is startling how light can shorten distance. The Rest House – now a grid of hard white with a diadem of coloured lamps – has leapt towards the townspeople. Every face at the window of the inner room is distinct. Every word is clear. Even the far fields have closed in, defined by the stipples of illumination at the school, the hospital, the police station, and on Nepruolo land. The town has shrunk. Only the sky and dawn seem more distant. (134)

The party is a site of sexual intrigue as the Minister flirts with the policeman's wife, but its climax comes as the fan accelerates until its disintegrates, showering the room and guests with debris, mirroring the teacher's tale. The Minister and the policeman's wife clutch each other below its centre point for safety, but their fate is ambiguous. There are subsequently several plot reversals. Awni has become a shopkeeper and his Rest House has been displaced by the Huntsman Hotel, but it is the schoolteacher who has adopted a scientific view, perched in its bar. The story concludes on an ambivalent note, a bifurcation representing both the future and the past in conflict.

> 'The fan was too large and wilful. It ran too fast.' A saucer turns precariously on the teacher's finger. 'That little Rest House could not take the pressure. The fan disintegrated at speed, like a meteorite.'
> Visitors from the city see the logic of this – but the townspeople, avoiding those places where electricity is installed, cannot accept so prosaic an explanation. (138)

Again, there is not only the collision of two worlds, but also a repetitious pattern of movement and detail, the fan invoking the spinning disc. However, the meaning, viewpoint and overall register are ambiguous. Certainly, both books considered in this chapter exemplify the kind of notion of ambiguity and readerly possibilities that Crace sees as central to his work, an idea he clarifies.

> In larger terms something has got to be happening on the page with the meaning of the thing, the thesis of the thing, a massive series of constructed ambiguities which the readers have got to mix in their mind's eye. One of the chief ambiguities in my novels is this idea that I take an idea which is old and set it up against another which is new. The clash of the old and the new. The past versus the future. The idea that something new worth having is the loss of something old worth keeping.³

Of course, in one sense Crace toys with his readers, encouraging them to think laterally beyond the constraint of an immediacy of reality. This applies to the setting much as Judy Cooke in *Jim Crace* (1992) tentatively realizes in reviewing this first collection: "Is the location Latin American? Or African? The events challenge, and elude, interpretation." As Gerard Woodward comments in 'His Curse Is to Impregnate Every Woman He Sleeps With: Review of *Six* by Jim Crace,' (2003) "Craceland, however, is not so much invented as unspecified. It is an amalgam of domestic and foreign vistas that obey the laws of physics. It has gravity. Like Nabokov's Antiterra, or Kafka's America, it is at once recognisably familiar and confusingly strange." (13) As J. Hillis Miller posits in *Tropes, Parables, Performatives: Essays on Twentieth-Century Literature* (1990): "A parabolic narrative is . . . in some way governed, at its origin and its end, by the infinitely distant and invisible, by something that transcends altogether direct presentation. The correspondence between what is given in parable – the 'realistic' story represented in a literal language – and its meaning is more indirect than is the case, for example, in 'symbolic expression.'" (136) Crace's mythopoeic and parabolic storytelling has its own power to suggest a deconstruction of the causalities underlying a set of relations that lie in a fact, an event or an object. Each object extends beyond the co-ordinates of facticity and becomes redolent of a broader range of contexts and understandings. The parabolic meaning in "Electricity" is that the schoolteacher's hometown will 'disappear,' potentially its world so transformed as to become unrecognizable, its rhythm and pattern accelerated so much that its traditional forms will shatter, like the fan and the electricity disc.

The narrative and parabolic possibilities in 'Talking Skull' emerge partly through its structure and its layering. Lowdo, the narrator, is a country-born student of biology, an only child, who mixes with friends whose parents are rich and influential. Initially it is a hypothesizing address to his absent friends as he leaves the city to return home for the vacation. He imagines their response to the secret of his origins.

> I love so much to meet your fathers. They are unhurried. They are gently inquisitive. 'Do I detect a forest accent, Lowdo?' they ask me. 'What are your family? Timber or farming? Who is your father? How many men does he employ? How many acres?' We sit and contrive between us answers, which invent a wide flat valley, a leisurely shoulder-deep river, a contented village of a thousand compounds ... From the airstrip a modest Cessna takes off for supplies. A pretty maid serves iced mint-water and honey cake. In the paddock my mother and sister canter on thoroughbreds. (4–5)

The suggested intersubjective complicity in such lies is a Cracean touch, the implication being that the individual always creates certain deceptions as a social and narrative response, as readers also do in expanding the fictional world. Also the unconscious is at work. Lowdo's fantasy redresses certain aspects lacking in his life. He creates a mother despite his own mother's death, and a sibling. Not only does he socialize himself within his daydream, but also he challenges any closeness or debt to his father, expressing his oedipal response to the paternal negated by the lack of the maternal. The adept reader may observe a subtextual inference that this process of elaboration is similar to Crace's own fictionalizing, but the effect is not a vertiginous postmodernism, a reflexivity undercutting both reality and fiction, but an emphasis on the narrative instinct Crace insists subtends all balanced individuals. As he says:

> Human beings are narrative animals and even if you took away the formal activity of novel writing – in fact novel writing is very, very recent, but humankind's storytelling is not very recent – you would be able to establish very quickly that narrative is the central socializing aspect of humankind, written, read or whatever. In other words when we form relationships we need to be able to deliver anecdotes.[4]

Such is Lowdo's ability and innate propensity, drawn despite his reluctance almost instinctually, as the story makes evident, from the storytelling tradition of his origins rather than his scientific training, from a tradition so embedded that he evokes listeners even in their absence. He proceeds to confess his deceptions to a hypothetical audience of friends, conveying his embarrassment at his family's centuries-old trade, the sale of milk from freemartins to aid fertility. He admits changing from city clothes to a country smock, proceeding on a mule from the Rest House, adding: "The pretty maid I have described to your father's is not a complete concoction. She serves at the Rest House and sleeps with the lorry driver." (6) The student's reticence dissolves with his confirmation of his concealed origins. Paradoxically the villagers near his father's land are fascinated by his urban student life, highlighting contrasts traditionally explored by the pastoral. "They want to know about life in the city. I describe domestic refrigerators and air-conditioned stores, traffic and cinemas, tinned food and night clubs, golf courses and elevators. I offer American filter cigarettes. All – from the boy to the grandmother – accept and puff on them studiously." (8) And naturally, this reconfirms his narrative instinct, and the subsequent action of one of the villagers reconfirms the other family tradition. The old woman takes him to a freemartin which is described in terms of its grotesque body:

> She leads me out of the compound to a shed well away from the house and pulls back the leather from the door. The young heifer is brought into the open. I kneel to examine her. Her genitals are badly malformed, her vagina wide and exposed with an enlarged clitoris and a stringy tuft of vulval hair. Her udders are underdeveloped. A fold of skin – a rudimentary penis – runs from her udders to her naval. She is a freemartin, the malformed, cursed, and sexually disruptive twin of a bull calf. She is the warped demon of fertility. I tie her lead to the saddle of the warped demon of fertility. I tie her lead to the saddle of the mule (she tries to mount him, to excite him) and set off for my father's compound and his herd of ninety freemartins. (9)

The sexual ambivalence of the creatures reflects Lowdo's own concern over his status in the two worlds that he inhabits, rational urban and superstitious pastoral, and suggests the different concepts that dominate each one. Lowdo's training cannot suppress the emergence of the notion of a 'demonic' quality, as if the superstition he rejects cannot be abandoned completely. Following tradition his father is offered such cows by local villagers so famed are the effects of his product. Lowdo contrasts his own scientific knowledge and view of the world with the implied ignorance on the part of his illiterate father who admits openly to being uneducated. The father appeals to a different way of assessing the world citing the observed outcomes of his medication to encourage his customers. According to Lowdo's view,

"My father touched his chest at the spot where his unscientific prejudices imagine his heart to be located and gives thanks. He walks forward to exchange the money for jars of grey milk." (12) They argue as Lowdo attempts to dispel the notion of the "'strange or magical or ill-omened about these cows,'" (10) insisting on the biological explanation.

His father's response is to relate the story of the talking skull. Their narrative abilities link the son and the father, the latter compulsive although unoriginal and formulaic. Nevertheless his efforts are filtered through his offspring's hostile account. "It is a folk-tale so familiar to every schoolchild in every continent that even hard-pressed teachers no longer tell it. But the man inhabits a less complicated universe than the schoolroom. He is committed to his tale. Nothing can stop him now." (13) The tale within a tale is very clearly intended to serve as a parable for his son, and by implication so should Crace's story for his reader. As V. George Shillington comments in 'Engaging with Parables,' (1997) allegorical elements are intertwined in the parabolic structure (6); furthermore: "Parables give a sense of direction without a detailed map. They create a different world from the accepted world, a tantalizing new world not unlike the old world, yet radically unlike it . . . Four words in particular in this definition capture the genius of the 'parable' form of communication in the speech of Jesus: metaphor, arresting, strangeness, and tease." (15) Crace's own technique derives from such cultural precursors, as inferentially Lowdo draws upon traditional structures to layer his own tale. For as Shillington insists, narrative plot does not simply lead to the "moral of the story" (16) but is "polyvalent" and is open-ended and without a single effect (17). Originality is irrelevant to parable and its characteristics subtend both Lowdo's and his father's performativity, linking them, especially as the structure of both their stories is hinged upon reversals with comedic elements, significantly so as John Dominic Crossan explains in *Raid on the Articulate: Comic Eschatology in Jesus and Borges* (1976):

> The term *parable*, then, should be used technically and specifically, from ancient to contemporary example, for *paradoxes formed into story by effecting single or double reversals of the audience's most profound expectations*. The structure of parable is a deliberate but comic reversal of the expected story. It is not a literal reversal . . . It lays bare the relativity of plot, of any plot, and because it is paradoxical it also precludes the possibility of having its own plot taken literally or absolutely. (98)

In this light, consider the essential features and details of Lowdo's father's tale. A young man drawn to the city claims to his family, and sweetheart, to have found enlightenment there. They insist all wisdoms are old. He tells of finding an old skull hidden in bushes which admits that talking brought it to that state. For a storyteller to centre a tale on the abjuration of the act of talking is to be already paradoxically inclined. The young man returns to the village to talk of his "marvel" and is rejected by both the villagers and his family. "But the young man was insistent. What did they know about the big, wide world? He'd show them up for what they were! Ignorant bumpkins. He'd bring the skull to the village. Then they would eat their words." (14) On rediscovering the skull it is silent and without support he becomes a crazy stranger talking to the bones until he dies:

> 'Dropping to the ground next to the old human skull. Now, at last, it opened its yellow jaws and asked, "What brought you here?" What do you suppose the young man's corpse replied?'
> 'Chatter,' says my father.
> ' "Talking brought me here",' I recite dutifully. (14–15)

The parabolic meaning suggests first one should neither abandon one's origins, nor forget those who are in support of one's development. Second, ties of loyalty and a sense of intuitive scepticism override the rational, the chattering explanation of aspects of the world beyond words. The point of comparison is emphasized when the father and his old friend, visiting to acquire freemartin milk, respond to the son's questioning by likening him to the dead skull.

The narrative appears to diverge tangentially. The wider world intrudes. Lowdo's secret is revealed when a Swedish television documentary-maker arrives. "She is, she says, interested in living folklore." (17) Significantly the team arrives by helicopter, disturbing the natural order, agitating the air and disturbing not only the community, but the foxes, owls and night owls, a peculiarly English selection of creatures. The documentary gives Lowdo and his father a degree of fame and their trade becomes a *cause célèbre*, the subject of public debate. It ends Lowdo's denial of his origins and his inheritance, if not his uneasiness as to the spurious nature of his father's trade. Back in the city, the father of one of his friends believes Lowdo's attitude is misguided, advising him to value his current lifestyle and its benefits such as jackets and expensive jewellery. He analyses in effect the commodity fetishisms, surplus value and capital accumulation subtending capitalism:

'You want to be a city boy with an office, a bank account, and a Peugeot. You admire scientific curiosity, business initiative, modern industriousness. But all our business fortunes are based as much as yours on superstition. What is superstition but misdirected reverence? Your clients overvalue bogus milk. Ours overvalue transistors, motor cars, fashionable clothes, travel. This is the key to business. Unearth what is overvalued, amass it, and sell at inflated prices. Your forefathers were the first of the modern businessmen. They grasped this basic principle of trade.' (21)

Lowdo's dream towards the story's end is of modernizing his father's trade, the fusion of such belief and profit with a pristine commercial process. But visiting his father at "the Harvest Vacation" (23) increasingly he is referred to as the 'Talking Skull' and his father seems to strengthen and age less. Enigmatically the tale ends like some perverse fairy story. "Has he grown a little taller, even? He has no grey hairs. His back is square and straight. His teeth and eyesight have not deteriorated. I fancy that he fears his heirs and has determined to live forever." (23) The fanciful contests the scientificity of Lowdo's beliefs, having to even contemplate the very impossibility of the reversal of aging. Certainly it is as if his very self-confidence ebbs in the rational and scientific, ineffably faced with the inexplicable, another Cracean device.

Another enigmatic story follows, offering tragicomic possibilities, with its underlying theme of family ties and their failings. "The World with One Eye Shut" is narrated by a young male prisoner, a legal clerk, arrested some time before. In retrospective sections recalled from his cell we find that in a bar he has criticized the totalitarian state after a young soldier has flirted with his mentally challenged sister, Freti, and taken her off for seduction. After their departure the clerk is bullied by other soldiers and responds with a drunken bravado that seems meaningless, but is portentous. "'Protect us from the despots who tyrannise our sisters and make recompense with beer.' There was no laughter now, except my own. People turned inwards." (32) Ironically it is the seducer, Corporal Beyat, an unremarkable country boy, who guards him in the barracks, a symmetrical and ironic Cracean gesture. His arrest is bathetic,

> A car door had swung open as I was walking from the market with a newspaper and a bag of manac beans. They were expert at abduction. I was pulled onto the back seat and the car was in motion before I had a chance to cry out for help to the old men who sat in the shade of the

porches and watched the traffic pass. The beans spilled on to the floor and cushions as expert blows to the chin, hardly hurting, kept me dazed and silent as we drove out of our gaunt and pungent streets to the wide catulpa'd avenues and to my cell. (33)

There is no suspense, simply a retrospective account which mirrors his generally muted and dazed response to life, an underlying fatalism, as if the cell were his predestined fate. The invented elements and words, "manac" beans and "catulpa'd" imply an exoticism of sorts, an otherness. One detail of the young clerk's imprisonment becomes crucial to the his perception of his situation and greatly shapes the story. By pressing against the cell wall he obtains "a view of the outside world, the medley, careless, trading town from which they have removed me." (27) His restricted vision allows a view that includes the women who gather outside the barracks, apparently including Freti, protesting for their missing male relatives in a manner reminiscent of South American dictatorships. Ironically Freti is there to glimpse Beyat. The clerk spies Beyat going off duty and listens to the rumours of the prisoners, fearful of "the kitchen" where inmates are purportedly tortured. He hopes naively that Beyat might mention him to his sister. A voyeuristic sense pervades the narrative, removing him doubly from the world.

At the suggestion of other prisoners, but not knowing whom to trust, he places his hopes in passing his name to the women so a lawyer might be alerted, attempting to persuade Beyat to convey a message to Freti. Ironically the clerk's confidences to his fellow inmates are betrayed, troubling Beyat because his Captain has heard the rumour that a soldier has contact with a prisoner's sister. Hence he agrees to a message that appears designed to shut her up, while alerting family and friends of the prisoner's plight. The intricacies of the minutiae of the plot offer an insight into the conspiratorial world of oppressive incarceration, and of the paranoia of repressive regimes. Despite its delivery, the message is found and literally stuffed into the prisoner's throat by the Captain, almost killing him. His frantic struggles to expel the obstruction result in a final desperate burst of strength and energy. He shatters a window attracting the women with his cries.

> I pushed my head and shoulders out and screamed at all the people. The air, the voice, the paper, the pressure of the window frame upon my chest, the consternation of my lungs, conspired to produce a sound of

such velocity and volume that the letter to my sister shot out into the air high above the yard, heavy with saliva, pink with blood, and bounced far beyond the puddles of shattered glass. (43)

The naivety of the clerk makes his plight, although horrific, full of understated and yet layered ironies, a naïf in a nightmare. Rushing forward the women's noise stifles his cries to his sister, who ironically holds back, as witless as Beyat's description of her until she calls out, but Crace ends on a moment of enigmatic irony, a poignant note of resignation. "Whose name I cannot say. There was too much passion, and too much noise, and I am far too distant from the gate." (44) The reader is left to imagine and fear the worst.

Irony and family ties are central to "On Heat," the fourth story, in which there are three time periods (and these represent overlapping phases of memory and experience, a recurrent Cracean device), one of which precedes the birth of the narrator who is the spinster daughter of a Professor Zoea, a specialist in Natural Science who died in 1940. Arthur Schopenhauer in *Parerga and Paralipomena, Short Philosophical Essays: Volume Two* (2000) says, "the intellect does not constitute our original and true inner nature," (47) which observation summarizes the crux of Crace's story on several levels. The seventy-two-year-old daughter relates first her initial memory which is the second period chronologically, recollecting a moment in the 1920s when as a child she assisted her father's fieldwork on a solstice beach collecting tiger crabs. She refers to a photograph in the second edition of her father's monograph, *The Secret Life of a Tiger Crab*, a work concentrating on the mechanism which results in its mating on a single day, where she can be seen "standing at father's side – an awkward, bony twelve-year-old in a torn and spermy dress," (68) after collecting swabs of sperm for her father with her siblings. The procreative urge and a sense of Darwinist selection define the images.

Her recollections are of a third period in 1986, initially tending her aging mother with her sisters after being called by the doctor, and left behind to piece together the implications of her mother's earlier frank conversations with her offspring by which time she cannot recall them. The details are redolent of an earlier age, the father's plate camera, of his willingness to dissect a jungle women's corpse in his quest for knowledge, and the automatic deference to him of his young bride.

The daughter also weaves her tale from elements of her mother's sick-bed confessions, "the cantankerous memories of a nonagenarian," (87) which suggest the mother fell out of love with her husband,

and from details drawn from the daughter's own research from her father's photographs, letters and archive, which reconstruct the past. In one suggestive photograph her parents are surrounded by pregnant forest women labelled by the father with the pun, "All Pregnant and Correct." (69–70) His levity dehumanizes the women and conceals his obsession for control by ordering or notating. Both the focus of enquiry and the implied suggestion of a weakness or subordination to either primordial urges or scientific processes are implicitly directed towards women. The professor represents the intellectual faculty, suppressing his lust for his new bride as determinedly (and yet unsuccessfully) as he can.

What compels the daughter is not immediately evident, except to the close reader. She tells next of the second period around 1914, reporting her mother's account of her father's sexual ardour after their marriage, and of their earlier fieldwork in the forest after the professor encountered a forest tribe who procreate collectively and whose pregnancies are as synchronized as menstruation. She describes a young forest girl, 'Puppy,' who follows the couple back to the city and becomes both a servant and the subject of the professor's scientific attention. Informed and guided by a trapper, who "claimed to understand a little 'forest', a tongue so labio-plosive that linguists titled it vapid-vadap," (72) the professor decides to spend an extra six weeks monitoring the tribal pregnancies, while the wife teaches Puppy and the wife recalls, "'I taught her cat's cradle and hopscotch. It was foolish, perhaps. But she was sweet – an awkward, bony little thing – and I was bored beyond endurance.'" (73) The repetition of "awkward, bony" is a textual clue as to the spinster daughter's quest in retracing the experiments her father conducted on Puppy and the mother to chart menstrual and other synchronicity.

In the forest the natural order has produced death as well as life. Crace details the phantom and ritual pregnancies of the forest men, mimicking birth with "stones and dolls," in which the professor sees simply a social, anthropologically observed purpose. As Meletinsky observes: "The structure of mythological thought transforms all reality into metaphor. It is only art, according to Cassirer, that resolves the contradiction between image and meaning, since only in art is the image accepted for what it is." (35–6) This artistic view or impulse, the professor lacks. His wife is sceptical of his view, perceiving his regulatory, controlling aspects, and she recalls the event when he was ready but unwelcome with,

'His callipers, camera and notebook . . . The births themselves seemed relatively easy; labour was short – as if the stones and dolls now produced by their men had freed the women from a punishing confinement. Or so your father said . . .
For every bereaved mother there was an orphan child. 'Left to its own devices, nature is cruel but tidy,' my father noted. (75–6)

Both his faith in recording nature as if dispassionately and the tribal male ceremony are juxtaposed by the stillborn, the fatal bleeding, pain and slow death for some of the women, and his inaction towards such suffering is not made any more acceptable by his final comment above concerning what he sees as an ordering principle found within a poignant balance of nature, where he implies an almost Darwinian principle governing their pain and tragic demise.

This tale involves recurrent Cracean themes: the juxtaposition of nature and scientific concerns, their opposing accounts of the world, the parent–child relation implied in the narrative responses of the tale-telling children, and the power of instinct and humankind's capacity to draw upon innate characteristics to shape life. The development of ideas, scenes, details, time sequences and nuances offers an example of Crace's growing confidence. Initially the professor sees human sexuality as unlike that of animals, a matter of civilized choice (71), and is fascinated by the more primeval possibilities, but also wishes to conceal his research for fear of rivals and notoriety. Before concerning itself with the outcome of his return the narrative turns briefly to the mother in the present,

> My mother slept, while my sisters and I, made self-conscious and dutiful by her illness (her madness) aired and tidied the house, polished the cluttered sapwood tables of the reception rooms, threw out old papers, dry plants and bad food. And (as if she was already a corpse) we opened her unanswered mail, checked the contents of the family box which she kept beneath the bed, and leafed through the albums of cards and photographs. (82)

Beyond the literal facts, strong underlying aspects include families, secrets and parental death. The daughters discover an unseen photograph which includes the thirteen-year-old Puppy, dressed as a maid. In contrast to her smile her father's notes convey a listlessness in charts compiled from daily tests and swabs from both his wife and Puppy, and in what the daughter hypothesizes as a bizarre household ritual.

> His daily readings measured the presence and absence of vaginal acids secreted during ovulation and that period of sexual excitement titled estrus amongst the lower mammals. The first column – Poppy's? – recorded unbroken torpor. The second – my mother's? – showed a conventional monthly cycle, the acids increasing towards the middle of the cycle and then decreasing. (84)

The two charts appear to synchronize, although he is apparently frustrated according to his wife's recollection by her use of douches of potash soap, but Puppy's responds after fourteen months by achieving sexual readiness matched only by his own "unusual turbulence, his breathlessness, his solicitude as he sat her at the chair of his desk and drew from its drawer his thermometer and his stethoscope and his speculum." (86) The details are suggestive, but as the daughter records according to the archive and journals the experiment seems unfinished, the recording of evidence 'thin' and later the disappearance of the forest settlement. His note of his plan to take his wife and three girls to the coast, the site of the daughter's initial 'spermy' memory, leads her to reconsider the image of herself, 'thin and dry' in the photograph on the beach, contrasting her broad, tall, heavy-hipped mother and siblings. The realization sends her back to the photograph of the maid and her father's charts whose dates the daughter matches with her own birth, imagining the natural sexual regularity of the forest and the final image of "the closing of a study door?" (89) This is a manner of epiphany, a realization of self which otherwise would have been denied her without her mother's aberrational behaviour. Her previous lack of personal understanding is significant in that the facts have been denied her, but she has understood the truth intuitively. As Schopenhauer says, practical or technical knowledge is insufficient, and,

> To understand anything really and truly, it is necessary for us to grasp it *in intuitive perception*, to receive a clear picture of it, if possible from reality itself, but otherwise by means of the imagination. Even what is too great or too complicated to be taken in at a glance, must be conjured up in our minds through intuitive perception . . . But what does not even admit of this, must be made clear at any rate by an attempt at a picture and simile from the intuitive perception that is so very much the basis of our knowledge. (48)

The humour and ironies have led to a poignant moment, but also a subtext of the hubris of science or the scientist when pitted against nature, given human's own complicity with that which it seeks to interrogate, exteriorize and quantify. The professor has been compelled by instinct and sexual arousal, and his 'inner nature,' just as much as the forest tribe, all of them driven, both the men as much as the women. As James Hamilton-Pearson says in 'Voyages Out,' (1996) "The story is a wonderfully truthful account of the intersection of private pathology with Western natural science, and Crace's strength is that he knows not to moralize. There is no need to contrive denunciations." (38) Clearly the tensions in the tale are sufficient.

'Cross-Country,' the third story, is lighter and yet ironic, full of contrasting self-images and desires. It is more positive about the western subject. This reworking of the fable of the hare and the tortoise exemplifies Crace's debt to archetypes and traditional tales. Eddy Rivette a Canadian volunteer teacher runs daily along a path winding through the valley in a remote area accessible only on horseback. He achieves a curious fame which leads to a local rival 'Isra-kone feeling displaced. 'Isra, a famed horseman, is the favourite of the brotherhood, a group of older men, the repository of traditional values and of the Siddilic language. They are hostile to other young men who have acquired Western ways, such as the mayor's son after his travels to England and Italy.

'Isra's horseriding skills saved the mayor when 'Isra rode to fetch assistance when their leader suffered a heart attack. The episode has become part of the mythology of the place, and yet has been undercut since the mayor had to be airlifted by helicopter and saved by modern medicine. "Four foreign doctors had slaved to quiet his heart and keep the mayorship with this fearful old man and away from the wild ideas of his wild college son. And 'Isra had returned to tell of his ride and that the chief would be well. Even the smallest children will say it. 'Isra-kone is the finest horseman in the valley." (51) The attention paid to the jogging teacher forces 'Isra to spread word of a challenge to him, ironically his opponent the last to hear of this "Great Race" where on horseback 'Isra will compete with the runner. During the race, too superstitious to look back, 'Isra does not know that the teacher deviates from his usual route which would have resulted inevitably in the teacher losing. Rather the runner takes the longer valley route to avoid the treacherous descents. Both are exhausted, but the unnerved horse falls upon 'Isra, and his shame is complete. This story combines the elements of the African tale Crace had encountered and recognized in his travels, fleshing out the details with a poignancy and juxtaposition of elements, such as the two men and the horse at the race's end. "Not a whinny from her, too tired and breathless. Not a cry from 'Isra, too shamed already. One small gasp from the teacher, a cry of victory suppressed through experience until the line was crossed. A great whoop from the villagers, from the cackle of Loti to the yelp of the schoolchildren, as the winner of the race crossed the line of shadow marked at the side of the store by a low and sinking sun." (62–3)

'Sins and Virtues,' the fifth story, is the first-person narrative of an old calligrapher who possessed the traditional franchise to inscribe people's Sins and Virtues – capitalized throughout the tale to stress the generic, archetypal qualities – which are sealed in a bamboo tube and ritually burnt at death. This is a tradition that draws upon the mythical world that is fading. The calligrapher recalls adapting to changing times, the business initially overshadowed by religiosity, but later producing shop-fronts, parchments, posters and letterheads. Having made his fortune he has left his marketplace stall and in semi-retirement ponders his longevity, symbolized by the acacia planted at his birth by uncles in their village which is finally almost leafless, "Only one branch draws sap. The rest is the home of ants." (94) He revisits the acacia every birthday. The image is one of decay. His pride in his past achievements contrasts with his current condition: "I am the last and certainly the most distinguished of calligraphers in the old Siddilic script but I am done with weaving and ennobling letters, of chasing their edges into the corner of the page. I am a doodler." (95) There is an avoidance and complacency in the acceptance of the calligrapher that reminds one of Ricoeur's reading in *Figuring the Sacred* of the tone and quotidian emphasis of *Ecclesiastes*, most especially his self-conscious air of wisdom and modestly, together with his plain living mostly outside the flow of the world:

> The everyday of Qohheleth [*Ecclesiastes*] is the everyday as rediscovered by someone who has looked death in the face and renounced knowing. It is the everyday under the sign of not knowing. Made modest, divested of its pomp, wisdom is then tempted to an excess of humility. The wise person who does not know feels discharged of the responsibility of carrying history on his or her shoulders. Hence that person is tempted to reduce the space of life to an everyday round deprived of historicity: 'There is nothing new under the sun.' (178)

The calligrapher has no other responsibility than to himself; and one suspects that his 'inner meanings' are less important than the routine of work and meals, changing of clothes, working only "three shifts from habit, from boredom and to exercise the arthritis in my hands. My mind is elsewhere, searching out material for my last work, to be burned at my funeral." (95) His is a ritualistic, relatively decontextualized world, with its quasi-mythic routine. Ricoeur describes what constitutes the overall mood of the calligrapher's voice, but it is disturbed by other more dynamic and intrusive forces, his habitual nonchalance shaken by events. Modernity in the guise of the western market intrudes, first simply with the collectors' mania for buying shop-fronts which has produced numerous forgeries, and second with the visit by a head of protocol followed by his government minister to force the calligrapher to produce "'Canvases decorated in Siddilic script. Ornamental pieces, works of art, not shop signs and the like.'" (100) Two central contexts of different chronological perspectives are essential to the story. The calligrapher's transition, a slow, deathly time, his literal move from active life towards death, collides with the urgency of modernity, the insistence of a public determination of meaning defined solely by present needs. A comic parable emerges much as Crossan describes since "Parable is paradox formed into story." (93) Using Crossan's chronological distinctions, the individual and private time – what the doodling protagonist refers to as his "inner meanings" (95) – finds itself subsumed and overwhelmed first by what Crossan calls *experiential* time, in Crace the immanence of the calligrapher's death and his torpor, and second by epochal or public time, represented by the market created by modernity and more particularly the corrupt, bullying and commercialized political process (134). The epoch of Siddilic and its mythic meaning seems anachronistic and uncertain, and clearly although *sidereal time* (that established by clocks, calendars) has become less relevant to the calligrapher, impending experiential and sidereal times are paradoxically conjoined so as to produce his apparent equilibrium, and impel him to retrace his past and the meaning of first his work, explicitly, and second his life, implicitly. In this he confronts a broader problem that is perhaps left unanswered, enigmatically balanced. As Crossan says:

> There is also the more problematic phenomenon of epochal time. How are the empty slots of sidereal time filled and fulfilled on levels that go beyond simple individual preoccupations. And what are those levels? ... Are these epochs of shared and communal fulfillment *disunited* and without mutual connection or are they somehow *united* each with the other in some overarching design. (134)

It is his own Sins and Virtues that have preoccupied the calligrapher in his previously undisturbed dotage, and he is unconcerned that Duni, the ironmonger, has profited from his shop sign, watching the dismantlement helped by his servant, Sabino, with both amazement and equanimity.

> In the market place, as in Chicago, the ancient characters of Siddilic have lost their meaning. The only care the forgers take is with my signature and, because their hands are young, these signatures are now better than my own.
>
> Sabino is growing rich on pickings from my wastebasket. Dollars cannot tell doodles from the name of God. (97)

The threat of the Minster's Head of protocol and that of the minister himself contrast with the calligrapher's studied indifference. His reflections are even disturbed on a visit to his uncles' acacia. The air-conditioned ministerial car put at his disposal symbolizes his submission to authority and its blandishments. The tree represents him as not impervious to the modern world, but as barely alive, a dying and fading symbol of traditional ways. He ties a strip of cloth to the tree as on every birthday until it:

> was now a ragamuffin of flapping tatters, from white to grey to nearly black. There was more linen than leaf. In the old days I came by donkey and then later by bus and now by air-conditioned limousine. In the distance, beyond the walls of the acacia wood, I could hear the stereo cassette of my driver and the shrieks of the children. A touch of reality amongst the reveries. (102)

This practice is part of a totemic tradition, part of a mythopoeic world, where, as Meletinsky says, "By attempting to explain the nature of man and the universe, myth reinforces the status quo. One of the ways this is accomplished is by enacting myth in rituals that are continually repeated." (156) The remnants of this world seem likely to finish with the calligrapher. The dreamlike condition of continuity with the past and the spiritual is marginalized and even in prayer his celibacy, required by custom of his calling, seems to offer his only true reward which is expressed in his wish for a 'Lily Death,' an image implying a gregarious afterlife like that of the wider world, for the plant like the community sends shoots among its own kind that will outlive it. This is despite his solitariness in life which as he ruminates more reflects, in their tradition, a 'Moon Death,' since "The moon is solitary and childless. It has no offshoots. But when it dies, it rises to live again. I had lived a moon life. Was I to die and rise again? Was the reward of solitude on earth immortality of some kind?" (103) Another underlying conflict is the pastoral tradition, an intrinsic conflict between the life of the town and of the country, and as Kegel-Brinkgreve says, in that tradition nostalgia and a sense of loss generally play their part in the world-view (136–9). The calligrapher's prayers combine a sense of loss, regretting missed opportunities, and hints of alternate pathways. The very immanence of the calligrapher's death, which haunts the text, and the dying tree both represent what Bruno Damiani and Barbara Mujica describe in *Et in Arcadia Ego: Essays on Death in the Pastoral Novel* (1990) as part of the pastoral tradition's view of the country life, where "Death often serves the purposes of providence, for awareness of their own mortality returns to reason some of those characters who have gone astray. " (160) Unable to work according to his instructions, the head of protocol first threatens the calligrapher, demonstrating his cruelty with cigarette burns on his servant's head, and second tosses him a fortune in notes, but still the old man dreams of young women. These threats of sudden death do affect the calligrapher, who begins to meditate on matters more metaphysical and spiritual than in the past.

He cannot replicate his past talents, but a Syrian bar owner recounts a failed attempt to sell without export licenses forgeries of the calligrapher's work, when both he and his American purchaser were threatened and insulted. After the calligrapher dreams of a beautiful woman and his own rebirth as a young man in western clothes, he decides to buy the Syrian's fakes, secretly passing them off as his own. Ironically, the last genuine piece is his Sins and Virtues, "which was intended to be sealed in a tube of bamboo and burned at my funeral, is now to go instead to Vienna, Paris and Chicago," (110–11) and is left unsigned. He balances his Lust with Virginity, Selfishness with Self-Awareness, admits misanthropy, but claims Tolerance, and states, "Talent shares its box with Deceit, the same word in Siddilic for Forgery. 'ALL THIS WORK IS FALSE,' I have written and decorated in gold. Now my sins and virtues are complete." (111) He refuses to tour the world with his art, apparently unworried by questions of authenticity, by claiming infirmity. Ironically he tells the minister that the one unsigned item can be sold cheaply: "'That is good practice in business, too, to have something cheap amongst the more expensive.'" (112) This scene teasingly subverts western values, but undermines his own value system equally. He has encapsulated his life on the parchment's grid, but finally he denies these failings when he leaves his instructions for burial with Duni, hiding behind the customs of their religion to claim, "'My conscience is clean.' The sinlister, I reminded him, must be free from sin. It is the custom and the regulation." (113) He returns to a more primeval, mythic frame of mind, concerning himself with the issue of death as a metaphysical image, exactly where Meletinsky situates it in terms of mythological thought, where "Myth is fundamentally about the transformation of chaos into harmony, and primitive man defines harmony in such a way that it includes all the axiological and ethical aspects of life." (156) Finally, he simply contemplates death and rebirth. He concludes, "I am not interested in letters. The quest for Meaning in Form belongs to an age long past. I often draw a forest of trees, almost bare and leafless, with the moon hovering on the horizon. Is it dawn or dusk? Soon we all shall know." (113)

The final seventh story is described by Crace as different from the others: "It's the one piece I've written that I've done in a complete reverie. All the other pieces were cunningly conceived by me – I don't use the word *cunningly* to polish my own medals as it were – but *consciously* conceived would be a better word. Whereas I was possessed when I wrote 'The Prospect from the Silver Hill'. I'm very fond of the memory of the writing of that piece."[5] Certainly it possesses a hallucinatory quality. It concerns the madness of an employee of a mining concern.

> The company agent – friendless, single, far from home – passed most days alone in a cabin at Ibela-hoy, the Hill Without a Hat. His work was simple. Equipped with a rudimentary knowledge of mineralogy, neat, laborious handwriting, and a skill with ledgers, he had been posted to the high lands to identify the precious metals, the stones, the ores, that (everybody said) were buried there. (141)

The agent suffers from phrenetic insomnia and sleeplessly he invents a family for himself, telling the survey gangs "about the companionable life, which he had concocted in his daydreams." (143) Talking non-stop he antagonizes the men since his voice offers only sadness and failure. His behaviour is bizarre. He daydreams of friends at Ibela-hoy, of finding the "newest mineral in the world," (144) and begins to hug boulders. He attempts to replace drill cores into the earth, seeing in each stone a landscape, planets, continents and other topographical features. As Crace explains, "His condition, of being hollowed out, was actually just mirrored by the condition of the landscape that he himself was required to hollow out."⁶ Remembering his father's death the agent has transposed his trauma and loss into empathy for the stones severed by the gravedigger, tearful at any rupture of the earth. His madness mutates and:

> When at last they left him in peace he turned to the samples on his bench and sorted through them with unbroken attention. A stone of apple-green he removed and walked with it into the valley where in a cave there were lichens of the same colour. A fistful of grit he scattered in the grass so that it fell amongst the leaf joints like sleet. A round stone he placed on the river bed with other round stones. (147)

His reports and samples invoke no interest from the company, even a fragment of low quality platinum or some graphite, so he begins to perceive a different dynamic. "Now he wrapped a piece of damp clay and placed it in a sample bag. Its colours were the colours of pomegranate skins. Its odour was potatoes. He sealed the bag and sent it to the company. Urgent, he wrote on the label. Smell this!" (148) His continued eccentricity alarms them, but it masks his perception of an underlying different order of things, a reversion, for as Meletinsky says:

> There is a kind of feedback between the mythical 'explanation' of the world . . . and its pragmatic function of reinforcing the social and natural order that continually re-establishes universal order. In a word, the power of myth to reconcile chaos with order lies in the properties of the mythological vision of the world – in primitive ontology, in other words – and not in mere repetition of rituals. (157)

The latter is what the calligrapher attempts in 'Sins and Virtues,' his last vision more like the primitive ontology to which the agent returns. In the latter's failure he seeks an ordering principle. In his isolation he has returned to a mythologizing consciousness. He is pursued by the company, after ignoring the discovery of silver, stolen to reunite it with the ice at the top of the mountains, a symbolic fusion. At the end, naked, he escapes, hugging stones, imagining himself at one with the landscape and his imagined family. "He conjured in his dream a world where the rocks were hot and moving, where quakes and volcanoes turned shales to schists, granite to gneiss, limestone to marble, sandstone to quartz, where continents sank and rose like kelp on the tide." (151–2) Finally, ignoring the helicopter and jeepful of men sent to retrieve him, he enters his vision of his family and child, reverting to an earlier principle of understanding. As Meletinsky says, "A few characteristics of mythological thought derive from the fact that primitive peoples were not yet able to differentiate themselves fully from the natural world. By projecting human qualities onto natural objects, they imbued them with life, human form, and passion, will, economic activity, and a social dimension." (152)

Kearns may be correct in concluding that "Crace's stories are delicately inventive elegies for the local, the odd, inefficient, the native as they give way before international junk and its economic and ideological bases." (487) And yet, more than this, *Continent* remains important because it allowed Crace to explore crucial themes and stylistic issues. He admits, "I feel that *Continent* has marked me down for the kind of writer that I subsequently became. I think the main things are there, particularly in the early novels, which are the theme of society at a time of change, a moralistic view of the world, and all presented in prose which is or attempts to be beautiful." He adds: "I remember one of my publishers, Jeff Mulligan, saying that this book will be in print in twenty years' time. It pleased me someone bothered to say that, but I thought frankly that it was a ludicrous prospect. Yet here we are twenty years later and it's still in print throughout the world and that's pleasing."[7]

The Gift of Stones

The Gift of Stones is more conceptually structured than *Continent*, its central premise that a Stone Age community has to respond to both physical and technological challenges, which undermine the community due to its dependence on one economic activity. Set in an unspecified location, seemingly northern European, Crace's novel is more emphatically concerned with landscape, much like 'The Prospect from the Silver Hill.' Although it shares the prehistoric past evoked in the company agent's hallucinations, *The Gift of Stones* has less emphasis on a mythological consciousness, exploring folkloric possibilities of the oral narrative tradition, but as Perry Glasser notes in 'A Stone Age Storyteller Speaks from the Dawn of Narrative Art,' (1989) "Plot isn't what Crace wants us to care about." (6) As Brad Leithauser points out in 'Not Written in Stone' (1989) the language of the villagers is profoundly modern, the narrative deploying "an elevated tone that, in its open artificiality, dismisses as beside the point any reservations we might have about the authenticity of his re-creations." (x3) Leithauser does object that this very grandiloquent tone serves to contrast certain apparent grammatical infelicities so that:

> the book's occasional relaxations of grammar ('My father was the wisest of the two,' 'she was more diligent than me,' 'His arrow was more swift than her') jar the ear. In our loose age, a phrase like 'more swift than her' may not be deemed a solecism, but in the pure linguistic air of Crace's ideal prehistory, it rings troublingly, like the stroke of a cracked mallet. (x3)

The central tenet, of the transition from a flint-based economy to a Bronze Age one, suggests a modern parallel in the pre- and post-Thatcher years. For Crace it loosely serves as an allegory for the traumatic changes endured by his adopted hometown of Birmingham when Thatcher painfully restructured the British economy. He explains its provenance:

> I was at the British Museum with my son, looking at the worked flint heads, some of them incredibly beautiful. I remember saying how lacking in sophistication that world must have been, but I was deceiving myself. Those displayed in front of me were beautifully worked, sometimes brown, sometimes flint grey, sometimes white-flecked. These highly worked arrowheads and scrapers and knives were perfectly symmetrical and done with immense skill. You know any damn fool could make an arrowhead out of metal by pouring some hot metal into a mould and then letting it dry, but to actually find the stone – and I seem to remember in this exhibit there was an example of un-worked flint – and to see the possibility within that flint and then to make a worked flint that would be light enough to fly through the air and kill a man or a pigeon or a deer struck me as exactly the opposite of a lack of sophistication. It was actually evidence of greater sophistication than we have. So that interested me, first of all because there was a metaphor there between the un-worked piece of flint and the worked piece of flint. That's always interesting: the natural world un-worked and worked, and the ability of humankind to make so much of the natural world. The other thing was that this was the post-Thatcher period when Birmingham itself was going through a huge collapse of the one certainty it had enjoyed in the past. You might think we were a bloody awful city, an ugly city with a widely mocked accent, but we always had the certainty of work. Birmingham was the city of a thousand trades. If you wanted to buy anything in metal from a bronze elephant to a teaspoon, it probably came from Birmingham. This gave the city a real sense of pride and

identity. People might laugh at Birmingham, but the world would always want metal bashers. And then what happened? Along came the moment of the Japanese motor car, and metal bashing went somewhere else, so that single certainty was robbed. So at the time of my visit to the British Museum I was wondering how a city that has lost all its pride and self-esteem at being a working city, not a cultural one, would reinvent itself. I remember looking at these beautifully worked stones and being able to imagine the stone-workers saying at the time, 'Well, they might laugh at our village centre, they think we've got a terrible accent, but the world will always want stone-bashers.' I'd then moved along to the next little display case and there was bronze, bronze arrowheads so fine and light that you felt that they could float to the ground like leaves. The spiel is that those two display cases delivered to me the perfect metaphor for Birmingham, reliant on the certainties of industry, having to reinvent itself when overtaken by progress. Because I'm exactly the kind of writer that would not set a novel in Birmingham in the 1970s and have a real family living in Longbridge, because I'm not a realist writer, I needed that kind of gift of the metaphor in order to allow that book to happen.[8]

As Begley says in 'A Pilgrim in Craceland,' "*The Gift of Stones* (1988) is set at a precise historical moment (in the split second before bronze made stone-age weaponry obsolete) but the seaside village he describes could be simply out of time. Change comes suddenly, irrevocably, and the human response to it is captured with wonderfully uncluttered intensity." (231) Crace's world is predicated on a universal quality of trans-historical values, much like Bataille in *The Accursed Share; Vol. II* who insists: "In reality, there is no profound difference between the reactions peculiar to rudimentary civilization and those of advanced civilization." (67) The flint allows Crace to incorporate centrally a functional object, foregrounding the material and external aspects of the world as operating upon humans, representing trans-historically how people humanize themselves from the substance of their unmediated, pre-civilized origins. Humans come from this past as the arrowhead from the flint. With bronze that analogy of man being shaped from nature is disturbed; it suggests the impulses towards modernity, whose detachment Lane sees as embodied in the daughter, in her "increasingly suspicious, questioning perspective." (29) Crace makes the parameters of the community clearly recognizable, running parallel to that of modernity. As Bataille explains in *The Accursed Share; Vol. III*, objects demonstrate a crucial transition from the beginnings when the *object* became detached from an initial inner experience, which at first did not differ from experience that animals apparently have.

The tool, the 'crude flint tool' used by primitive man was undoubtedly the first positing of the object as such. The objective world is given in the practice introduced by the tool. But in this practice man, who makes use of the tool, becomes a tool himself, he becomes an object just as the tool is an object. (213)

The stoneys' world is oppressive and harsh, its ordering principles a kind of stolidity derived from the stone with which the community has affinities. Perhaps this explains or mediates Pei's sense in the *Boston Review* (1989) that "the world it chooses to invent, rather than being 'fresh,' is consistently, aggressively sour." (23) However, the artisanship, the stoneys' very act of grafting, stresses a visceral interconnection with substances and as Leithauser indicates, Crace enhances such relations:

> *The Gift of Stones* displays, for all its brevity, a delight in elaboration. Crace is fond of lists and processes. Since his novel takes place in a prehistoric community – a flourishing village of stoneworkers who live by an unnamed sea – his lists include a good many simple tools and wild plants, and his processes center on the intricate, cumbrous manipulations by which, at the craftsman's anvil, useful designs are released from the raw, chance shapes of nature. A commendable respect and affinity for physical labor radiates from *The Gift of Stones*. (x3)

However, this very labour fails them. Initially at the margins is the storytelling facility of the central characters, the father and daughter, which is ameliorative (or redemptive) when the story and world become interfused, a necessary synthesis since it dissipates this world's dense, stolid facticity, which seems incommensurably unpleasant and threatening. As the daughter reflects, "The paradox is this – we do love lies. The truth is dull and half-asleep. But lies are nimble, spirited, alive. And lying is a craft." (62) And as the father points out, a story told by someone as stolid as Leaf, the most talented stoneworker, is flat and tedious (63). As Gary Krist explains in 'Serendipity' (1990) the father "ease[s] the monotony of the stonecutter's mundane labors. He performs the same role, the author implies, that Crace himself does, providing his fellows with imaginative fictions through which and by which they can live a fuller existence." (659)

The novel opens vividly describing the storyteller's injury. "My father's right arm ended not in a hand but, at the elbow, in a bony swelling. Think of a pollard tree in silhouette." (1) The daughter describes the pus that oozes like semen and recollects his accounts of his severed limb which, less variable than his other accounts, she takes as truth. "It was less fantastic than his other tales and his expression, in its narration, lacked the usual mannerisms of the story-teller, the floating eyebrow, the single, restless hand, the dramatic contours of the voice." (1–2) This sense of narrative form and the fantastical resonate throughout the novel and Crace's work generally. Here it contrasts the bleakness of the environment, but significantly already in both *Continent* and *The Gift of Stones* it does more, since the storytelling extends itself parabolically, and the very act and movement of the story becomes an overarching structural motif in Crace's narratives. As Lane says, "The relationship between the two narrators in *The Gift of Stones* is crucial: it is not a blood relationship as such, although stories bind them; rather the relationship is about the *repetition* of stories." (30) This repetition emphasizes the recurrent universality of storytelling rather than any fundamental *differentia*, and its compulsive quality. The unhealed wound evokes Crace's father and his influence. Crace explains: "If the truth of the matter is told, the book is deeply imbued by the experience of my childhood. Also you have to love landscape, you have to have the natural history background, you have to have been on the left, you have to have been, for some reason or other, hostile to commerce and industry in some respects in order to write that book."[9]

Crace's narrator draws from her father's own words, alternately summarizing and quoting them verbatim, an echo of the past. Lane believes the text

> mediates the storyteller's stories, partly by placing them in quotation marks. This simple act is one of repetition and difference, losing the immediacy (of performance and the social circuit) that Benjamin laments, but also complicating the temporality of narrative (the past is brought into the present, repeated in the present, and repeated as versions, rather than absolutely factual accounts of events). The result is a temporal montage effect. (30)

The daughter recounts her father's tale of the threatening arrival in his childhood of horsemen at their coastal village at dawn demanding flint implements. "He rehearsed for us the scripture of our village –

Continent and *The Gift of Stones*

that we could not be touched because we possessed the gift of stones." (2) This repetition is sterile, with its insistence on an apparently unchanging relation, encouraging them to disregard the sea, encouraging insularity and arrogance.

In contrast the seven-year-old storyteller already exhibits an affinity with the landscape and its littoral nature, but he neglects its warning concerning the horsemen. "He liked the springy, bracken path that led up from the crusty boulders of the shore, with the wind and spray at his back, spitting and whispering, 'Go home to your house and fire. Go home.' So he was in no mood – and of no age – to treat the horsemen with suspicion or to roll into the undergrowth when they called him over to them." (3) He escapes as they try to steal his scallops, and yet his disobedient and dreamy face antagonizes them as he scampers away. One dismounted rider shoots a poisoned arrow into the seven-year-old's arm. Fearful the young boy cuts himself below the wound, thus saving his life and he flees clutching the arrow, which later he would pass like a trophy to his audience. The tension and suspense derived from retelling these events become part of his craft. The narrator's affinity with her father is evident from her report of the story's reception: "Give us the details, we, his audience would say. Tell us once again how your blood flowed like a cliff spring down your arm, into the sling, onto the scallops, how the landscape turned from bracken-brown to red, how the bracts on the under-leaves stuck to the thickening blood as you toppled from the rock." (4) The novel articulates a reflexive sense of narrative, the relationship between the narrator and listener variously multi-layered. As Glasser indicates the father as "primordial storyteller" represents the true artist, transcending the vision of the artisan. (6) Nevertheless, importantly the daughter's scepticism situates him as an unreliable narrator, who remains central to the future and its ambiguities.

Realizing the boy requires an amputation, the villagers choose a stone for Leaf, who is reluctant to perform this act. Finally the horsemen return to trade, unabashed and unashamed. Both the narrative and its sequence of events are replete with paradoxical symmetries. Object, event, action, intention and necessity converge in Cracean fashion, typified in the climax of the novel's first phase. The crux of attention shifts and the villagers circle with a strange fascination those who previously threatened death and are now mollified, their compulsion stronger than their desire to trade:

> Everybody there was drawn towards this knot of men. The villagers were hypnotized, and for a while the trade in borers, burins, sharpeners, harpoons, stone wrist-guards, sickles, fire-flints, sling-stones, scrapers, hand-axes, arrowheads and tangs and barbs came to a pause. Women stopped their basketry. Small boys who fashioned string by rubbing buckleaf fibre on their thighs finished early for the day. The man who sold coloured dyes which came, he said, from snails and molluscs, bark, insects, the waste of certain birds (but which, my father claimed, were lightning dust) ceased for once to sing his wares. (23–4)

The horsemen represent the outside world which the villagers have avoided, turning inward. "My father's ornateness as a story-teller cannot obscure the one plain truth that needs no hawk for decoration – that the village was obsessed with work, with industry, with craft. It made the people purposeful, wealthy, strong. It made them weary too, and a little jealous of the outside world beyond the hill, beyond the warren of mine-shafts, its drifts of unworked flint." (9) Lane compares the relationship of daughter and father to Benjamin's notion of storytelling being superseded by the novel form, but rather the storytelling is extended and problematized. The father's parenthetical comment above concerning lightening dust demonstrates the fabulist instinct of his art, bifurcating towards the absurdity of the imagination, abandoning briefly the everyday and the concrete. This partakes of what Maurice Merleau-Ponty describes in *The Visible and the Invisible* (1968): "*Chiasm*, by which what announces itself to me as being appears in the eyes of the others to be only 'states of consciousness' – But, like the chiasm of the eyes, this one is also what makes us belong to the same world – a world which is not projective, but forms its unity across impossibilities such as that of *my* world and the world of the other." (214–15) Crace's text foregrounds the interconnection of the tangible and visual, and the chiasmic. The transformative power of imagination becomes a central theme, and this capacity allows the father to redirect the villagers, taking them beyond the limits of experience through a wisdom that is not simply contextual. There is something more than Lane's chiasmus – which remains too secular and overly concerned with rhetorical styles – something at least residually transcendent. The very details of the father's narrative engage in the performativity found in parable, which as Miller notes, emerges from an underlying tension originating from its evocation of heavenly parallels that can only exist beyond words:

A true performative brings something, a 'meaning', that has no basis except in words or something about which it is impossible to describe whether or not there is an extralinguistic basis... Secular parable is language thrown out that creates a meaning hovering there in thin air, a meaning based on the language itself and our confidence in it. The categories of truth and falsehood, knowledge and ignorance, do not properly apply to it. (139)

Craceland embraces such dualities and contradictions thematically, its irrealist, fabulist tendency challenging rationality, extending the structure and referential grid of language. As Bataille says in *The Accursed Share; Vol. II*, "Intellect fails, in fact, in that with its first impulse it *abstracts*, separating the objects of reflection from the concrete totality of the real." (112) Although storytelling relates to the actual, it alchemizes the mundane, coherent, apparently self-evident perceptions. Crace's objectivity indicates an underlying transcendent possibility.

Reluctant anticipation of the amputation is used to create dramatic expectation, resolved ironically when the horsemen bring the skills necessary to operate while using a tool exemplifying the fine artisanship of the stoneys. Stunning the boy through drink and a mallet blow upon his chin, the bowman who has injured the boy performs this act. Subsequently his childhood is unpropitious since he is functionally useless, unable to dig for, carry or work the flint. "So I grew up like some wild plant, ragged, unattended, not-much-use." (34) After these events the stoneys withdraw again, neglecting the landscape that will seduce the boy.

Eight years later, an epiphany occurs when at the end of summer the boy chases a boat on the horizon. "'That ship would soon be out of sight. Unless, of course, I followed it. Why shouldn't I? I had no stones. I simply filled my chest with air and took off down the coast.'" (37) He embarks upon an adventure along unknown coastal paths, a littoral expedition, tracing the edge of his world until the landscape changes as does his own nature. For Crace landscape represents an opportunity for the reorientation of human wonderment of the world. "The New Age, atheistic post-Darwinists are saying the narratives of landscape are stronger and more powerful and more awe-inspiring than the narratives of creationism. And in doing so they're kind of imbuing the natural world with a mysticism and with a spirituality. That's very much what I do, I think. That's so different from my father's level of atheism, which was political atheism."[10] This sense is tentative in *The Gift of Stones*, but an awareness of the potential of the natural world subtends the narrative, focused upon apparently unprepossessing objects. The crumbling red stone he finds while sheltering from the rain symbolizes the difference not just of the terrain, but the horizon of an alternative experience, one challenging the stolidity of his familiar world:

> 'I had encountered there a rock unknown to all my neighbours. A stone so soft – I soon would learn – that the sea could break it. A stone so soft it couldn't crack a skull. Was this some illness, some disease? Imagine if the illness spread, if it made its way along the coast to infiltrate the flint pits on the heath. A picture came into my mind which left me smiling and breathless with its implications.' (41)

Such changes alter one's relation to the world. Eva Feder Kittay comments in *Metaphor: Its Cognitive Force and Linguistic Structure* (1987), "Metaphor is not merely one 'among endless devices'; it is the paradigmatic device for pointing out analogies and making comparisons which cross the bounds of our usual categories and concepts," (19) and adds that it does so through *perspectival incongruity*. Crace emphasizes such incongruities in moments of premodern consciousness, exploiting such attitudinal naivety. The father acquires his role as a storyteller only after this transformation, his abandonment of the familiar, his *rite of passage* in hostile conditions. He encounters Doe and her baby daughter, in a meagre, ramshackle dwelling beside the salt-land heath. "She was a beauty in decay." (46) Abject and solitary after the disappearance of her husband and sons, Doe's hopes and conversation dwell on the annual arrival of geese, another symbol of the natural impulse towards both rhythm and change. She barters herself to passing men for food. Unable to satisfy his passion, or even kill a chicken for her payment, the storyteller is frustrated by her indifference. He liberates the chicken and returns to his village to be mocked by his uncle. He responds by reworking the facts of his journey, embroidering his escape, displacing the mundanity and abjection of Doe's condition, and thereby the tedium of the stoney village.

> 'That ship would soon be out of sight. Unless, of course, I followed it. Why shouldn't I? I had no work to do. I simply filled my chest with air and took off down the coast.'
>
> My cousins had stopped eating. Their eyes were turned on me. Those phrases – 'filled my chest' and 'took off down the coast' – had made

them hopeful in a way they could not understand. Those phrases were like perfume. They had dramatic odours. They promised more. I knew at once the truth could not be told. No love, poor food, a woman – thin and naked, with breasts like barnacles – who sold herself for chickens. What could I say to make it sound attractive? They wanted something crafted and well turned. I wanted their applause. The truth would never do. It was too fragile and too glum. It offered no escape. (54)

The tale displaces his redundancy, depending upon his flourishes, upon variation and repetition, upon untruths. From his adaptation – of himself and of reality – he creates the narrative 'embroidery' to which the daughter refers, initially as a survival technique, but later acquiring status and purpose. His gift ultimately becomes functional since in the final episode only he can lead his tribe of flint-workers and flint-traders from their failing village, guiding them through the transition in technology from stone to metal.

Equally importantly his perambulation, this carrying of elements of one world to and from another, creates an extension of experience that has similarities to the metaphoric process, the yoking together of disparate elements. Christopher Tilley in *Metaphor and Material Culture* (1999) stresses the artefactual origin of metaphoric thought, describes a process which "Involves a transfer of one term from one system or level of meaning to another (*metaphora*: carrying over)." (4) Such elements of transfer recur in Crace; frequently too he conveys a pleasure in comparative imagery, often innovatively and comically used. The bowman's leather face is "a leather purse with teeth," (3) a horseman's buttocks between Doe's knees in copulation are "double-dumplings." (50) He describes the "juice-red rocks" (72) of the shore, and the stones of the house Doe built on the edge of the stoney village, "like the shyest snails which never showed their heads, but moved when no one watched. Her stones had life. They crept. They nestled. They muttered in the wind and heat." (117) Crace sees storytelling as an evolutionary element, part of a central concept of adaptation. Earl R. Mac Cormac concurs in *A Cognitive Theory of Metaphor* (1985):

> metaphorical truth could be viewed as completely relative if it were not for its participation in this evolutionary process in which the stability of the ordinary, banal perceptions and expressions of the world in literal language provides an objective base for metaphor. Metaphorical truth and literal truth exist on a continuum; one does not necessarily need to reduce metaphors to literal language in order to assess their truth value.

> Truth value arises from the new possibilities and new insights that metaphors provide. (224–5)

The storyteller's truths synthesize the two, the literal and the metaphorical, both essential to the Cracean style, for as Tilley says, "without metaphor human communication would be nigh impossible." (4) The inherent conflict of differing world-views creates the ambiguities of Craceland.

After the storyteller's discovery of the salt-heath, an odd, far from idyllic relationship with Doe emerges during his periodic visits, creating a separate life from that of being "the minstrel-king of lies, the teller of wide tales." (82) After a drinking session with Doe his sexual advances are physically and finally rejected. The site of the source of his narratives is destroyed when inland farmers gather to slaughter *en masse* the geese who are threatening their livelihood, and incensed by their frenzy of killing, they attack Doe's meagre home, leaving her dog dead. The father leads her back to the stoneys and she is far from welcome.

At this point the daughter reveals herself explicitly as Doe's daughter, adopted by her new father. For her the village offers respite after the trauma of the battle of the geese, providing "A world of symmetry and composure." (103) On his return the storyteller reverses his earlier lies, calling upon another manner of persuasiveness, by being literal or truthful. Questioned about Doe by the hostile villagers, wary of a newcomer who has to be fed, he declares:

> 'This is a story made by life . . . It's true in every way.' That caused some cautious laughter and some shouts. 'You know that when I want to make your eyes stretch wide, I stretch my stories wide to match. You know that when I want some fun, I let my stories tickle truth. You all know that. You are not fools. Well, now, here is a tale that's meant to make you weep. There is no need for camouflage. The world out there is sad enough. So this is not a dream. This, to a hair, is fact.' He'd never heard an audience so quiet. (105)

Soon, however, he returns to his synthesis of supposition and facts, creating versions of the story of the disappearance of Doe's husband and her sons, turning their lives into conjectures with various endings – abduction, abandonment and murder – all equally unpleasant for Doe, each version an unpleasant, potential truth she has to re-experience viscerally. "My father had released three breeds of grief to gnaw and tumble in her gut." (119)

Crace's adept and yet elusive mode of storytelling reminds one of Benjamin's dictum arrived at in describing the writer Leskov:

> Actually, it is half the art of storytelling to keep a story free from explanation as one reproduces it . . . The most extraordinary things, marvellous things, are related with the greatest of accuracy, but the psychological connection of events is not forced on the reader. It is left up to him to interpret things the way he understands them, and thus the narrative achieves an amplitude that information lacks. (89)

Crace amplifies his narratives by focusing largely on the visual, creating a free play of referential possibilities that are not diminished by his recursive style of writing. As Cooke comments: "He utilises rhythm and metaphor and strong visual imagery to convey his major themes: the tenacity of the human spirit, the irreducible energy of the physical world." And yet human activity in intersecting with nature discovers its potential indifference to the human world, as with Doe's comic attempts to create a home:

> Our house was like no other. My mother found that stones, however flat and heavy, were not keen to lie at her bidding. Her stones were like the shyest snails which never showed their heads, but moved when no one watched. Her stones had life. They crept. They nestled. They muttered in the wind and heat. And so she built four living walls which would not stand like all those other village walls made out of more quiescent stones. Her walls were wayward, unsubmissive. They toppled in the wind. They barked her ankles. The fell down on my leg and did not move despite my screams and tears. (117)

The instability extends as a motif and metaphysical reality, a disorder in a world of temporary stasis that itself is threatened. The symbol is phenomenological. As Tilley points out, humans often "are inattentive to material metaphors." (264) Crace's highlights them. Cooke's 'tenacity' drives their adaptation when the stone and their associated skills have become worthless. Crace is ambivalent towards their craft, because its stolidity is both a virtue and a curse. As he says, "I'm romanticizing the activity of cutting the stone, and at the same time I'm romanticizing the importance of Birmingham as a workshop of the world. It's unquestionably a romanticization because I've never worked in a foundry, I've never come home, having to wash the swarf out of my hair. So, on the one hand I want to romanticize the activity of working stone because it is beautiful, its products are beautiful, but on the other I feel that there's something very humdrum, and very destructive about the world of commerce and industry."[11] Doe destroys herself, out of necessity, by joining that world, sustaining a temporary dignity. Doe's dogged transformation is somewhat ironic, since eventually she is faced with hunger again, only to die, struck by a bronze arrowhead, murdered while momentarily recovering a sense of freedom.

Doe and the storyteller are precursors to and symbols of change. Although the male stoneys turn to Doe for illicit sexual pleasure, she is shunned and her ramshackle dwelling remains marginal, essentially outside of the main settlement. In both worlds, Doe objectifies herself, and as Bataille explains in *The Accursed Share; Vol. II*, "The prostitute is . . . an object whose value is assessable." (140) A further symbolic and thematic significance is that Doe is intimately associated with death and corporeality as a kind of symbolic interfusion. Consider the circumstances of her life in terms of Bataille's comment:

> What then is the essential meaning of our horror of nature? Not wanting to depend on anything, abandoning the place of our carnal birth, revolting intimately against the fact of *dying*, generally mistrusting the body, that is, having a deep mistrust of what is accidental, natural, perishable – this appears to be *for each one of us* the sense of the movement of the sexual functions and of death. (91)

The storyteller's ardour for Doe declines in the period when she appears to have been integrated, digging out and hauling raw flint before it is worked, becoming much like the other stoneys. He even prefers the time when she serviced passing horsemen so complete is his antipathy towards stoney life. In the final scene before the exodus, to survive Doe must revert to prostitution.

> Doe led the way into the bracken, and – that painful, reminiscent lifting of her smock – she stood ready to receive my cousin and his shells. She might have been upon the heath once more. Her thighs were punctured water bags. Her breasts were flat. Her face was reddening with hidden sores. Her eyes were beaten and appalled at the prospect of her task which made her both the trader and the labourer. She was the merchandise as well." (150)

An attack by horsemen follows, mirroring both the earlier attack upon the storyteller as a child, and the warning of the wind that comes too late. Doe's own demise is both definitive and yet provisional. The fact of her death is acknowledged, but towards the end of the novel there are three versions of Doe's death, leaving the possibility of the culpability in a jealous rage of the storyteller, a gossip's story he finishes for his audience, although the daughter confirms, "I owe it to my mother and to him to tell you only what is known and not what he would wish us to believe. Doe had bled to death for sure and father had, indeed, found her beneath the shadow of the hawk. He had wiped clean the arrow-head, and placed his ear against my mother's chest. She was entirely cold and still. In that my father told the truth. She was no more than stone." (156) In the final chapter, after a harsh winter, he leads the bulk of the villagers on their exodus along the coast, familiar to them from his stories, revelling in their discovery of his fabled red stones. By the end of the novel they reach the end of his experience when pure imagination has to take over, but this is daunting.

> At last his lies had caught him out. He knew what no one else had guessed, that this salt heath was the limit of his knowledge of the outside world, that all he knew of better days was those few times with Doe. He looked out at the night beyond the heath where, next day, we would go. The stars were just the same, the moon, the wind. No doubt they had a sun there too. The stories that he'd told were now our past. His task was to invent a future for us all. He closed his eyes and what he saw was the shingled margin of the sea with horses wild and riderless close by. He tried to place a sail upon the sea, but could not. He tried to fill the air with human sounds. But all he saw were horses in the wind, the tide in loops upon the beach, the spray-wet rocks and stones reflecting all the changes in the sky, and no one there to notice or applaud. (169–70)

Mark Kamine claims in 'A Prehistoric Tale' that "Novels about growing up traditionally end when the hero is about to head out into the world beyond. This one is no exception." (20) True, but the daughter's narrative testifies to the survival of both the tribe and the act of imagination. Further, arguably, the significance of the storyteller's narratives is that nature and the evolutionary, historical sweep become both his subject and the judge of his storytelling. Something transcends. This is no longer a discrete 'human' narrative, but potentially a broader one. He can become an agent of evolutionary change, an agent of history, the conduit for greater forces than himself.

Notes

1. 'Crace–Tew: Telephone Interview 1.'
2. Ibid.

3 '1998 Westminster Interview.'
4 Ibid.
5 Ibid.
6 'Crace–Tew: Telephone Interview 2.'
7 'Crace–Tew: Telephone Interview 1.'
8 'Crace–Tew: Telephone Interview 2.'
9 Ibid.
10 Ibid.
11 Ibid.

3

Parables of distress: *Arcadia* (1992) and *Signals of Distress* (1994)

Arcadia

Crace says *Arcadia* "has less of a hidden life than the other books; it's less open to interpretation. It's less ambiguous, less ambivalent."[1] The novel is divided into four parts, 'The Soap Market,' 'Milk and Honey,' 'Victor's City' and 'Arcadia.' The novel opens with the planning for Victor's eightieth birthday celebration and the party itself. Subsequently it describes the commercial redevelopment and destruction by Victor of his past, demolishing the Soap Market with its medieval scrubbing stones and gargoyles, creating a globalized shopping centre selling a homogeneous, and according to Teske trading a postmodern, experience as much as its goods, which certainly as Teske says "cater[s] for tourists and middle-class suburbanites who have no local bond with the city." (177) In the final short section, the completed project is characterized by steel and glass, high rents and by regulations all in stark contrast to the apparent chaos of its predecessor. A third narrative element is Victor's past, the description of his struggles around the time of the death of his mother in a tenement fire in the impoverished Woodgate quarter seventy-four years previously. Fourth, there are sections concerned with Rook and Anna, two of Victor's middle-aged, senior employees, and a new arrival to the city, Joseph, who comes into immediate conflict with Rook. Echoing Crace's early career, the narrator is the "Burgher" or gossip columnist and political satirist, who by the final section in a demoted post compiles in advance Victor's obituary, and the implied conceit is that this narrative reflects his notes, drafts and ruminations for a biography of Victor for which he has been commissioned.

This world is in transition; Crace's city exhibits a chaotic dynamism that Raymond Williams identifies in *The Country and the City* (1985

[1973]) as a "sense of possibility, of meeting and of movement." (6) Cooke says, "Arcadia is a rich brew, a novel of ideas which probes the nature of civilization and apportions some blame for its manifold discontents. As a study in corruption it has an almost Jacobean intensity, yet the overwhelming impression of the book is its sensuous celebration of life. Cities urgently need to be reinvented and Crace has been prepared to make that act of imagination." Francis King in 'Nostalgia for the Mud' (1992) is impressed with Crace's descriptive and metaphoric skills, and wonders, "How could any judge of a literary award . . . not at once be captivated by the manner in which an image expands, becomes nebulous and solidifies into another, which then in turn undergoes the same process; by the abrupt, dislocating but always impressive transitions from one scene to another; by virtuosity with which the realistically particular keeps acquiring the looming generality of myth?" (34) Crace's use of description is, given its topic, appropriately verdant and lush. Edward T. Wheeler in a review in *Commonweal* (993) says, "This is a carefully crafted book, one that seems as symmetrical and patterned as a globe artichoke. The prose runs continually to unmarked blank verse, so rhythmic and alive is it to incantation." (26) In contrast, Geoff Dyer in 'Word Salad' (1992) is more dismissive, describing the style as progressing from "a sort of cockney baroque, moving to within a beat or two of a constantly thwarted iambic tattoo." He adds, "*Arcadia* reads as if translated from some earthy register of yore into a mordant modernism." (45) Crace's "vegetative" quality, which so irritates Dyer, interprets the city through a neo-pastoral lens, attempting to understand the rural and its interrelationship with the urban where the allure rests with the latter. The city originates in the marketplace, satisfying what King calls "that atavistic yearning of even the most hardened of city-dwellers." (34) As Teske outlines the changes to the market transform an open public space to a more controlled, quasi-privatized one, thus rejecting the "communal, truly political sphere in the physical space of the public *agora*." (166–7) Throughout her analysis Teske outlines emphatically the impersonal and elitist character of the new development. In responding to the advancing modernity of the city, Crace indicates that one key influence is the work of activist and theorist Jane Jacobs:

> Jane Jacobs's ideas are so close to what I've expressed that sometimes I wonder whether I've simply raided her work and stolen from her. However, actually the order was like this. I had certain attitudes towards

cities and town planning before I started writing, but once you start writing, you then look into what books deal with the subject, and you get all the usual classics. Jane Jacobs was always being mentioned, so I read her after I had decided I wanted to write a book making those points. And there she was making them so fully and thoroughly, so I think she bolstered my situation rather than being a springboard for the book. However, she certainly expressed in non-fiction exactly what I wanted to say in fiction, so I won't pretend I didn't raid her cynically and thoroughly.[2]

Jacobs's study, *The Death and Life of Great American Cities* (1993), attacks the destruction of neighbourhoods by "monopolistic shopping centres and monumental cultural centres," (14) precisely the outcome of Victor's interventions. In *The Economy of Cities* (1972) Jacobs also describes the necessary adaptations of cities which she sees as providing "A country's basic wealth [which] is its productive capacity, created by the practical opportunities people have to add new work to old." (206) As Crace admits, "More than any of my books, this was one I was writing outside of my natural frame," adding that "Everything was a symbolic image in that book."[3] Crace, like Jacobs in her narrative exemplifications of individual responses to the city, humanizes these forces and illustrates the social text of the city, described in contrast to the rural landscape by Lefebvre in *Critique of Everyday Life, Volume II* (2002) as contributing towards human understanding through "localized and condensed" urban symbols. (308) Jakub Stemporowski in *The City and the Country, the Myth and the Reality in Jim Crace's Novel 'Arcadia'* (2004) points out that despite apparent postmodern features, *Arcadia* lacks any significant reflexivity (8), concluding that such a generic categorization would prove unfruitful (9–10), particularly as "Crace's metaphoric lyricism" is far more revealing, indicating an Arcadian possibility. (12) Ironically, Victor's life is intimately tied to the rhythms of the city and its commerce, yet he hankers after the mythic rituals of the countryside of his infancy, nostalgia for an illusory version of the life that rejected both himself and his mother. Crace explains his own impulses:

> All through my life there has been a tug between the joys of the countryside and the attractions of the town. It's easier to justify the countryside because of its association with the virtues. You always feel a little shabby for wanting to stay in the town, and this has been a debate throughout our married life. All of our married life we've been trying to persuade ourselves that living in the town is an admission of defeat, because we could

have easily at any time moved into the countryside, claiming our Arcadian vision for ourselves. We imagine that the city doesn't allow us to be *complete* people. But I think this is a false imagination.[4]

A similar pastoral tension recurs throughout this novel, establishing the antinomies animating modern pastoral. In 'The Soap Market' Rook, one of its former stallholders or "soapies," promenades among the democracy of passing strangers, towards his old market haunts, seeking the greenery to garland Victor's birthday chair, "Just like the chair in Leyel's Calendar of Customs: Plate XVII, a fogged black-and-white photograph of a small boy from the Twenties, beaming, tearful, overdressed in breeches and a waistcoat, amid the birthday foliage of a high-backed seat." (4) The idea derives from tales of Victor's mother who seeks solace in a composite fantasy of the village home she had abandoned out of necessity. This migration towards the city mirrors a historical process Jacobs identifies in *Cities and the Wealth of Nations: Principles of Economic Life* (1984) where peasants flee to the city drawn by its economic possibilities (33, 35).

Like Jacobs, Crace exemplifies the true nature and necessity of the city for modern culture. She argues in *The Economy of Cities*: "Cities simply cannot be 'explained' by their locations or other given resources. Their existences as cities and the sources of their growth lie within themselves, in the processes and growth systems that go on within them. Cities are not ordained; they are wholly existential." (136–7) The actions of Crace's characters, his plot and his narrator's thoughts convey a similar sense.

> This is the sorcery of cities. We do not chase down country roads for fame or wealth or liberty. Or romance even. If we hanker for the fires and fevers of the world, we turn our backs on herds and hedgerows and seek out crowds. Who says – besides the planners and philosophers – that we don't love crowds or relish contact in the street with strangers? We all grow rich on that if nothing else. Each brush, each bump, confirms the obvious, that where you find the mass of bees is where to look for honey. (263)

Like Lefebvre who in *The Critique of Everyday Life: Volume II* describes the city as "bursting with cars" (310) and dominated by signals and symbols, Crace identifies the control of the urban populace by signals and rules amid its flow of population and vehicles. Nevertheless, he is not hostile to the urban environment itself, or the lives led within its confines. Crace says,

> In many respects this book affirms the town because it says that although the countryside is loosely associated with closed communities and with the virtues, and cities are associated with the vices, nevertheless cities are the driving force for change. You would never have had the great hospitals, the great universities and the great scientists if it wasn't for what cities provided. But my feeling, mirroring Jane Jacobs main point, is that the things cities are good at and that cities should triumph at are those very things that people think are wrong with them – crowds, streets, parking, traffic, noise, pollution: all of those things need celebrating in the cities – but, bigger than that. Amongst the things the city is good at are sin and anonymity. That's the point that *Arcadia* wanted to make.[5]

Crace's narrator comments rhetorically: "We townies are the only creatures in the universe to benefit from chains, to make our fortunes from constraint, to wear the chafing, daily harnesses of city life as if they are the livery of plutocrats." (263) Throughout, in opposition to Em and Victor's bucolic fantasies, Crace revels in the heterogeneity, the energy and even the misdemeanours of the city. Dyer's notion of Crace's vegetative register, or "vegetablisation," in fact establishes a central tension of modernity, that of its pastoral myth and, within that, modern subjects' unease with their collective self. Hence, the poignant isolation of both the central characters and of the narrative perspective, what Joseph Olshan in 'Meet a Despotic Octogenarian and His Utopian Marketplace' (1992) describes as its "weird introspection." (3)

The novel's opening tone attempts to establish complicity between narrator and reader in understanding the limited emotional range of Victor and the importance of his childhood. "No wonder Victor never fell in love. A childhood like the one he had would make ice-cubes of us all. He lived on mother's milk till he was six, and then he thrived on charity and trade." (3) It simplicity is significant; as Stemporowski comments, "*Arcadia* is not a novel that requires an active reader in that it is fairly simple formally, lexically, and in terms of ideas." (23) Rook works closely with his boss, whom he cheats by accepting payments from the soapies. Ironically Rook formerly represented them in a protest against changing conditions in the market, before changing sides and accepting Victor's offer of employment on.

> He saw himself as lean and black, a cliché creature of the night. Indeed, that's partly why our Rook was known as Rook: the black clothes that he wore when he was young and on the streets. The rook-like nasal cawing

of his laugh, too, his love of crowds, his foraging, his criminality. But more than that: the puff-chested, light limbed posture of a bird. (9)

Victor's celebration means a change of routine for Rook, who chooses to walk to undertake his errands, drawn in part by what Jacobs describes in *The Life and Death of Great American Cities* as the "drama" (49–50) and "the heart-of-the-day ballet" (67) of the streets. Rook remains the archetypal market trader and city dweller, and as Crace comments, "His deviousness is what makes him interesting; it's what makes him powerful, and what makes him conflicted about himself."[6] Almost immediately Rook realizes a young countryman is following him, concretizing the city–country conflict. Following city instincts, Rook walks into the maze of streets in Woodgate where he grew up, where an earlier fire had led to previous redevelopment. Hurrying through the labyrinth of medieval streets he reaches the market where the insane self-appointed "Man in Cellophane" directs the traffic and where "The place was open to the sky, and could have been a medieval harvest fair," (16) set apart from the towering "Big Vic," the colloquial name for Victor's tower-block headquarters.[7]

The market is a profusion of activities, smells, colours, and even "the living things that make a living out of market fruit and market crowds. The roaches, bugs and weevils that share our meals and beds." (17) Among the cornucopia of products, several soapies surreptitiously pass bribes or "pitch payments" to Rook. "A third – the soapie known as Con – shook openly and tauntingly a sealed envelope in Rook's face, with Rook's name written large and red on it for all to see. Others saw the payment as a trade. They paid, then mentioned problems that could be fixed, if only Rook would talk with Victor." (21) In the bar with the soapies Rook sucks in error on the poisonous laurel he has picked for Victor, suffering an asthmatic attack, clearly unknowledgeable about the natural world, the converse of his anonymous young stalker. Town and country oppositions multiply. Ironically a true young countrywoman serving at the bar has no knowledge of this supposedly traditional rural birthday garland, part of Victor's fantasy of authentic origins. Its provenance is spurious.

Such rural authenticity, contrasting Victor's illusions, are related first in the retrospective narrative of Joseph, the young countryman, who toils in the fields, saving for a cheap summer suit, one he has seen modelled in a catalogue. His ambition is a slick urban life, but as Stemporowski observes, "Joseph's idea of the city is also a myth" (33) derived from cheap catalogues and magazines. Drawn by this desire, weekly Joseph loads produce destined for the city onto the "Salad Bowl Express" train. His blemished face is unattractive, so habitually he hides behind a box allowing him to show off his stripped, muscled torso to the rich women passengers on their way for urban weekends. "His was a rural face. But his body, give or take a scar or two, was smart enough for town." (33) He dreams of city life, his fervent and narcissistic desire for individualism drawn by the idea of urban privacy and anonymity. As Lefebvre says in *The Critique of Everyday Life, Volume I* (1992 [1947]) "Towns tell us of the almost total decomposition of community, of the atomization of society into 'private' individuals." (233) For Joseph, the petty thief, this is especially attractive. "No one there would know his name, or where he lived and worked, or who his family were ... In town he'd flourish in the privacy of crowds, in the monkish cells of tenements, in streets. His neighbours would be strangers. They'd hardly nod. He'd be a mystery to them. They'd only know the things he chose to tell." (33) Jacobs in *The Death and Life of Great American Cities* describes the indispensable nature of "privacy" in cities (69) also commenting, "Impersonal city streets make anonymous people." (67) Joseph's actions are both transgressive and naive. He stows away with his final load, a plastic tank of ten perch ordered for Victor's birthday meal, into which he urinates during the journey. On arrival he gravitates towards the Soap Market where he is caught stealing by Con, who retains his identity pass and induces him to attack and rob Rook, guided by an old photograph. Angered by his previous asthmatic attack, Rook retaliates and overcomes Joseph, retaining his pen-knife, which he uses to trim Victor's birthday laurel. There is an uncanny symmetry in such minor intersections.

Victor's party for the older traders from the market is a sterile lifeless affair, much like Big Vic, a high-technology environment plagued by an artificiality that permeates both Victor's celebration and his life. As Crace comments,

> Here is a man who is destroyed by his lack of emotional relationships, and so harks back to the times when he can remember when it was good, which is why he wants to imprint those final emotionally secure times, even though they were troubled times, onto the city. Of course in doing so he destroys the past. He's not only destroying his own past, and nostalgia about his own childhood, but he is destroying *The Past*.[8]

Despite Victor's rooftop garden, where he spits on the soil mimicking the ritual of a countryman, he cannot transcribe anything of the unpoetic realities represented by Joseph, but rather relies upon a version derived from the mythic tales and stories told in childhood by his mother.

> Victor's simple dream of celebrating eighty years in country style could not come true. The air inside Big Vic lacked buoyancy. It was heavy and inert. It was soup. Dioxides from the air-conditioning; monoxides from the heating system; ammonia and formaldehydes from cigarettes; ozone from photocopiers; stunning vapours from plastics, solvents and fluorescent lights. What oxygen remained was drenched in dust and particles and micro-organisms, mites and fibres from the carpeting, fleece from furniture, airborne amoebi from humidifying reservoirs, cellulose from paper waste, bugs, fungi, lice. (54)

The brief assertive sentences and lists reinforce Crace's rhythmic percussion, a foregrounding of style and structure, so derided by Dyer. As Crace says to Vincent, "That's what I'm going for. Drawing attention to the form of what I write, rather than the content. Some people hate it, but it's my obsession, my compulsion." (44) As Teske notes, "Even as an 80-year-old presiding over the vegetable market in the pose of Mumford's prehistorical ruler-kings Victor rejects the urban reality around him in favour of a dream of the countryside. At Victor's eightieth birthday celebration his secretary, Rook, a thoroughbred city person, tries and fails to reproduce the cliché of a rural harmony uniting rich and poor, old and young, human beings, animals and nature." (170) Moreover, the passage above typifies how Crace's content is naturalized by the dominance of his stylistic resonance, allowing his narrators to declare apparently self-evident truths, and the narrative to sustain repeated undercurrents or subtexts, and underlying mythological and symbolic possibilities. The rhythmic effect evokes certain culturally embedded patterns, including fairy-tales, parable and the poetic. As Harrison explains, parable sets up a tension between the layers of effect and structure, of the narrative form and its determinant "body of underlying conceptual material in terms of which, if at all, the narrative has to be construed *as a narrative*, and the tension reveals a way of structuring the narrative." (238) Allusion to a common experience is implied variously in Crace's tone, repetitions and assumed familiarities. In what is finally the unknowable world of the story this creates an ambivalent tension, and Crace periodically alludes to his own storytelling function, thereby refusing a reductive relationship with reality. Craceland is never directly mimetic, and yet Crace attends to objects and events, offering a density of detail, emphasizing the symbolically potential.

In *Arcadia* the worldview of the narrator dominates, focusing on the immediacy of love, trade and personality. Crace renders complex the apparent simplicity of each action and event, with a plethora of inner motivations. Thus the reader is invited to amplify the text's potential almost in spite of itself. As Miller states: "The paradox of parable is that it is a likeness that rests on a manifest unlikeness between what is given and what cannot by any means be given directly. A parabolic 'likeness' is so 'unlike' that without interpretation or commentary the meaning may slip by the reader or listener altogether." (136) In Crace, conciliating various marginalities renders a thematic and structural unity, where different individuals, opposing fields of vision, different forms of expressiveness, and a sense of *mythos* and place all intersect. As Miller concludes this is appropriate to parable since "parable is a mode of figurative language which is the indirect indication at a distance, of something that cannot be described directly." (136)

As a result of Joseph's actions, Victor's fish are "bladdery" (57) and his habitual discomfiture with others is only alleviated by the inadvertent revelation by a guest of Rook's illicit payments. Instantly Victor's decides to rid himself of his assistant, chiefly because of Rook's resistance to the redevelopment. "The market was as good as gone and so was Rook. Decisions had been made, that day. The skyline of our lives was changed." (65) Unaware of his fate, Rook initiates an affair with Anna, inducing some empathy for a difficult, ambivalent character. As Crace reveals, "One of the tricks with someone hard to like is to see that person in an intimate relationship, so we do see him intimately, with his trousers off."[9] In contrast to the couple's newly discovered domestic intimacy, Joseph seeks company by joining the homeless who sleep in the market. The journalist narrator reveals he has published the story of the fish, which is read by Rook and Anna between bouts of lovemaking. The novel is replete with intersecting moments implying communitarian possibilities. A series of elements are intertwined at this point. The sexual climax followed by the "recklessness" (67) of the couple's sleep contrasts with the brief sleep on cobblestones of Joseph, who watches Victor's light as the latter wanders through his apartment in Big Vic full of wind, deciding how to honour his mother, unaware of Joseph's destitution (69–70). "He'd put her back. He knew exactly where she should sit and beg in bronze, between the Soap Market and the garden." (70)

All of the major elements of the narrative have been initiated and the second section, 'Milk and Honey,' returns to Victor's relationship with his mother, whose very name 'Em' signifies archetypal motherhood.[10] It undercuts his dreams of the past. "Victor was a townie almost through and through. He was not as soily or as leafy as he claimed. He'd fled the countryside when he was three weeks old, when this brusque, gymnastic century was also in its infancy. His dad had died. An epidemic of sweats had seen him off before his son was born." (75) Em is unable to sustain herself and her infant in the countryside despite the myths of plenitude, and hence she sets off for the city while breastfeeding Victor, seeking her younger sister. Looking naively for a *poste restante* address at the Postal Hall, she cannot even recover her own uncollected letter to her sister. She encounters both the city's indifference and its rapaciousness as she fights to free herself first from a stranger who attempts to persuade her to give up Victor for adoption, and subsequently refuses offers of money for sex. Crace reworks a series of cultural clichés, commenting: "That section is very Dickensian."[11] Em both becomes a beggar and succeeds in this by chance, by following her first two women benefactors to the Soap Market and finding a pitch under a discarded parasol. Despite her naked breast passers-by offer money.

> You could study scenes more intimate in churches or galleries. Madonna and her Child. The infancy of Christ. First Born . . . Em and Victor made a wholesome sight when Victor was asleep and on her breast. Coins dropped into the mother's palm or on her shawl were tribute tithes for family. Em understood. To earn pity and the cash of citizens she had to seem respectable and, more than that, serene – a living sculpture labelled Motherhood. (88)

Gradually the novelty diminishes. Em's experience and that of the market reflects what Lefebvre observes in *The Critique of Everyday Life, Volume II*: "Like the everyday, the street is constantly changing and always repeats itself. In the unceasing shifts of times of day, people, objects and light, it repeats itself tirelessly. The street is a spectacle, almost nothing but a spectacle, because we are in it, walking, stopping, participating. If you are in a hurry you will not see the spectacle, even if you are part of it." (310) This sense is accentuated when after

Arcadia and Signals of Distress

almost dying because of Victor splitting her breasts, destroying the image of a serene Madonna, Em rediscovers her sister, a more successful beggar. Unable to accept the discipline of service, Aunt has embraced the streets, wearing a jaunty straw hat, and offering her own story to counter the dejection of her sister:

> Em told her story of how she'd come to town, and how the town had almost beaten her. Then Aunt replied with hers, and how the town was better than a friend. It took more care of waifs and strays than any village in the land. 'If that weren't so,' she said, 'the countryside would be the place for girls like us. The trees and fields would overflow with widows and orphans. But look around you, Em. Look on the streets. It's cities take us in.' And then she added, 'City air makes free.' (102)

Aunt's final remark *exactly* replicates a medieval saying as reported by Jacobs in *The Death and Life of Great American Cities*, which maxim Jacobs argues still holds true (458). Polemically the novel resonates Jacobs's insistence that cities animate the economy and offer opportunity even for the abject, and that "Cities are fantastically dynamic places." (24) Nevertheless, as Teske indicates, Em rejects the city, withdrawing into an idealized view of village life (170).

Crace enumerates their lives in a Woodgate tenement. At the Aunt's suggestion they use Victor to beg, training him like a dog (111) to be docile, feeding at the breast on honey (the second element of this section's ironic title which displaces the first) until his mother dies in a fire. Chapter 5 describes in detail Em's narrative retreat to a mythic countryside in the tales for her son where "She had made a tinseled paradise of it." (116) Em in her 'city-country contrast' reduces 'complexity' to 'simplicity' and after her disillusionment rather than escape the city literally, does so through her bucolic fantasy.[12] The promised Arcadian return is impossible, as is Victor's wish to recreate this illusion.

> She told these stories to her son. He took them in, eyes shut, laid out across her lap. He did not understand the half of what she said, a quarter of her words. What could it mean, the key was wiser than the stool? The knives are boys and scissors girls. And rain was pips and pods. And sea was saddle? A normal child of four or five would think it all a strange and – finally – a tiresome game, to bend words in a way that was confusing and not funny . . . But as we know, Victor was no normal child. For him the words his mother spoke were two-dimensional, a sheet of sound, a shallow wash of stories from his mother's village and the past.

He had no role to play except to keep his head and body still, and listen hard. (120-1)

According to Stemporowski, "Thus, Crace demystifies the mechanics of the myth." (33) However, unlike Crace's reader, Victor cannot understand the realities of life because of the tales' permeation of his psyche, the bucolic *mythos* as a surplus of language, transforming the literal and material. Furthermore, Victor comprehends instinctively the mythic resonance of childhood and motherhood that are the stories subtext. And yet his impulse remains a pastoral one, for as Poggioli says, "The psychological root of the pastoral is a double longing after innocence and happiness, to be recovered not through conversion or regeneration but merely through retreat." (1) Poggioli describes Victor's maternal legacy as "The bucolic ideal." (1) Structurally his old age intersects with the earlier times, and yet by manufacturing 'lost' realities from an idealized storytelling, paradoxically he destroys the essential qualities of the past. "The irony was this, the richness of the past was richness second-hand. His mother's childhood and her adolescence in the village landscape was made shiny and intense by distance and by time. It was Victor's milk and honey now." (122) The influence is so comprehensive Victor adopts this myth as part of his identity, guided by an illusory essence of himself.

Fire destroys the district; Victor's mother dies as she sleeps late because of illness. Her death mirrors an underlying theme, for as Wheeler notes, "In the most fundamental way, this novel places at its center the struggle between life and death." (26) Given the police appear to be at hand immediately to force back the crowds, rumours of its conspiratorial origin circulate. "The police, the politicians, the nobs and profiteers who wanted all the city to themselves had come before the sun was up to make a furnace for the poor." (132) Jacobs reflects that "a deliberate conspiracy" can be often used by profiteers to clear property (288), and certainly the riot that follows, and the one towards the novel's end, reflect Jacobs' observations about "public peace" in that "It is kept primarily by an intricate, almost unconscious, network of voluntary controls and standards among the people themselves, and enforced by the people themselves," (41) which temporarily disintegrate in both cases. For Victor the aftermath is an epiphany when he finally realizes "that this was his first unfettered image of the town, [and] that up till then he'd only glimpsed the

Arcadia and Signals of Distress

city streets." (135) His Aunt retreats to the market, dragging the child, at six years old almost unable to walk unaided so long has he played the role of the infant in their begging. There instead of her sister, she finds a lover in a pickpocket, Dip, a neo-Dickensian characterization of life on the streets. Crace invokes Jacobs' commentary rhetorically in addressing the reader.

> Now do you see the charm of cities? None of this adventure could have happened on the village green where Aunt and Em had first played tip-and-kiss with boys. There was no flirting, pocket-picking strangers to encounter there, in patent shoes and collar studs, with private rooms. The only available men were cousins all. Or neighbour's sons. Or daft. They were as solid and passionate as trees, as heroic and original as farmyard hens. That is to say they were all dull and without sin; their only privacy was sleep and shit. But city air makes free – and country pullets can become street cockatoos or fighting birds or songsters once they've shaken hayseed from their wings. So, Aunt and Dip, two village souls gone free and wild in city streets, could no more pass each other by than cats pass a dish of cream. (144)

During their passion they send out Victor to sell eggs, which initially his aunt steals. Very nearly caught she works out with matchsticks how to profit from them legitimately. "The street kids did their best, with threats and brittle charm, to make Victor one of them. They had their gangs." These are very much like those observed by Jacobs in her study of American cities (85–6). Soon Victor becomes self-sufficient in his trade, and thereafter first Dip and then Aunt disappear. A crucial scene follows with the resolution of a quarrel between two soapies by one of Victor's customers in a Soap Garden bar, a huge man who dips his eggs in sugar. "They said he was a landlord of some sort, a pimp, a man who'd been a consul in the tropics and had made a fortune out of gold or slaves or running guns, an impresario, a counterfeiter, an opera star who had not sung since some scandal or some love affair had silenced him, an undercover cop." (163) This urban myth exhibits the anonymity and the possibilities of the city. The customer tears in half "A blue five-thousand note," (165) giving the two disputants half each, thus hypnotizing Victor and inspiring the early ambition which would lead to his successes.

The third section, 'Victor's City,' represents an elaborate sequence of interlinked events, returning first to the Monday after Victor's celebration. Rook and Anna walk together to Big Vic, and discovering that the normal schedule is cancelled, Rook concludes Victor must be dead. Anna, in the note instructing her to dismiss Rook, misinterprets Victor's allusion to his "out-of-work contacts and activities are not morally compatible with the trust invested in him." (183) She imagines this refers to her affair, although Rook understands intuitively Victor's arcane reference to the illicit pitch-money. At midday Rook is ejected and subsequently inhabits a *demi-monde*, drinking, fantasizing revenge, and increasingly resentful. As Richard Eder says in 'The Phantom of the Market,' (1992) he is somewhat of an "elliptic figure" who "takes poisonous refuge among the roots he has poisoned." (12) Crace depicts the man's self-destruction as intense, describing his daily returns to the Soap Garden bar and the market, initially hoping to see Anna. He re-encounters Joseph, and mimicking Victor's story of banknotes torn in half, Rook offers some half-notes to Joseph intending to make use of him.

Five months after Rook's dismissal an architect arrives, Signor Claudio Busi, a "figurehead," (210) from Milan who regards the old market as "squalid" (211) and dislikes the way in which shopping becomes an "expedition." (210) "He was elated that the Busi Partnership of New York, Paris and Milan might be the ones to introduce some Order and some Uniformity. A modern, regulated city should be governed not by the impulses of the crowd but by the dictates of its tramlines, pavements, traffic lights, timetables, laws." (212) Crace's implicit critique of unresponsive architecture and planning – typified in the underlying anti-humanist and anti-historical tenets of Busi's architecture – mirrors that of Lewis Mumford who, in *The Highway and the City* (1964) says, "There is hardly a single great innovation in building this last thirty years – total air-conditioning, all-round fluorescent lighting, the all-glass wall – that pays any respect to either the meteorological, the biological, or the psychological knowledge already available, for this knowledge calls for radical alterations in their present use. And still less do these innovations heed human activities or human desires." (154) Such deficiencies are exhibited in Busi's design, nicknamed "The Glass Meringues" by colleagues. It is ironically called "Arcadia," a utopian vision unrelated to the past, and "For Signor Busi, the outdoors which they planned to bring indoors was more than just a scheme to shield the market stalls from wind and rain and temperature. The 'outside' meant the countryside as well, the world beyond the margins of the town." (213) Crace describes undertaking detailed research:

When I was writing about cities, particularly when I referred to the plans that were being presented to Victor in the third section, there were many building terms and much theoretical satire that were not natural to me. I wouldn't say it was the most researched book that I've done, but it was the book in which I relied on outside sources more thoroughly, because I didn't have the background to write this book without undertaking that kind of reading.[13]

Busi flirts and charms Anna, while ironically "Arcadia" works its magic on Victor, unconsciously conjuring an illusion similar to his mother's stories. "Plans were strewn across the desk and carpet. Victor stood amongst them, a reference dictionary in his hand. *Arcadia* – a rustic paradise, he read. *Arcadian* – of pastoral simplicity. *Arcade* – a covered row of shops." (217–18) And yet curiously Victor's misunderstanding mirrors the pastoral impulse, for as Poggioli says, "the pastoral ideal shifts on the quicksands of wishful thought." (2)

After the flirtation Anna is conscious of her middle-age. She shops in the market with an acrid funereal smell from the lettuce leaves, both a symbol of nature and a presentiment of death. She re-encounters Rook and blurts out the details of the redevelopment plans. His compulsion for revenge inspires a renewed passion, suggesting later that Anna agree to share dinner with Busi so Rook might obtain the plans. "This was unadorned revenge, and revenge is next to lust in its single-mindedness, its self-regard. So Rook did not care that Busi, Anna, Joseph and yes, Con and Victor, too, were mostly innocent of blame for the malfunctions of his life." (227) Rook's negativity allows him to walk Anna like a willing cuckold to the Excelsior hotel. Impassioned by the idea of Anna's seduction, he consorts with a young prostitute from the country, another migrant to the city, another imperfect Arcadian exile.

Armed with Victor's plans, Rook uses Con to engineer public objections and on the day of the press conference to celebrate the new project, a protest march leaves the old market. Drawing on experience of activism and protest, Crace details its *jouissance* and communality. "The closer the soapies got to Big Vic, the unrulier they became. To see their faces you would think that they were mutinous and angry. In face, these men and women were having fun." (250) The crowd below attracts Busi and Victor, the two at an almost godlike remove, their decisions changing lives.

Later Busi offers his credentials to a press conference attended by the narrator, the Burgher. "'I introduced the notion, as you know, of "building as event". That is to say, that when we use a building we should experience narrative and drama in the way that on a mountain walk we experience the textures and elements of landscape.'" (253) His appeal to narration echoes Lewis Mumford's claim in *Art and Technics* (1952) that "All buildings speak a language, and this language must be understood by the people who use it," (132) but Busi neglects its aesthetic and communal qualities. The press draw attention to the protestors' objections and Victor descends reluctantly with Anna to persuade the crowd they have been misled. As Stemporowski says:

> He feels bothered that he must go out of his air-conditioned, safe, and weatherproof tower block to speak to the crowd of insignificant soapies. Here Crace employs another of his ingenious metaphors: 'How long since God last descended from the heavens to stand with mortals on the ground?' . . . It is Victor who asks the question and this thus reveals the feeling of omnipotence and power that he believes he wields. (18)

Victor placates the protestors by offering them a consultative exercise. Rook descends, destroying his relationship with Anna, and consorting with the market's vagrants after the bars close. Increasingly marginalized, Rook's bitterness compels his sarcastic tirades against Victor as the market moves to the Big Vic carpark, for what Rook describes as two years in the wilderness. In the last week between Christmas and New Year closure approaches and a new middle-class "valedictory clientele" (277) contribute to the party atmosphere that culminates on New Year's Eve when Rook persuades Joseph on promise of payment to set fire to the stacked stalls and awnings. History repeats itself first with a fire and second, after the Chief of Police's cursory decision at dinner to deploy a rapid response unit, with a widespread riot. Teske comments that "the contrast between the private New Year's party, from which the urban elite of Mayor and Police Chief do not want to be disturbed, and a grass-root coalition of disappointed citizens rioting together shows a basic conflict in the understanding of urban community." (177) It symbolizes the disparity Elizabeth Wilson articulates in *The Sphinx in the City* (1991): "The urban crisis is a crisis of inequality, and of authoritarianism." (158) Police respond to a cascade of vegetables with tear gas, and with a single victim: Rook suffers another asthma attack, only to be attacked by Joseph for the promised half banknotes. Ironically, in a Cracean series of reversals Joseph's attack saves Rook's life, only for it to be finished off by a beating from two policemen in the final onslaught against the rioters. Crace recalls that "When the idea of a vegetable battle came around, it was one of the most pleasing deliveries that a novel has ever given me, because I didn't know it was going to happen at the time, and I think that this pitched battle at the end of *Arcadia* is one of my favourite scenes."[14]

After hiding in the boot of a car, Joseph uses Rook's keys to enter his apartment and illicitly achieve his anti-Arcadian vision. "This was the dream he had when he was loading produce onto trains: the day would come when he came home to his apartment in the city. He closed the door on everything. He'd never known such perfect carpentry or such a calm as this." (305) Joseph is arrested for burglary. Given the outcry against the police anti-riot tactics and the martyrdom of Rook, the authorities claim Joseph is a leader of the riot. The narrator reveals proleptically that he is tried for Rook's murder, his defence – the genuine account – interpreted as "deranged and farfetched explanations." (308) On the day after the riot, Victor takes Anna on a private pilgrimage to the market, to the site of the yet-to-be-named victim, as if finally paying homage to Em. The reader's knowledge of Rook's identity makes Anna's presence poignant. For Victor the rain on the umbrella reminds him of a phrase used by his mother, once more evoking in him a nostalgic sense of the power of the past, cutting him off from the present despite this ritual.

In the final short section, 'Arcadia,' the project has been completed, and the reader encounters a version of what Wilson's terms "the ultimate postmodern experience. As popularly described, it combines kitsch architecture – and kitsch nature for that matter – a whole 'inauthentic' lifestyle, in fact, with a population of transients." (136) As Crace comments, "When you have a new building like the Arcadia at the end of this book, not only does it not allow you to know what is north and south, to tell spring from winter, to tell night from day, not only does it not let you know if you're in Birmingham or Buenos Aries or Brisbane because it could be anywhere, because it's so homogenized, but it also filters out the sin."[15] Rather than what Teske interprets as examples of *flânerie* (175) *Arcadia*'s last section comprises effectively two 'visual surveys' of adjacent environments in the city – Arcadia and Woodgate – especially when correctly understood in terms of the concepts Kevin Lynch defines in 'A Process of Community Visual Survey' (1990) where he is concerned with perceiving urban locations via questions of a "sense of special identity" integrated with "a sense of general location." (297) Crace's spatial sense of neighbourhoods evokes Lynch's insistence on understanding such environments by deploying a full range of perceptions, commenting, "While this is a survey of *visual* character, it would logically be linked to studies of all other sensory qualities of a place – sound and climate in particular, but also touch, smell and other senses." (263) Teske, however, correctly identifies something in these promenades that contrasts with Victor's view from above which is "visual, panoptic and theoretical," (175) rather than visceral. Ten years have passed after the riot. Displaced as the Burgher by a young woman journalist, the narrator prepares Victor's official biography, uncovering the story of his subject's early years. He visits on his first 'visual survey' the centre now nicknamed "Fat Vic." This homogenized, characterless zone is patrolled by uniformed guards, and patronized by an upmarket clientele. Its restaurants, garden court, trading corridors, patios, terraces and balconies constitute one of the "self-isolating projects" (xiv) Jacobs refutes in *The Death and Life of the Great American Cities*. They resist Jacobs's concept of humans and cities integrated in nature itself. However, Arcadia cannot resist nature entirely. One side is an aviary designed for exotic birds, invaded by the city sparrows. The narrator's responses to this litter-free, regulated and thoroughly commodified environment are ambivalent. The statue, *The Beggar Woman and Her Child*, is caged to prevent people touching it, negating their ritualistic urges in response to its presence. Crace says of such a centre, "It has its seductions, and someone like me would always be welcome, but it homogenizes the city. It takes away all those things that Jane Jacobs says are so important. It robs you of any sense of landscape."[16] There remains a lack of conviction in the narrator's ironic conclusion: "Arcadia is a triumph. Let's admit it. It weathers as I watch; it settles in. There is no complacency, just the swagger and ambition that cities flourish on." (333) However, it lacks the meaningfulness Lynch asserts the visual environment ought to possess for observers where "its visible character should relate to other aspects of life: the functions and activities of places, their history, their future, the structure of society. Human values and aspirations. People will 'read' a city landscape." (296) The narrator offers the first line of his book, which reiterates that of *Arcadia* the novel, linking the two narratives. On leaving, he contrasts himself with Victor's skyscraper isolation, lost in his fake bucolic mythology. After his "Press Club Buffers" lunch, the narrator in his second 'visual survey' wanders in Woodgate where a chaotic street market, Soap Two, has sprung up, home to the traders forced out of Arcadia by its economic demands and standards of presentation. As Teske says, "The community of the market, however, presents itself not as the harmonious remnant of an Arcadian past, but as a political organism. In a counter-vision to Victor's urban citadel or acropolis, the city is seen as an *agora* in every sense of the word: As a market in which traders convene and as a multifunctional place in which citizens communicate for the common good." (177-8) There is a seductive anarchy, echoing the force of the riots, a historical impulse that subverts even the postmodern. Unregulated, the ex-Burgher can toss a paper bag upon the ground and eat as he walks. The weather links him to nature and reality. "I cannot escape the rain, despite the umbrella my neighbour holds. My suit is sodden at the shoulder. My socks and shoes are wet. My forehead sweats with rain. The weather is a ballet for the streets. But then there is a more substantial dancer too. Cellophane is kicking water in the air." (344) The ballet refers to Jacobs's notion of the elements of the city street "miraculously" composing a whole through various improvisations (65). In Soap Two the narrator finds what Jacobs describes as "This order [which] is all composed of movement and change," (65) and is akin to art. He participates in this living, typically urban ritualistic 'ballet.' He reflects, "My rainy footprints on the pavement will soon dry, but footprints and the thousand sodden paper bags which held a thousand pears, the eyes, the cores, the stalks, the rinds of daily life, are more substantial – are they not? – than shadows. They swell the middens of the town." (345) In his first 'visual survey' there is no sense of community, failing to satisfy Lynch's question, "Is the viewer presented with a memorable sequence?" (297) In contrast, the second market's haphazard evolution does, for despite its apparent chaos and disorder, Crace's narrator finds a congruity where a sense of community clearly emerges. The novel finally affirms a humanistic sense of space, whereas Victor inhabits an artificial domain.

Signals of Distress

Signals of Distress is a highly complex novel. As Field comments, the novelist "has, he says, the kind of Puritanism which puts everything in a story for a purpose." (49) Hence the following analysis charts key elements in the text's development, juxtaposing the often interdependent features of each chapter. According to Robert Wilson in 'History on the Rocks' (1996) this is a "muscular novel" that vacillates between nature and a demotic democracy of the ordinary person, but finally is sympathetic towards its protagonist, Aymer Smith (x9). For Lane, "the protagonist is a humanist, someone who thinks he cares, but is revealed to be a pompous prig out of touch with the world he wants to save." (27) Aymer's pomposity and apparent do-good intentions can be interpreted radically differently, given his self-evident vulnerability. He is acted upon and mocked. Crace implies that an ethical judgment is required in facing the complex human interactions of everyday situations, recognizing even in the mundane what Ricoeur in *The Symbolism of Evil* (1969) calls the "possibility of evil." (3) Aymer is an unthinking thinker, for as Emmanuel Levinas says in *On Thinking of the Other: entre nous* (1998 [1991]): "A particular being can take itself for a totality only if it is unthinking. Not that it is wrong or thinks badly or foolishly – it simply does not think." (13) Aymer significantly misinterprets agency in others, but importantly without malice. This is Crace's most conventional novel in terms of idiomatic style, chronology, but also its specificity. However, although set in November 1836 in Wherrytown, as Hamilton-Pearson comments, "Unlikely as it seems, the settings of *Continent* and *Signals* have much in common. This makes sense if one remembers L. P. Hartley's dictum that 'the past is a foreign country,' because it is evident that Crace's imagination is mobilized by confrontations between various kinds of foreignness, and that 1836 is quite as foreign as his seventh continent." (38)

Crace's imaginary community by the sea, and Dry Manston, a tiny hamlet further down the coast where two kelpers live, are both located near Cradle Rock, a huge rocking stone set above the sea, whose balance is a symbol of the ethical engagement of the text, representing a wavering between different senses of the world. According to Begley this setting is in part "anchored by a 'real' geography," (184) but not an urban one. If the new arrivals to the city in *Arcadia* manifest uncertainty, they are nevertheless migrants drawn by the 'sorcery' of the urban mass and its economic benefits. In contrast in *Signals of Distress* the arrivals in Wherrytown are more numerous, and their reasons contingent, and heterogeneous. Wherrytown seems microcosmically small.[7] Unlike *Arcadia*, its locations remain remote and rural, distant from the violence that occurs in the brief glimpse of the town at the novel's end, a chthonic and threatening addendum. The novel's chief concern is the disturbed balance of a small community and the fate of individuals literally in transit.

Seascape and landscape feature strongly. The sea delivers or attracts a range of visitors who then explore both themselves and the littoral nature and possibilities of the coastline, a theme present in *The Gift of Stones*. Generally the characters represent traditional (recognizably Shakespearean) archetypes: a radical male virginal puritan, an unsympathetic ambitious brother, two young lovers brought together by fate, a Rabelasian female innkeeper, and a grasping merchant. Cracean elements persist, for as Crace says:

> The critics who said it was a dismissal of my previously established style, in almost every respect were wrong. Because it was set in a named place, they presumed it was a realist novel, set in west Cornwall, near Penzance. Actually the landscape is just as invented as the landscapes of the other novels, something I've dreamt up in order to fool you that it's real. The use of stones and the use of landscape, as metaphor and as character, are exactly part of my usual kind of plot. And it's very much part of my overall agenda to that point, which is concerned with communities on the edge, undergoing change. However, there were significant differences from other books. Undeniably it's set in a named year and a named country – even if you don't want to specify whether it was exactly Cornwall or not – and what this meant was for the first time I had an idiom I could use, one I was almost obliged to use, because in the 1820s and 1830s people spoke in a certain way, which is a matter of record.[18]

The impulse for historical specificity, exploring social nuances, allows the characters through idiomatic dialogue to experience a gamut of emotions and epiphanies, often romantic. The shaping force of nature is recurrent, partly conveyed in a further symbolic aspect of the Cradle Rock, representing the delicate equilibrium of forces that constitute the ontology or being of the world, a fragility reflecting the situation of many of the characters. In disturbing the social balance, small decisions and actions have unintended and yet substantial consequences. The power of the sea and of the elements can mould human lives. Crace choreographs the disparate events around a series of repeated journeys along the coast. As he explains, "The main journey is Wherrytown up to Cradle Rock, which is a place where you would rest, and continue to where the women live and the boat was wrecked, Dry Manston, and subsequently the walk back."[19] As Meletinsky comments, "Modern mythification uses the cyclical aspect of myths and rituals to express universal archetypes and to structure the narrative." (312) At the end Crace's narrative is resituated, first in imaginary dream locations, second in the city and finally briefly in the ocean. The preceding pattern is displaced by fantasy, by violence and death, a social and metaphysical disruption. Crace's historical impulse expresses a contemporary mythical consciousness.

The force and presence of nature is established early as a motif. The opening chapter is tumultuous; 'The "Belle" and the "Tar,"' two ships, battle a storm that is so strong that "A few miles down the coast from Wherrytown, the Cradle Rock, which normally would take the efforts of two strong men before it began to seesaw on its pivot stone, teetered, fluctuated, rocked from just the muscle of the gale." (1) Having suffered seasickness, Aymer Smith is aboard the paddle-driven steam-packet, the *Ha'porth of Tar*. As a puritanical moralist he had undertaken personally to represent his family soap business, intent on explaining why the company's new process based on developments by Leblanc makes the local kelp collectors redundant, although in reality this virgin seeks a country wife.[20] Aymer is central, and his rites of passage constitute much of the novel. Certainly through him the novel becomes, in part, an ironic self-conscious reflection by Crace on his particular brand of secular Puritanism. *The Belle of Wilmington*, a sailing barque, crewed by Americans under Shipmaster Comstock, with Otto, a slave, chained below with the four hundred cattle loaded at Montreal, suffers from the storm's violence, and is beached on a sand-bar with the loss of four sailors. This is a crucial event, significant in terms of the kinds of juxtaposition it creates, and its origins lie in Crace's own experiences of the West Country and the Isles of Scilly:

> There has been for many generations a family of photographers called the Gibsons, who photographed shipwrecks in the Isles of Scilly and the West Country, mostly the Penwith Peninsula of Cornwall which is the far west part. Those photographs are immensely powerful black and white pictures, all of wrecked ships, sometimes ships still in the sea and being broken up, sometimes beached. They were my companions while I was writing, providing stimulation for the book. The photographs represent something about an isolated community at that time, way out of contact. Suddenly one day wrecked on your beach is a boat; something almost inexplicable and unprecedented is delivered on your shore. One of the reasons for setting this book in the nineteenth century is that this is the last time you can have such inexplicable, sudden interfaces between things you haven't heard of or things you haven't encountered before, in this case a black man and American sailors.[21]

As the *Belle* is wrecked, the narrative juxtaposes the cautious packing of Aymer with Otto's injury aboard ship and the fate of the ship's bitch, Whip, cast into the sea with a 'signal of distress' that Ralph ties around her neck. The dog's name symbolizes the realities of slavery and oppression, ironic since it is one of the few English words that Otto can articulate. This ensign is found hours later by seventeen-year-old Miggy Bowe, a kelper from Dry Manston, and the alarm is raised by her mother, Rosie. The rescuers, local fishermen, are amazed by the African, a result of their cultural isolation, their innocence.

Miggy's desire for Palmer Dolly, a young fisherman, is displaced when a young American, Ralph, playfully attempts to retrieve the ensign from Miggy's neck. As if through calamity and rescue, another Shakespearean motif, the two are drawn together by fate. By this point Crace has established the major locations, the inn without name where they lodge being a focal point. As Crace says, "Most of the main players are out of place. They're either waiting to be dislocated entirely – they're going to the New World as emigrants – or they are dislocated because they are washed up on the shores of this place where their culture, and their attitudes and their responses don't really gel. The American sailors, Aymer himself, certainly Otto, and even the cattle themselves, are all dislocated."[22] The novel's intricate plot maps the nuances of characters' encounters and their underlying responses, replete with the minutiae of such interactions between this isolated community and their visitors. Begley identifies the consequences of a typically Cracean strategy of deceit:

> Critics praised the book's 'period precision,' and certain rustic details are particularly striking, like a tilled field at dusk smothered with the town's surplus of herring: 'a shoal of pilchards staring at the moon, their eyes as dead as flint, their scales like beaten tin, their fraying fins and tails like frost, their flesh composting for the next year's crop.' Crace delights in announcing to interviewers that this detail is wholly invented – fake folklore: As far as he knows, no nineteenth-century farmer ever fertilized fields with unwanted fish. (Think of it as the author's intertidal fantasy.) (231)

Crace delights too in the poetic incongruities of these false images, his uncanny symbol of fertilization and renewal. The generic landscape and knowledge of local detail are synthesized through the medium of Crace's fabulist inclinations.

In the second chapter, 'The Journey West,' Aymer, who prides himself on plain speaking, is escorted to the inn by George. He dislikes Aymer's bookish and opinionated reasoning. Tim Parks in 'On the Rocks' (1994) considers "Aymer Smith is the only fully and satisfyingly created character, but far too foolish and minor to constitute any comment on the whole obsession with holding liberal points of view." (36) Aymer's radicalism is deeper than Parks suggests. Throughout Aymer rationalizes and interrogates everything in a manner that is disengaged from the underlying realities of situations. He is awkward, evoking hostility with his hectoring manner, but it is through him that Crace can engage with one of the underlying possibilities of the book. As Crace indicates Aymer's characterization should not be regarded as fundamentally negative and represents a knowing critique of the radical left in Britain, combining elements of self-criticism and self-awareness.

> People think that the book is hostile to Aymer. I am shocked when people ask why I decided to sustain a book with such an appalling character, because actually I'm fond of him, in the way that only a person of the left could be. To some extent it's a fond critique of the left, and equally of my own political posturing. I was always aware that I was a person with an implacable, unmovable political stance on just about everything that I would be pleased to share with anybody. I wouldn't give an inch or listen to other people's points of view, something unfeeling and heavy-handed and roughshod about my political position, and it's still there. And this reflects a criticism that you can make of the left, which can't see a good deed for the principles, missing out on all their good deeds in order to find such principles. Poor old Aymer is very much like that. And, of course, we need people that are highly motivated by principle, but maybe it's a good idea to be reminded that they're not necessarily doing anybody any favours on the way.[23]

Aymer remains distant from the common person, a separation encountered variously. Initially, he regards the villagers as uncouth, especially Mrs Yapp, the innkeeper. "He had, he felt, been treated with hostility. The woman hadn't even stood to greet him. That was not behaviour to admire. And George the parlourman had seemed to find his conversation comic, except when he attempted jokes. He hadn't even shown gratitude when Aymer had presented him with a bar of white soap by way of thanks." (17) Superficially Aymer appears to negate others, imposing his understanding as a kind of violence in Levinas' terms, not completely in opposition to Ricoeur's possibility of evil since that is precisely what it will evoke. However, at one level his impulse represents a more deeply empathic, if confused mutual understanding, and he is partly redeemed by his attempts to think through the meaning of things, however inadequate his understanding.

Aymer writes to Howells, the local agent for the company that his brother, Matthias, has transformed with its "ninety adult hands." (19) Their products do not interest Aymer. His affinities lie elsewhere. "He was a Sceptic, a Radical and an active Amender," (20) thought foolish by his sibling. Despite Aymer's interventions on behalf of the workers "He didn't have an easy manner with the factory hands. He wasn't even liked. But he could fight on their behalf." (20) The little-travelled Aymer, unlike his brother, feels a moral compunction to notify Howells, and the kelpers, in person, a matter of "Duty" and "Conscience" that compels him to take the voyage. "He was surprised how travel unleashed him, how he could talk to sailors on the boat with a freedom absent from his home and city life." (22–3) As George and Mrs Yapp read and appropriate the letter to Howells, Aymer encounters lodgers at the inn, Robert and Katie Norris, emigrants about to leave for Canada. The curt Howells returning from the site of the wreck alerts the inn to the imminent arrival of the sailors from the *Belle* and insults Smith, creating an ongoing antipathy.

In the third chapter, 'Shared Beds,' not knowing that in the flurry of excitement George has not handed over his missive, Aymer engages in various acts of imagination. He hypothesizes about how to address Howells and fantasizes about Katie Norris. Rather than being grounded, his world is unconsciously both chimerical and creative. An underlying desire is the motivation for offering to share his room with Norris and his wife as a solution to the overcrowding, establishing opportunities for his sexual fantasies. On arrival Otto is an object of curiosity, exotic to the locals. "What did they know except what they'd learned at fairs or from sailors or in farthing pamphlets they'd bought from pedlars? That Africans were ruled by dogs or smelled like dogs? That Africans didn't wear clothes and had no tongues, no names, no navels? That black men didn't dream? The Wherrytowners did their best to catch sight of a navel or a tongue, to find his oddities." (33) Otto finds this harsh environment equally odd, an important juxtaposition by which Crace humanizes him. Aymer exhibits empathy despite his often ludicrous, ill-adjusted manner. Drawn to the tackle room where Otto is locked, he attempts to feed him and insists to

George that Otto's wounds be treated. Finding that the preacher, Mr Phipps, tends to the sick, Aymer summons him. Phipps suggests baptism rather than medicine. Aymer's response is equally idealist or ideological, for as he later writes to his brother, "'I think it is my task and obligation to serve the sacred cause of Negro emancipation by visiting upon this man the benefits that Mr Wilberforce has brought about in our own land but which, alas, do not yet flourish in America.'" (41) For all of his awkwardness and ideological insistence, Aymer is a symbol of progressive change. As Robert Wilson concludes, "Aymer has new, democratic ideas about work, class, slavery and religion, which both the sailors and the townspeople meet with skepticism and even derision." (x9)

In the fourth chapter, 'Aymer's Duty,' Comstock, the inn's guests and the *Belle*'s crew are fed on 'squab' or leftover pies in the main two rooms, and the occasion signifies a shift of Aymer's consciousness, creating in him a sense of wellbeing. Ralph Parkiss is teased by his shipmates for admitting his attraction to Miggy and in the more formal room Aymer parades his erudition to the annoyance of Comstock. "Here were two universes, the solemn and the jubilant, the reverential and the scurrilous, connected by an open door." (45) Aymer's lack of self-awareness creates much of the novel's tension, humour and pathos. Partly to silence Aymer, one of the crew, John Peacock, is encouraged to intervene with a tall tale of three men frozen crossing the St Lawrence, one of whom is revived when the boat is retrieved in the ocean five months later. Aymer objects to the irrationality of the account. In *Signals of Distress* the rational and the acquisitive are dominant discourses, and the imaginative becomes transient and peripheral. Sanctimoniously Aymer refuses treacle pudding because of its sugar, or "'Slave dust, that's my name for it,'" (53) only to be reminded by George that he sleeps on another slave product. "'They's cotton sheets. And cotton is the consequence of what? I'll have your bed stripped back to the bolster, so you can sleep in peace. Just say the word.'" (54) The juxtapositions highlight various significant themes, with George's bluff comments contrasting Aymer's pretentiousness. Crace explains, "Finally I could have characters who were saying things that were unintentionally funny or were funny on purpose. I could set someone who is not educated but smart against someone who was educated but not very smart and have some fun at both of their expenses, as when George talks to Aymer."[24] Later, Aymer's sexual dreams of Mrs Yapp are interrupted

Arcadia and *Signals of Distress*

by the sound of Katie Norris urinating into a chamber pot, and the sight of her buttocks and her embrace with her husband in the early Sabbath light.

Aymer escapes outside, and motivated by Howells' incivility, he decides to walk along the coast to inform the kelpers of their plight. He releases Otto whom he encourages to flee. This pivotal moment seems impulsive, almost unconsidered, unlike Aymer's polemical thoughts and interventions. Otto's flight is an ambivalent symbol of freedom, and demonstrates with its consequences the limits of Aymer's introspection and rationality, especially when compared to George's more instinctive interventions that follow. There is something constrained in Aymer's sense of commonality and freedom. As Crace says:

> Comparing Aymer's relationship with Otto to George's relationship with him, all the higher ideals are adhered to by Aymer. He comes up with the idea of releasing this man, setting him *metaphorically* free. What he's physically done is to take a man, who's been shipwrecked, and is lost – but at least he's in a warm store and he's being fed – and turn him out, into the cold landscape of Cornwall where he has no friends, no means of feeding himself, and no language to negotiate his own future. Aymer had made things worse for Otto. However, George who hasn't set him free, who as far as we know hasn't got an opinion about black people, is the person who nevertheless displays good sense, and secretly goes off and feeds and helps him. Actually without any principles, without any introspection, he is the person who helps Otto.[25]

At the end of this chapter the essential dynamics of the plot have been established, and much that follows is concerned with how the displacement of individuals allows new perspectives, the romantic undercurrents that result, and the confrontations brought about by different worldviews, much of which results from Otto's presence and the opportunities for short-term profit offered by the *Belle*.

In the fifth chapter, 'Dry Manston,' on the Sabbath by the site of the wreck, Miggy and her mother attempt somewhat comically to catch one of the shipwrecked cattle for illicit meat. After her mother's return Miggy encounters first a heifer on the coastal path and then Ralph who "was honouring his sailor's boast, to see what she'd got hidden in her breeches. He's volunteered to walk the six miles to the ship to discover how it had fared since it had beached, but he was looking for the girl. She made a din – in case he passed her by." (61) The interactions are comedic, an interlude after the intensity of the preceding confrontations and events. Returning home they encounter Aymer on his mission, nonplussed by the kelpers' indifference to his news, not aware that previously Howells had taken so much of the profits that most are relatively unaffected. Aymer's innocence is further exemplified by his shock at kelpers who offer daughters for his care if he can advance them. For Miggy, Aymer typifies a certain kind of traveller, those she has seen in more temperate months drawn to the Cradle Rock:

> Miggy knew the type of man he was, though he was out of season, a winter cuckoo. From time to time, usually in the spring and the summer, she'd come across such pale-looking fellows walking the coast, with knapsacks on their backs, and walking sticks. These were the only people that she'd ever met that were more than a day's walk from their homes – apart from Ralph. (66)

Thereby Crace confirms Aymer as a radical, quasi-romantic archetype. His arrival disturbs Miggy who flees home, escaping his overstated polemic concerning handshaking, "talking like a sermon" according to Ralph's account to Miggy's mother before Aymer's arrival. His offer of soap and a shilling is rebutted by Rosie who is concerned for her daughter since, unlike others, the Bowes depend almost entirely upon kelping. Finally Aymer is confronted with the consequences of the family's business decisions, the logic of new trading practices.

In the bare earth-floored cottage an embroidered passage from 'Jeremiah' passes proleptic comment of both Ralph and Miggy's fates: "Weep sore for him that goeth away:/ for he shall return no more,/ nor see his native country." (74) After his offer of two shillings is dismissed, Aymer fantasizes about the possibilities of Miggy as a wife, triggering one of the daydreams that characterize the book, hypothetical scenes of friendship, love and marriage. Subsequently Aymer aids them in recovering one of the dead cattle. He suggests it might be regarded as flotsam, since his scruples will not allow him to aid stealing a live one. "Aymer Smith was not a Revolutionist." (77) The episode results in knowledge and experiences being challenged by external realities. Nauseated by the flurry of gulls and fish feeding on the blood and meat, Aymer encounters seaweed familiar from his books, but is shocked by the very colours, surprised by its ontological intensity. His limitations represents those of an often copious and yet unworldly knowledge. Promising to return, ironically with his fantasy of a country wife offset by Ralph's reciprocated ardour, Aymer requests Ralph's initially reluctant company back to Wherrytown. Such ironic juxtapositions of desire create a recurrent motif in the novel, a disharmony of natural passions. The two divert to the Cradle Rock which Ralph attempts to set rocking, "But Cradle Rock was so exactly poised that Ralph's weight only deadened it. He couldn't make it move." (81) This landmark derives from Crace's local knowledge:

> I have climbed up many times to the Logan Rock on Treen Cliffs in West Cornwall. This thing used to rock quite a bit. But at the end of the Napoleonic Wars a lieutenant and his men went up there one night drunk. They got a great wooden tree trunk and they shifted the Logan Rock until it tumbled to the ground. Next morning they were all arrested, and the local magistrate said to this lieutenant, 'You have to put it back.' And he spent the next eighteen years working out ways to replace the Logan Rock. It bankrupted him, and when he got it back up, it never rocked again; it was so delicate he could never make it rock again. So you imagine how that, as a true story, an absolutely unexaggerated story – well, it might be exaggerated over the years, but that's exactly how I heard the story – made me recognize what a wonderful image the idea of a rocking stone was. In other words, the natural world delivers to humankind something which is big and impressive and joyful, but very, very easily toppled. Everything hangs in the balance, the delicate balance of nature. If you stand below a huge stone, which might weigh as much as a bus, and with your own shoulder you make it move, you have a physical counterpart of the arrogance that people on the left feel when they think that their leaflet is going to change the world. That appeals to me: the Logan Rock as an image that a mere human can change something with his or her weight alone was central to my understanding of the kind of person that Aymer Smith was.[26]

Of course in a sense, this equilibrium, the bonds of love and friendship, the feeling for equality that Aymer instinctively feels, are all part of a human balance that contrasts with the forces of greed and shortsightedness characterized by Mrs Yapp, Walter Howells, Captain Comstock and the preacher. Abandoning his sling, Aymer helps Ralph, their rhythm setting it in motion, a movement away from its equilibrium, and nature restored to its own violent rhythm, its trajectory symbolizing change. As they return struggling back through the snow, fishermen set out at midnight, since "On this God-flinching coast it was bad luck to catch or eat a Sunday fish." (83)

The sixth chapter, 'Evensong,' describes the Sabbath in Wherrytown, and reactions to George's report of Otto's 'liberation.' Mrs Yapp and Comstock assume that Aymer has disappeared with the slave leaving his own possessions. Their intolerant negativity is revealed. "Who should they blame but Aymer Smith, the meddler with the soap, the sugar abolitionist." (84) Flirting with Comstock, Alice Yapp removes Aymer's sheets and his possessions, another appropriation. The Captain meets Howells, who suggests taking care of the repairs and other problems Comstock has listed, and arranging retributive justice for Smith. "'I'll see he gets a beating. There's fellows that I know will gladly break a bone or two and only charge a sovereign. I'll write a letter to a man I have up east. He's in my debt and has a decent fist.'" (88) For Levinas, violence against otherness represents "Life of the living in the struggle for life," (xii) but finally reduces possibilities, atavistically negating civilization. In its microcosm *Signals of Distress* configures a layer of potentially malevolent manipulation which underlies apparently normative interacting social forces. Of course, given Crace's ideological proclivities, this is exhibited by those most associated with profit and control. Howells confirms Comstock's impulse to violence, his reduction of being to will and struggle. As Levinas writes, this entails a reduction of both otherness and being: "In a sense, the only thing at issue for the event of being is the being of that very being. To be as such is, from the first, to be preoccupied with being . . . To be: already an insistence on being as if a 'survival instinct' . . . were its meaning." (xii) As if unconsciously although only momentarily escaping Howells' malevolent influence, Comstock leads the Americans towards the chapel through the warren of the town, delighting like innocents in the snow, a contrast to the preceding machinations. Addressing his expanded congregation, Phipps' sermon concerns images and concepts of return, by which Crace stresses both the inevitable and imminent departures, and the flux of natural events. Without acceding to religiosity, Crace confirms the failings and common humanity of any such gathering, a temporarily extended community.

> Here in his congregation were a hundred hearts, in love, or grieving, or resentful, or simply fearful of the midnight fish, or palpitating with the guilt of failing to be saints. There were no paragons. Were Mr Phipps to go round as his congregation sang its final hymn ('Our home in Thee, Our Lord') and place his hand upon the hair and hats of thieves and adulterers and bullies and those who failed to love their neighbours as themselves, then there wouldn't be a head untouched. (92)

Arcadia and Signals of Distress

Man is less fallen than imperfect. The chapter ends with a reversal of its beginning: Aymer discovering an empty inn, and the absence of his bedding and possessions.

In Chapter 7, 'Sitting on Blisters,' with Katie inflamed by the beauty of her husband's singing, the two return to the inn after chapel. Ironically, her family in opposing her impending marriage and emigration conjured an oppressive image of sex:

> Her elder married sister and her Ma, not pleased to lose their Katie to the colonies, had warned of 'duty' and 'indignities' and 'getting used to manly ardours'. They had not mentioned that manly ardours might be shared by wives. Perhaps they didn't know. So no one had prepared Katie for how satisfying baby-making would prove to be. (96)

The waking Aymer interrupts the attempted passion, trying consciously to be humorous despite the news of Yapp's pre-emptory seizure of his goods. Advised by George to flee because of public suspicion concerning Otto's liberation, Aymer refuses and a confrontation with Comstock ensues. The public mood vacillates, initially making Aymer a figure of fun. However, after cuffing Aymer the captain has to be conciliatory when his victim finds a persuasive voice. Comically and yet perversely, Mrs Yapp attempts to blame the slave for the purloined goods. News of the escape troubles the Wherrytowners whose fears are exacerbated by some of the Americans after Comstock's departure. Although pompous, and not always accurate, Aymer's defence of Africans challenges the underlying ignorance, even appealing ironically that the loss of sheets and soap indicate an aristocratic nature, much to Mrs Yapp's discomfiture and George's amusement. Otto's presence persists, and according to Crace, "For me, Otto was never absent from the book. Maybe I didn't sufficiently stress this, but he was always the driving narrative force, because he represents the future and he represents dislocation. This novel is about dislocation."[27] In recounting the episode to the Norrises, a tearful Aymer finally comprehends Otto's predicament, and he is consoled by Katie who "pressed Aymer's head against her stomach and cotton nightdress as if he were a child and not a man," (113) a register of his vulnerability and underdeveloped emotional capacity.

In Chapter 8, 'Rankin's Dollar,' the Dolly family find the bloated corpse of one of the lost Americans among their catch of pilchards, and Palmer uses the opportunity to attempt to ingratiate himself with Comstock, hoping to volunteer for his crew. "He was dreaming distantly, though he hadn't got a landscape for America, or any idea how cruel the voyage there would be. He couldn't guess the span of the Atlantic, nor how the ocean, far from land, would scarp and dip like wolds, the *Belle* a wind-tossed wooden hut amongst the water hills." (120) Taking a dollar from Skimmer who searches the dead man's pockets, Palmer risks his life to take the news to Comstock, whom he finds in Mrs Yapp's room. "The American Captain was standing there, and naked too, but for the blanket round his waist and pillow cotton in his hair." (124)

In Chapter 9, 'Star-Gazy Pie,' Howells enthusiastically writes a letter "on behalf of Shipmaster Comstock, to William Bagnall, debtor, rascal, bludger, footpad, horse-thief, pugilist," (128) arranging a beating for Aymer on his return home. Subsequently Howells joins the community gathered on the beach for the pilchard catch. He insists its size means a glut, and lower prices, representing profit disturbing the world's balance. This carnivalesque scene symbolizes industry, a social cohesion, and ingenuity with every part of the pilchard used. However, not all is harmonious. Rosie is only too aware of the impending loss of her daughter given Miggy's eagerness to seek out Ralph. The Wherrytowners resent Howells' tithe as he oversees from his horse.[28] Aymer is peripheral. "Where did Aymer Smith fit in? He was, of course, the Smith & Son who Walter Howells no longer needed. Who Rosie Bowe would learn to do without. Who Shipmaster Comstock took to be a kidnapper. Who was a coward and a weeper. Who was (his own assessment now) an apostate not only to God but to himself. Who had abandoned Otto to the snow." (137–8) He converses with George concerning the nature of the pilchard, a 'pelagic' or 'surface' fish, Aymer obsessed with classificatory nuances that evoke in George a deep suspicion of words. George regards Aymer's usage as divorced from any common reality, although George's ripostes mean Aymer regards him as an intellectual equal. Addressing her mother Aymer's proposes marriage to Miggy, but is interrupted by the arrival of Rankin's body, a reminder of death, and subsequently the public embrace of Miggy by Ralph, a symbol of passionate love, unavailable to Aymer. The world is indifferent to his desire and his concept of truth.

Howells responds malevolently, since conversing with Comstock he remains unmoved by Aymer's apparent innocence, unconcerned about the consequences of the letter he has dispatched. Ironically, during the evening's festivities, after recommending Lyell's *The*

Principles of Geology to Robert Norris as shipboard reading, another sign of his objectifying and classificatory impulses, Aymer explains one of his beliefs. "'Amendism is the scientific view that every offence – Mr Phipps might call it sin – should be settled only by reparations of an equal force,'" (153) emphasizing the disproportion of everything concerning Howells, including his tithe on virtually all activities in the locality. Clumsy as he is, Aymer offers a sense of proportion and equity. The rest of the day is engaged at Dry Manston in the corralling of the cattle and the removal of the *Belle* from the bar, followed by a night-time celebration with dancing. Excited by dancing with Katie, and slightly drunk, Aymer "lay awake and tried to picture Otto going home, the stone and sand of Africa, the moon and sun, the trees perspiring in the night." (155)

In Chapter 10, 'The Faintest Voice,' after a sexual dream involving Miggy, Katie and Mrs Yapp, Aymer decides against his better judgment to stay until the following week and the return of the *Tar*. "This was a symmetry worth waiting for," (157) ostensibly motivated by a desire to explore the countryside. His first encounter is with Phipps who tells him of the hunt and reward for Otto. As far as Phipps is concerned, using scripture to support slavery, the African "'is a savage. Dangerous. Unbaptized!'" (162). This indicates Phipps' true nature. A gravedigger offers evidence of Otto's presence, citing occurrences the reader knows to attribute elsewhere. Determined to find Otto, Aymer takes food and goes with Whip towards Cradle Rock, fantasizing about offering Otto employment, thus satisfying his social conscience. He visits the Bowes, listening to the dispute between mother and daughter concerning Miggy's intention to travel to America with Ralph. On Aymer's return to the rock the food has vanished and in his eagerness he tramps across country towards what he thinks is the napkin, another 'signal of distress,' only to find his own discarded sling. This is a pivotal episode. Aymer's certainties vanish, as the world impacts: "There were no granite stepping stones. The ground refused to take his weight. His boots sank in. The earth expired its brackish coffin smells." (171) Escaping this sense of death that periodically haunts the book, Aymer finds a wall-top path from which perspective he appears absurd, exaggerated and comic, as is the world itself. "The whole length of his body was reliefed against the sky. He looked as if he was ten feet tall, a comic, skinny stilts-man at a fair, with performing dog. A stringy hedgerow ghost. A diabolic scarecrow on the move." (174) He is lost in himself, thinking guiltily of Otto. In a landscape with Hardyesque resonance, crossing a field Aymer finds himself amid fertilizing fish which "had frightened him. Where was the order in the universe? How long before the sky was tumbling with frogs and rats. How long before the ears of corn had fins? He had never known such superstitious, concentrated fear, nor ever felt so far from home." (175) He finds refuge in a hut that he discovers, resurrecting the remnants of a fire on which someone had cooked a meal, an echo of Otto. This is confirmed in the morning when George arrives carrying food and a jacket, so Aymer is "happier than he could say to have the parlourman and the lantern as companions home, and to have his conscience liberated by the happy certainty that Otto had an unexpected friend." (179)

In Chapter 11, 'Gone to Ground,' rumours of Otto intensify among the increasingly uneasy locals as a chicken and eggs disappear. At Rankin's funeral Phipps refuses Aymer access to "blessed ground." However, much to Phipps' fury, since he too is drawn by Katie's attractiveness, the Norrises stay outside with Aymer signifying their friendship. Informed that George is leading the hunting party for Otto, Aymer unsuccessfully pursues them. As Howells and Comstock drink rum, predictably the search party returns empty-handed. In Chapter 12, 'Amor,' the work continues throughout Sunday on the *Belle*. Miggy, who flees to Wherrytown each day, encounters Palmer on the quay as he helps with the repairs. Ironically, Howells finds him so useful he conspires to prevent him from departing. Palmer reveals to Miggy his dollar, the figure of Liberty symbolizing their ambitions, and he confesses his desire to become a sailor. Aymer decides his promised payment to Miggy and her mother will be made on the day of departure, and lovesick he seeks Katie among the seaweed, but irritated by his obsessive attentions over the past few days the couple avoids him, another rejection.

Finally, over an evening meal of beef pie with music the inn celebrates completion of the boat. Phipps warns his diminished congregation of "'Master Sacrilege and his bloody uncles, Mr Cant, Mr Sin and Mr Cynicism,'" (203) which they take to refer to Howells, the sailors, Sabbath-breakers and the African. Subsequently, Phipps' dream of friendship with the Norrises and Aymer reveals his underlying isolation. Throughout the novel unconscious desires surface, expressed in aggression, or alternatively in dreams. The world seems precarious and restive, and in the thirteenth chapter, 'Cradle Rock,' any apparent equilibrium achieved vanishes. The younger sailors are

Arcadia and Signals of Distress

sent to recover the cattle, led by Ralph and instructed in dealing with the horses by Palmer. While Ralph departs to see Miggy, who masturbates him in their first sexual encounter, the rest become drunk on treacle rum and brandy purloined from the stores. After their arduous struggle with the livestock and the wagons, Palmer reveals his wish to stowaway. In their drunkenness the sailors dislodge the rock from its fulcrum, before they retreat to Wherrytown, sobered by their feat, with the coast unalterably changed, a symbol of a world altered. For Paula Burnett in 'Ocean Views' (1994), "This is a bleak book, its emblem the Fall, as enacted in the Americans' toppling of Cradle Rock." (36)

The fourteenth chapter, 'The Last of Wherrytown,' Crace describes both comically and poignantly the partings at the departure of the *Belle*. An underlying sense of portentousness and loss is confirmed by the fate of the ship indicated in a mock news-cutting as an addendum to the narrative. Lotty Kyte, an emigrant who is to join her brother in Montreal, so fears the sea's potential that she arrives with an opium bag around her waist and blindfolded, as "some Madame Haruspex from a traveling fair had warned the family that if Lotty ever saw the sea she'd die, 'and not by drowning'. So that is how she'd lived her life. She'd stayed inland for thirty-seven years." (220)[29] Reinvoking the theme of the intolerance of reason for faith, Aymer fulminates first against such "blind superstition," and then at Phipps' suggestion that he should pray for the Norrises. Both Aymer and Phipps demonstrate a lack of empathy or any capacity to accede to the view of others. Aymer points out to Katie that one might read in Lotty a parable or image of blind hope, but tired of his lectures Katie seeks simply his good wishes. To crown Aymer's sense of loss Comstock insists on the return of Whip despite Aymer's offer of twenty shillings. Unseen, Palmer Dolly stows away without farewells, again ironic and poignant given his optimism contrasts with his ultimate fate. Miggy and her mother receive three guineas each from Aymer, fuelling Mrs Yapp's suspicions, before the ship departs, dissolving into the fog.

> The coastal steampacket, *Ha'porth of Tar*, passed within fifty yards of the *Belle*. They rang their greetings across the water, and Lotty Kyte, reluctant to abandon the sea air and the deck, waved both hands into the darkness and had no fear. It seemed to Aymer that the tussling spirits of the age were passing on the sea; the old, the new, the wind, the steam, the modest and the brash. The future would be driven by steam, he was sure. It was a more compliant slave than wind. (228)

The accuracy of Aymer's predictions allows him a curious authenticity. Given the ending, the image of Lotty is almost bathetic since fearfulness would have been more appropriate, particularly as the prediction upon which she depends will prove fallacious, for if she never sees the sea, she will drown blindfolded.

Returning to the inn, in misery Aymer finds the energy to refute Mrs Yapp's scurrilous suggestions concerning himself and Miggy. He hears of the Cradle Rock, whose fate is blamed upon Otto, his name carved on a bench by Aymer cited as evidence. Wherrytown is reduced to a world of innuendo and parsimony. Aymer seeks hard evidence, joined at the rock by local fishermen searching for the stowaway Palmer. Aymer visits Rosie, whose evident sorrow contrasts with his timidity, although an underlying attraction creates an unexpected scene of passion. When Aymer's consoling words fail, finally he acts rather than hypothesizes, losing a broader innocence than simply his virginity.

> By Sunday she would be with child. The guess in Wherrytown would be that Rosie's new baby would be black. Everything unusual on the coast would, from that day, be put on Otto's bill. When no one could remember Aymer Smith or put a name to any of the Americans, or their ship even, the African would still be talked about. In fact, he gave a lasting phrase to Wherrytown. If anything went wrong – the harvest failed, the yeast went flat, a coin or button disappeared – they'd say 'Blame it on the African!' or 'Otto's been at work again.' (242–3)

Otto will achieve mythological status, but Aymer is to be forgotten. He scurries away shamefaced, his child his true gift to Rosie, who daydreams of her daughter's shipboard wedding and the consummation of her marriage.

Chapter 15, 'The Lands of Promise,' consists chiefly of Aymer's daydreams in the deserted inn as he awaits the dawn and his departure. In the first he imagines Miggy's future in Wilmington, heavily pregnant, with Aymer visiting under the Carolina sun, painting her portrait, which fantasy expresses Aymer's artistic desires. The second daydream is of seeking the Norrises in Canada and meeting Katie. "The Norrises hadn't gone to Canada for streets and market places. Their dreams had been a piece of land, a cabin in a clearing, privacy." (249) He imagines instead Lotty Kyte leafleting for her brother's firm, and finding the Norrises by the lakeside a few miles north of St Jean-Luc where he takes them furniture ordered from the Kytes. Of course

Arcadia and Signals of Distress

this is a romanticized pantisocratic view of the world, an outcome thwarted not only by the shipwreck, but by an impossible demand for harmony so contrasting with the realities of Wherrytown. In his imagination he becomes heroic, leaping logs to find the cabin where he confronts an image expressing his desire.

> He could see the aura of candlelight, and then the naked body of a woman, standing in a bowl of water. Her back was turned against the window and her hair was up. Her thighs were strong and freckled, just as he remembered them, although their toners were split in curving arcs of flesh, orange-warm from candle flame, pink-cold from the window light. She was the salmon and the thrush. Her hair was sand. She sang. She washed herself in Aymer's soap. (251-2)

This is an idealized vision of womanhood, but his memory of Katie singing "'For Death is but the Shaded Sea,'" (252) is a presentiment which disturbs his utopian vision. Finally he attempts to dream Otto back to Africa, but he cannot transcend reality or experience, capable only of imagining Otto at Dry Manston in winter.

> His eyes were tired, but he could recognize the frosty truth – that Otto's home was not in reach and never would be now. If he lived and had survived the snow, he could only be a ten-day walk away at most. He had his feet to carry him, and nothing more. Yes, Otto might be met again. Huzzah for that! He might be glimpsed. But it would only be on some English street. (254)

The daydreams, especially given the loss of lives at the novel's conclusion, emphasize the contingency of the future, and the limits of dreams and the imagination. Nevertheless, Aymer appears transformed, released from the over-literal and rational codes that have dominated his behaviour, and yet he remains an ambivalent character. He dedicates himself to searching for the escaped slave, fantasizing of their friendship.

Chapter 16, 'Good Boots,' is set in mid-January 1837. Aymer has returned home, wearing from his travels a tarpaulin coat and boots, symbolizing his transformation. Unlike his wife, Fidia, Aymer's brother, Matthias finds him more mature, less argumentative. Almost obsessively Aymer searches for Otto among the black inhabitants. Disappointed in a black drummer, Aymer on the advice of a black coachman he befriends, Scipio Jones, searches for Massa Hannibal, a prizefighter he hopes might be Otto. Ironically, Hannibal is an octoroon with an Italian accent. Aymer is followed by William

Bagnall, the recipient of Howells' letter, and his brother, Bagsy, who force Aymer into a stable yard where he is savagely beaten. "He stamped on Aymer's ankles and his feet. The tarsi cracked. Walter Howells had asked for broken bones. The Bagnalls had obliged. He'd asked for broken teeth as well. Bagsy found a cobblestone and brought it down on Aymer's mouth. Aymer had never known pain so fierce and concentrated." (269) The retributive force is shocking, the violence and evil of Howells realized vicariously. At his brother's town house, Fidia is reluctant to be disturbed, thinking Aymer drunk, but seeing his condition they care for him. Aymer feels dislocated, and thinks he is in Wherrytown before recognizing his nephew and nieces. He retreats to dreams restoring both the past and its apparent equilibrium. "He rolled it back on to its pivot stone. He set the Rock in motion. He made amends. He put the world to rights again. Helped only by the muscle of the wind, and by the charity of his dreams, the Cradle ascended and declined." (276) His desire is negated for only in imagination can the past and its apparent symmetry be recovered. As if to reaffirm that such a disrupted equilibrium can never be restored, the final page is an apparent facsimile of a fragment representing "A public announcement from Oliver's Register of Ships and Shipping Toronto, February 1837," of *The Belle of Wilmington* sinking in Cabot Strait of Nova Scotia. Wilson mistakes this as a factual element, stating that "Although the tale is fictitious, the *Belle* is not: On the final page of the novel Crace quotes from a real publication called *Oliver's Register of Ships and Shipping*, which describes the eventual destination of the ship's crew and passengers." (x9) In Cracean fashion the source, although it appears historical, is invented. The moment inverts the earlier recovery of the boat. "No soul survived save one small dog." (277) This final image is problematic, typically ambivalent, since it means the novel ends on two notes of negativity, subsumed into enduring transformations of life and death.

Notes

1 Dr Philip Tew, an unpublished telephone interview with Jim Crace recorded on an MP3 file, conducted from approx. 12:15 on 8 November 2004. Hereafter referred to as 'Crace–Tew: Telephone Interview 3.'
2 Ibid. Crace also refers to other sources. "*The City in History* by Lewis Mumford and a book called *Metropolis* by a chap called Jerome Charyn, and Jane Jacobs. Those were my ports of call really."

3 Ibid.
4 Ibid.
5 Ibid.
6 Ibid.
7 Such fairs are discussed by Jacobs in *The Economy of Cities*; see 128.
8 'Crace–Tew: Telephone Interview 3.'
9 Ibid. Crace adds that "Another trick to get you to like him is to see him in difficult circumstances, and of course he loses his job, and he is beaten up. So we feel sorry for him in that regard. It's the same with Joseph. We feel sorry for him because he's down on his luck, although he's difficult to like."
10 The same term is used by B. S. Johnson to refer to both his mother and archetypal motherhood in his last posthumously published novel, *See the Old Lady Decently* (1975).
11 'Crace–Tew: Telephone Interview 3.'
12 These antinomies are identified by Michael Squires in *The Pastoral Novel: Studies in George Eliot, Thomas Hardy, and D. H. Lawrence* (1974): 10.
13 'Crace–Tew: Telephone Interview 3.'
14 Ibid. Crace adds: "It's meant as a really obvious metaphor of the countryside being thrown at the town. An obvious thing is that a vegetable market is the countryside being brought to the town, and it actually is that."
15 Ibid.
16 Ibid.
17 Wherrytown Beach is near Penzance in Cornwall, but as Crace indicates the term is common, and therefore archetypal. MP3 file of a telephone conversation between Jim Crace and Dr Philip Tew, on 25 November 2004 from 15:00, hereafter referred to as 'Crace–Tew: Telephone Interview 4.'
18 Ibid.
19 Ibid.
20 Ibid. Crace indicates that his historical details for kelping derives from his own experience of the remains of the Kelp Industry in Scilly, commenting, "Every year, I clean out the kelp pits," and from Luke Over, *The Kelp Industry in Scilly* (1987). This explains the labour-intensive nature of kelping, the impact of Leblanc's discovery in 1787 so that "For many areas, including Scilly, kelping had declined and ceased by 1835," (3) especially since the Napoleonic Wars had delayed the first introduction of the Leblanc process into Britain until 1823 (22). Over comments of the process that "the smell, however, was both offensive and penetrating." (11) Aymer Smith's name may have been suggested by a new proprietor who arrived in Scilly in 1834, "Augustus Smith." (22)
21 Ibid. Crace refers to the 'Voorspoed Perranporth 1901' and 'Olympe Gunwalloe 1910.' See: www.gibsonsofscilly.co.uk

22 Ibid.
23 Ibid.
24 Ibid.
25 Ibid.
26 Ibid.
27 Ibid.
28 The dislike of Howells' method of extending credit rather than cash, and the fluctuation of prices both derive from Over's *The Kelp Industry in Scilly*, which describes the very instability of kelp prices, and the similar practices of tithes and credit rather than cash payment for both kelp and fish by local stewards and Scillonian kelp merchants (19–20).
29 Haruspex derives from a religious official in ancient Rome who interpreted omens by inspecting entrails in animal sacrifices. See Michael Quinion, 'World Wide Words.' www.worldwidewords.org/weirdwords/ww-har1.htm.

4

Death, belief and nature: *Quarantine* (1997) and *Being Dead* (1999)

Quarantine

Quarantine is familiar Cracean territory with its rhythmic prose and allusive qualities. Crace says, "It is most like a folktale of all of my work, and most like a scriptural text."[1] Kermode describes it as a "novel-fable." (8) As Gary Kamiya notes in 'Quarantine,' (1998) the central Biblical source is "Jesus' 40-day 'quarantine' in the wilderness, described in Matthew 4:1–11," (1) but as Richard Eder says in 'Cavedweller,' (1998) "Crace's portrait of Jesus is audacious and disconcerting." (2) According to Crace, "There was originally no intention that Christ was going to be a major figure. I was slightly embarrassed. I thought it was cheesy to say, 'Oh, and by the way there was a Nazarene called Jesus who was also in one of the caves,' just as a sentence in order to historically contextualize it."[2]

Crace undertook a trip to augment his sense of his chosen location; his account offers a brief indication of his writing method:

> Spending some time in the Judean desert gave me a sense of the landscape, which I could then misrepresent. But this was not the first desert I'd been into. I spent time in the desert around Khartoum when I was with VSO, and equally in the desert in Botswana which loans itself much more to intimate scrutiny than the rather dusty, old, baked, barren, not-quite-a-desert of Judea. So already I had plenty I could call upon, but I do think it made a difference. It reminded me of what the light's like and I came back with a book full of landscape notes.[3]

For Crace it remained "a hard book to write, but not a reluctant one," and his intention was that it should be both interrogative about its contexts and "to some extent didactic."[4] For Kermode the depiction of the wilderness "in obsessive detail: the geography and geology of the area, its birds and animals, insects and plants, its folk beliefs and superstitions," (8) creates a self-sustaining environment defined by its own vocabulary where "The effect is of an almost hallucinatory concentration." (8) Scott Bradfield notes in the *Observer Review* (1997) the importance of characterization: "In a story about the power of words to inspire people beyond their own limits, Crace's prose is clear, hard, resonant, and almost impossible to excerpt, since it generates a weird cumulative momentum." (16) Given Crace's emphasis on character interaction and plot, there follows a detailed critical explication of the interplay of such elements, although as Tobias Jones comments in 'A Voice Crying in the Wilderness,' (1997) "Whilst the story is deliberately orchestrated, and graced with a climactic denouement (with sex, storm and death) plot is never quite the point. It is somehow too meditative to be a page-turner." (39)

Given its setting, the original provenance may be unexpected – although perceptively Robert Irwin in 'Hiveward-Winging' (1997) realized that "*Quarantine* is about a handful of misfits brought together in a prolonged ordeal in the Judean desert" (21) – but helps to explain the strangeness and uneasiness of his travellers and to contextualize both their vulnerabilities and the novel's sense of liminality. Crace explains:

> In the Thatcher years near my home a place called the Palm Court was absolutely full of people receiving so-called 'care in the community' because they'd all been turned out of psychiatric hospitals. It was famously exposed on a television documentary, secret cameras showing how absolutely appalling it was. I visited on one occasion, and walking along a corridor, I encountered many tiny cell-like rooms. I was familiar with the inhabitants because they would wander around Moseley, having to hang around all day. They either looked like characters out of *One Day in the Life of Ivan Denisovich* or like the cast of *One Flew Over a Cuckoo's Nest*, very troubled people. They were often joyous, with a singing-in-the-street kind of trouble, but sometimes there was also aggressive behaviour.
>
> I was interested by people living on the edge, and impressed by the fact that otherwise they had absolutely nothing in common. It struck me as interesting to imagine another situation where everyone was living on the edge, with nothing in common save that their lives were teetering, either to fall into the abyss or to be saved at the last moment. At what point after that I realized that I could introduce Jesus, I'm not sure, and I'm not sure to what extent I thought up any other notions, but what is certain is that when I came up with Jesus in the desert, it was only to illustrate that initial concept.[5]

The transposition of madness and marginality to the Judean desert is both bold and striking. It adds a sense of a nullity, since the travellers' palpable fear of preterition permeates the text, their alienation transformed through their sense of the absence and failings of religiosity. Lane interprets the novel as a version of the Biblical narrative, one that is intentionally "out of control and, in its plethora of meanings, enriches a secular notion of the redemptive power of narrative." (31) The provenance suggests a pattern to these intersecting lives; their depiction, rather than augmenting narrative, explores the capacity concurrently to concatenate the literal and yet to propitiate, creating a narrative schizophrenia.

Crace's own scepticism concerning the spiritual and the miraculous influences his invented epigraph, ironically highlighting the scientific impossibility of the fasting indicated in his title: "The forty days of fasting described in religious texts would not be achievable – except with divine help, of course. History, however, does not record an intervention of that kind, and medicine opposes it." (iii) As Luke Timothy Johnson says in 'Jesus in the Desert,' (1998) "Like all good apocryphal authors, Crace seeks a gap or seam in the biblical narrative to exploit." (18) And yet as Crace concedes, "The book doesn't come across as an atheist text, and when you start adopting new scriptural modes in order to question those scriptural modes, it begins to sound exactly like the thing you are criticizing. It's full of invented biblical references that ape biblical references."[6] Crace's verbal repetition and recurring patterns of ideas mirror parabolic and evangelical accounts, culturally suggesting transcendence and poeticism. The contending dynamics of parable, including its contradictory 'extralinguistic' or metaphysical impulse, and what Lane describes as its "literary redemptive 'force'" (31), feature in *Quarantine*.[7] Moreover as with Biblical parable the focus is nevertheless the immediacy of the quotidian and mundane, a world bound by familiarities.

Kermode insists the novel's hallucinatory style "is deepened by the reports of dreams and by the shadows cast over the characters and events by the original story from which the new fable derives." (8) And yet it resonates with Crace's rejection of Christianity and its tenets; he insinuates his opinion that the Biblical source may simply constitute an earlier narrative. Crace outlines his view of Christianity's deficiencies in an interview with Minna Proctor in *Bomb Magazine* (2000):

> The Christian explanations for the scientific world are babyish, simplistic. That doesn't mean I sneer at people who believe in them, because of course such grand stories are very simplistic and straightforward, like the Icelandic sagas, Beowulf or all the Greek myths. Nevertheless, the simplemindedness of those narratives undermines the wonders of the universe. If you were to stand on the top of a hill – as you could have done in the 14th century – next to a religious practitioner and heard thunder and seen lightning, that religious practitioner might say, 'That is God expressing his anger at the sins of the universe.' It would have been the best available narrative. Indeed, the best available narrative of the time would have been that the world was flat. (3)

Crace's scepticism explains why initially he focuses not on Christ, but rather on the feverish Musa, dying in a desert tent. Expectations of grief and loss are refuted, since for his wife, Miri, her husband's imminent demise is "Good news," (1) which pun reworks the underlying original meaning of 'gospel.' The two have been abandoned by their caravan of traders, including Musa's uncles who take most of his supplies, leaving him alone with his pregnant wife, with only five goats and a lame donkey.

> It was Miri's duty to Musa, everybody said, to let the caravan go on through Jericho towards the markets of the north without her. It couldn't travel with fever in its cargo. It couldn't wait while Musa died. Nor could it spare the forty days of mourning which would follow. That would be madness. Musa himself wouldn't expect such waste. He had been a merchant too, and would agree, if he were only conscious. God forbid, that business should wait for funerals. Or pregnancies. (2)

This manner of reported speech recurs, and contributes to a layering, since various displacements and suppositions take the narrative beyond an immediacy of consciousness or any literal transposition of events. Similarly the caravan advises Miri to find a replacement husband, alerting the reader to Musa's horrendous nature: "A better one than Musa anyhow, they thought. A smaller one. An older one. One that didn't lie or use his fists so frequently, or shout or weep and laugh so much. One who didn't get so drunk, perhaps, then sit up half the night throwing pebbles at the camels and his neighbour's tents, pelting goats' dung at the moon. One who did not stink so badly as he died." (3) As Miri prepares a grave in the stony ground above the inhospitable, salty valley, five travellers approach. "The caves near Musa's grave, for all their remoteness, were known to be hospitable, much prized by those who sought the comfort of dry, soft floors, while they were suffering, much prized by desert leopards, too. Inside were the black remains of fires and, on the walls, the charcoal marks where visitors had counted off their quarantines in blocks of ten." (11) Each of the first four arrive: Shim, a blond man of Greek culture who is seeking inner spiritual meaning; Aphas, an elderly Jewish stonemason whose imminent death of cancer has inspired him to seek meaning; Marta, a Jewish woman who cannot conceive a child with her husband and is hoping for a miracle; and an unnamed badu villager from the southern deserts whose motivation remains obscure. Among many other pilgrims to the desert, "those who made it to the perching valley where Miri – half open-eyed – was sleeping, and where Musa and the fever devil were bargaining the final hours of his life, sought something more remote and testing than requiems and communal prayers." (12–13)

The fifth barefoot traveller is the most extreme: Jesus, a young Galilean obsessed with religiosity, whose arrival is announced fifty paces away by the braying donkey, another oblique and refashioned biblical reference.[8] He wishes to fulfil the quarantine without food or water, stumbling upon Musa in his goatskin tent while searching for sustenance before his self-denial begins. Even in his delirium Musa regards him as a thief, "A Jewish face, young and long and womanly. A Galilean face. A peasant face. A robber's face, for sure." (25) Jesus presses upon Musa's chest and moistens his mouth, thereby setting in motion a chain of events predicated on the apparent miracle of Musa's recovery. As Crace explains:

> I was writing that early chapter, where Musa is in his tent, and I realized that Musa must be ill, about to die. I had the playful idea of having Jesus stop him dying. I was writing the chapter with the intention of simply having a sideways mention of a character, Jesus, but by the end of that chapter Jesus had actually walked into the tent and performed a miracle.[9]

After Jesus' departure, Musa revives, but remains far feebler than his normal adult identity of the confident trader; this weakening allows him to inhabit his underlying weaker side, one suppressed since childhood. The doubling is significant, for as Miyahara Kazunari points out in '*Quarantine*: Jim Crace's *Anti-Christ*,' (2000) this indicates one of many perverse parallels between Musa and Christ since the latter also has a kind of double identity, the secular and the divine.[10] Kamiya notes that "Jesus' simple act sets in motion a plot that appears, at first, to be simply an ironic subversion of the orthodox Jesus story." (1) And as Bruce Bawer comments in 'Quarantine,' (1998) "That Jesus's miracle ends up benefiting a tyrant and harming innocents is typical of this novel, which, while making the Nazarene an authentic worker of miracles, refuses to imagine the circumstances of these miracles in any other than the most harshly realistic terms." (X05) The immediate outcome is Musa's rage, angry about Miri's absence, his abandonment, their lack of goods, and the beast's refusal to move. Musa is hardly spiritualized or enlightened by his survival. He bludgeons his ailing donkey to death with a pestle, ironically losing his footing and almost falling on his victim, a grotesque juxtaposition. "He had to start again, and use the pestle like an axe, chopping at the mortar of her head. Big men are often clumsy when they are violent. Their venom can seem comical and soft. They are too breathless and they have too many chins. Thin men, with bloodless lips and hollow waists appear more dangerous. But Musa's frenzy was not comical." (35–6) As Crace explains, Musa destroys the donkey that is a symbol in Christ's biblical narrative, and hence both the familiar and "the future narrative that you identify with Christ is being slaughtered early on and being dropped over the cliff. When Christ sees the donkey fall past him, he's seeing the two thousand years of Christianity also fall past him."[11] The violent meeting of incompatible elements is grotesque. The relationship of these two strangers is crucial to the novel. Crace states, "Musa is Latin for muse, and so named because he is Jesus' muse."[12]

As Bradfield says, "Like Milton's *Paradise Regained, Quarantine* is based on the biblical tale of Christ's temptation in the wilderness, and Musa, like Satan, provides the ultimate con-man and dissembler." (16) According to Kazunari, "Crace has carefully set Musa's age at about twenty-six, which is close to the age at which Jesus Christ allegedly started ministry on the road." As if to reinforce this sense of being spiritually chosen and his perverse negation of the Biblical Christ, in explaining his recovery to Miri, Musa ascribes his resurrection to a literal spirit. In contrast to his jubilation, "She was unwidowed and unfreed, the mistress of unwelcome lips, the keeper of a wasted grave." (40) Almost simultaneously, another woman reflects upon her imperfect life. Unhappy in her marriage for eight of its nine years, Marta reflects on her husband, Thaniel, and his threat to divorce her if no child is forthcoming, after his barren first marriage. Drawn outside by noises she is attacked by a scrub fowl that she kills, and then drinks water from the grave that has filled like a perfect cistern. Ironically this will allow Musa to control the others, and exert more power.

Drawn by Marta's screams, the other three travellers emerge, Aphas and Shim arguing over immanence and enlightenment, highlighting the lineage of mysticism that underwrites Crace's text, for as Shim comments, "'But here...' again he felt the cloth of words, 'what better place to look beyond enlightenment and god for nameless things than here, in caves, far from the comforts and distractions of the world?' Aphas nodded all the while, though men like Shim – scholars, mystics, sages, ascetes, stoics, epicureans, that holy regiment – were a mystery to him.'" (53–4) Bawer observes that "Crace gives us in Shim a Hellenist conspicuous not only for his physical attractiveness but also for a theology that secular and liberal Christian readers may find more sophisticated and palatable than that of Crace's Jesus." (X05) As Crace himself indicates, Jesus shares with Shim a more pronounced commitment to the esoteric and numinous world-view.[3] For him,

> Shim was intended to convey something similar to New Age beliefs. I was certain at that time, with so much religion around, and so few scientific explanations for the world, you would have young men who would buy in any number of ideas. Of course Shim is not the only one to do that, because Jesus is exactly that kind of person, a naive young person, but less pompous than Shim.[14]

Such obsessions are mirrored in the peculiarities of all of the travellers, and, despite what Kazunari misreads as a putative rationality on the badu's part, Marta recognizes their disturbed and dysfunctional natures. "Her three companions were absurd. Even the honeyhead. Perhaps he was the maddest of them all." (55) Returning to the cistern she glimpses a vision of nature gathering at the cistern which is typically Cracean, for as Kazunari comments, "Crace's landscapes are in flux, teeming with life, sensitive to interconnections between living things." However, Marta is repulsed, alienated rather then blessed by her sight of the natural order since her apparent infertility and her sense of being barren sets her apart not simply socially, but ontologically. She exists as if between birth and death, unable to replicate the former, and fearful of the latter.

Musa is fixated on making more profit, but equally obsessed with finding and naming his saviour. Weakened by his ordeal, he demands

Miri help his every step so that he might summon the four travellers for news of the Galilean. Together they constitute what Crace admits is a 'passing' or temporary community, and this and the geographical location heighten "A sense of loneliness, a sense of exposure." Crace says, "The novel is about landscape, about natural history and humans in the landscape."[15] One must be cautious in this respect, however, for as Irwin notes, "Crace does not proceed by turning reality into fiction and then commenting authorially upon it. He seems to prefer invention to research, making things look right to factual accuracy – and quite right too. It's more fun that way." (21)[16] Musa seizes the opportunity to claim ownership of the land and the water. Sensing their weakness he progresses instinctively to "The matter of the caves. Accommodation is not free, he explained. They wouldn't call in at an inn and expect to eat and sleep for nothing. That was not dignified or rational. This was not common land, and travellers would have to pay a tribute of some kind. A token tribute. Nothing large. A gesture only." (63) Of course, Musa's instinct residually echoes Crace's description of institutions prepared exploitatively to offer pitiful accommodation to the insane in Birmingham. And yet Crace says one must have some grudging admiration of Musa's virtuosity, however perverse:

> Musa is not without his attractions. When you're listening to him, when the reader reads how he manages to get rents out of these people, and the way he's so quick-footed, although physically slow, and yet mentally so agile so that almost in a few seconds he's come up with a way of squeezing money out of these people, surely the reader's response can't be just one of moralistic disapproval. It has to be one of impish excitement at the same time.[17]

Musa's instincts are basal. Waiting for the men's response, he both fantasizes about Marta and calculates the maximum he can extort for the accommodation. Thereby Crace critiques the archetypal mercantile instinct, especially given Musa's lack of guilt regarding his deception, and his exploitative impulses. As Bradfield comments, "Once he has established a system of commerce based (as most are) on lies, he tries to convince Jesus to come over to his side." (16) Musa even insists they labour when helping him throw the donkey from the cliff.

In Chapter 10 Jesus searches for an inaccessible cave. His childhood and an adolescent religiosity were so pronounced that "His mother feared she'd never find a wife for him, he'd never put on any flesh, not while he prayed so often and with such riotous solemnity." (73) Although later, as a priest advises his father, Jesus outwardly lost his fervour, even as a clumsy carpenter he sees God in everything. "Even with his father in the workshop, cutting wood and making frames, he found there was a rhythm to the bow-drill and the draw-knife and the plane which took the place of prayer. Every movement was a repetition; every repetition was a word. The timber and the tools took on new meanings. The knots in wood were sins." (74) Jesus perceives signs everywhere, so he reads the inhospitable scrub as an unfinished landscape, which induces doubts of God's presence, and the notion the he partakes of a hellish "devil's realm." (77) Such invocations of the spiritual are not Crace's, but part of his character's pathetic fallacy, for as Crace makes clear in his interview with Proctor, "There is no Holy Ghost, there is no God, there is no Son of God, and there are no ghosts. There is nothing of the universe which is not contained entirely within it, which does not – or will not – have a thorough scientific explanation." (4) In buoyant mood Jesus interprets the flight of a stork as a sign of God, climbing down the cliff face to a deep cave. His struggle creates an image of *regressus ad uterum*, a ritualistic isolation. "There was nothing else for Jesus to do, except to simplify his life. Repentance, meditation, prayer. Those were the joys of solitude. They had sustained to prophets for a thousand years." (81) There follows a comic, subversive episode, for as Jesus looks upwards he is first hit by a stone, then sees an angelic blonde face with mocking words, and finally a donkey appearing in mid-air. All these events he interprets as signs of temptation, although the more mundane explanations, available to the reader by overlaying the events from the preceding chapter, negate his spiritual impulse and explication. This striking moment contrasts, as Kazunari indicates, with the moment when "after Jesus Christ is baptized by John right before the fast, he encounters 'the Spirit of God descending like a dove' (Matt. 3.16, see also Mark 1.10 and Luke 3.22)."

In the following chapter, drunk on date spirit, Musa plans first to tempt the pilgrims with food away from their commitment to a strict quarantine, and second to seduce Marta. He is a malevolent spirit, watching Marta weaving with his wife on Miri's loom, a symbol of their female bonding and the intermeshing of their lives. As he cheats the others, Miri reflects on her husband's persuasiveness since, "If only Musa had been talk and nothing else, Miri thought, then he might have been mistaken for a tolerable man – for there was something admirable about him, on first encounter." (86) Her resentment is so great, so extreme the disparity between his promises and reality, that she fantasizes about killing him and disposing of the body aided by Marta. He offers them remnants of cloth, of orange and purple, for the birth mat they weave, telling fantastical tales to justify his meanness. Musa is fascinated by Shim's report of the boy in the cliff face cave, attacking him, twisting his toes and demanding that Shim bring the boy back to him. The impulse to violence in Crace generally signifies both limited vision and a propensity for evil. Although Musa's victim defies him, nevertheless, Musa entices Shim by revealing the spiritual possibilities of the Galilean, and thus in his perverse way Musa does become a disciple of sorts. "'He wasn't only someone looking for his sheep or hunting eggs. Some nobody. He is a healer and his flock are men. His eggs are . . .' No, he couldn't think of anything for eggs. 'There's holiness in him. If it's the man. He is the one who saved my life.'" (90) Musa's preaching and its rhetoric are adapted from the marketplace, a curious revision of the Gospel. He tells of Jesus plucking the devil from him like an olive stone. As the others set off for the precipice, Miri stays to weave. She possesses the ability to infuse the cloth with her own life and being, impervious to and sceptical of the search for miracles since "She knew that life did not improve through prayer or miracles. The opposite, in fact." (107)

In contrast to Miri, Jesus reflects on his belief in angels and his expectation of a divine presence or intervention. "If needs be, god would show Jesus how to turn the stones to bread and take his water from the clouds," (108) which conviction condemns him to his slow, painful demise, and the vocabulary is deployed to interrogate the Biblical canon. Crace de-romanticizes the image of the hermit, explaining, "It's not very well documented what happens to a body when you fast, because when you look at religious writers you don't get any sense of that, they only concentrate on their spiritual feelings, you don't get any sense of the way the body degrades," adding that the only research he found was from newspaper accounts by experts of the condition of IRA hunger striker, Bobby Sands.[8] Crace humanizes Christ's spiritual possibilities, banalizing Christ into simply a misguided boy. In 'The Devil Inside' in *Spike Magazine* (1998) David B. Livingstone remains unhappy with this reduction, or what he describes as a "religious revisionism:"

> A strong Christ figure would have nicely balanced the immense presence of the unappealing Musa, allowing for a clearer juxtaposition

between the 'good' and 'evil' – and the miscellany of variants between the two extremes . . . instead, Christ is relegated to the role of a distant and largely passive spectator, interacting and intervening in the events swirling around him only sporadically and unintentionally while Crace repeatedly turns his attention to the vile Musa and the minor subversions against his dominion propagated by Miri and Marta – an unlikely first-century *Thelma and Louise*. Divinity is perceived only through its absence.

When Musa and the travellers peer over the cliff for a sight of him, Jesus sees something demonic about the stick Musa has taken from Shim, and identifies Musa as the devil sent to tempt him (111–12). In a sense, Crace inflects the Manichean possibility and elusiveness of good and evil more subtly than Livingstone can allow, nuancing its ontological complexity.

In Chapter 15 Marta is disturbed at night while urinating outside by the badu, anticipating her vulnerability. Significantly, in another subversive biblical allusion, she fantasizes about an immaculate conception. She comprehends a "holy pattern" to her quarantine, hoping for the miraculous, convinced of the Gally's healing powers, as if "sent by god to put the world to rights." (117) Although she dreams passionately of Shim, conversely she is irritated by his ridiculing of Jesus, by his denial of Aphas' belief in the mysterious quality in the boy, and angered by his negation of their spiritual hopes. Marta perceives the jealousy that underlies his mockery, and through contradictory emotions Crace emphasizes the separation of one's desires and one's recognition of the external realities of others in the world. The next chapter details Jesus' struggles where he seems on the edge of reality, losing contact with the literal, telling himself that his hunger and pains are deceptions, and that spiritual nourishment suffices (129–30). The ongoing difficulties of such a bodily denial are essential to Crace's interrogation of unquestioning faith. During his suffering, Jesus mimics the naked self-denial of an 'achimite' hermit.[19] He imagines himself a child in Eden until his headaches force him to retreat to the shade of the cave imitating a resting camel. Later he imagines himself like a canker thorn on the bush outside the cave. He abjures his humanity before subsequently repeating the prayers of his youth, listing the attributes of God he had learnt as a child. "Most of all Jesus was disrupted by the silence of the cave, the depth of night beyond the entry, the scrub's indifference. Perhaps this silence was another test, he thought. Like hunger was a test. And boredom, too, and fear." (133) Subsequently he marks out letters in and around the cave with a stone, listing words.

> He would not want to read so easily as scholars, he told himself, for that would only help to split the meaning from the sound, to divorce the music from the shape . . . In his ignorance, he could both listen to the words of the reader and marvel, too, at the unspoken narrative of shapes, or concentrate not only on the script but also on the spaces in between. God was in the spaces, he was sure. God went to the very edges of the page. (134–5)

For Lane language functions as "a mysterious spiritual entity in its own right, permeated in its presence and absence by God," (32) and Jesus responds both with spirit non-instrumentally and with the world instrumentally. Rather than generating narrative, as Lane suggests, the mill-game unifies social practices, its repetitiousness reflected in Jesus' obsessive inscription of the cave, first abandoning the name of God, then language and finally seeing the world and God symbolically in the game, allowing him to forgo prayer. In both prayer and the game man has to imagine or inhabit the role of God. The mill-game is neither simply language nor a game, and Jesus in playing himself sustains an elusive role, where the game is not Lane's random winning or losing (33) but a coadunation where the two appear to coalesce.

Chapter 17 charts the growing friendship and intimacy between Miri and Marta, under the gaze of Musa who continues to fantasize about Marta. Already he understands Jesus' healing powers as something to trade, a trick to be learned (139–40). The women bond and embrace after Marta touches a bruise on Miri's face, empathizing in her womanhood, after which they share the abjection of their lives. They bathe together naked. "Once they heard the curtain drop. It was still swaying when they'd pulled their clothes back on. They knew that Musa had been watching them. But still they laughed. These were the fullest forty days they'd ever lived." (141–2) The group continue to argue over Gally's status as a holy man. Racked by pain Aphas desires to be healed, but is contradicted by Shim. Musa devises a plan to tempt Gally from his cave with food and water, becoming the archetypal devil. Whatever their dysfunctional relationships, and despite Musa and the hostile environment, a community is forged. As Bradfield concludes, "Crace writes about the ability of strange people to lose themselves in places that will never be their own, even though, ultimately, Crace's novels create a sense of location like nowhere else on earth." (16)

In Chapters 18 to 20 Crace reinterprets the temptation of Jesus, reshaping the biblical co-ordinates, adding layers of detail. "In my story it's some decent people trying to make sure he doesn't do any harm to himself."[20] Jesus is delusional, imagining a pigeon trapped in the canker thorn, scattering its leaves, but realizes that a leather bag is being is lowered on a rope, which literalizes the temptation of Christ. (149)[21] Musa's blandishments reassure Jesus he has the ability to heal, fulfilling his secret, previously unarticulated desire. This apparently uncanny knowledge confirms the devilish nature of his tempters. "Musa's offers were too crudely tempting; his summonses for Jesus to vacate the precipice and heal the sick were too bespoke to be remotely innocent." (150) He resists the seductive words, but in Chapter 19 Musa fills his dreams, initially in the marketplace and in the cave, transforming the devil into a priest. In Galilee's marketplace Musa offers him the chance of quarantine, an unconscious merging with Musa that prefigures the novel's end.

Crace describes the detail of the degeneration of Jesus' body: the loose teeth, swollen gums, swelling legs and suppurating wounds all come as a surprise to Jesus. "No one had said, there will be stomach pains and cramps, demanding to be rubbed and soothed like dogs." (158) He becomes sensitive to light, confused and inept, and at this point his spirit falls apart just as he is too weak to escape. In Chapter 20 there are three more attempts by Musa and his accomplices to tempt him, followed by the arrival of the badu with locusts and water after scaling down the cliff. This is a pivotal moment for up to this point Crace's Christ might be saved, especially since his resolve begins to weaken. He begs for his own lips to be moistened, mirroring his encounter with Musa, another doubling of the two. However, Gally finds strength in the badu's inarticulacy and frightens off his putative benefactor. Christ becomes elated. "Jesus laughed. How dull and unprepared the devil was." (164) However, only at this point does his temptation end, because he is so close to death.

In Chapter 21 Miri works at her loom on the purple-orange birth mat, but is forced by Musa to fill the water bags. Deviously he uses the excuse of fatigue on their return to rest near Marta's cave where he demands the honey given to the others by the badu. Pointedly rejecting the parables offered by Shim and Aphas, Musa tells his own story of a trader travelling across a desert to barter goods for a hundred monkeys so as to sell them in Nabatee "where monkey flesh was thought to be ... he winked again; he did not say the word ... an aphrodisiac." (172) Musa's tale within the meta-narrative of the novel has a curious status, since its claims are evidently absurd, especially the image of bunches of his caravan's monkeys hung from camels. Furthermore, it seems almost incomplete, ending with Musa and his party following thirteen dying monkeys as they instinctively trace water until the final fourteenth one succeeds. However, it serves him in attacking Shim's "learned commentary," (178) and subsequently the book moves towards its various climactic points. Musa feigns an illness, pretending to be near death again – another doubling of Christ – so that he might rest in one of the caves near Marta. Crace creates suspense in the following chapters after the storytelling interlude. First, in Chapter 22 Shim stays out on the promontory above Jesus' cave, fearful of Musa who has instructed him to look out for Gally, and as he peers in the darkness he hopes vainly for Musa's death. Without knowing, Shim perhaps temporarily prevents Musa's planned attack on Marta. Finally, Shim is driven away by "a cruel, defiant wind," (187) just as the storm rips apart Miri's tent which Aphas, sent by Musa to shepherd Miri, is unable to prevent, the forces of nature apparently malevolent rather than indifferent.

In Chapter 23 Jesus feels the wind offering transcendence, reviving him from unconsciousness. The power of the wind disturbs the equilibrium of this transitory community. The final decline of Christ precipitates various subsequent transmutations after his burial in Chapter 28. The fact of Jesus' death is charted by Crace as a peculiarly immanent union with the forces of nature.

> Quarantine had been the perfect preparation for his death. His body was quiescent and reduced; dry, sapless, transparent almost, ready to detach itself from life without complaint. A wind this strong could pluck him like a leaf . . .
> It seemed to Jesus, when he woke and put his hands out to the wind, that he was already dead and living it . . . There was no future there for him. No fleshy future anyway. He had surrendered food for dreams. (191)

The transformation of events into dream retrieves a theme from *Signals of Distress*, emphasizing the power of narrative and the imaginary. Bataille says in *The Accursed Share; Vol. III*, "The 'miracle' of death is understandable in terms of this sovereign exigency, which calls for the *impossible coming true*, in the *reign of the moment.*" (211) In preparing himself for death Jesus reaches for the power of such a suspended moment:

> There was a light, deep in the middle of the night. He tried to swim to it. He tried to fly. He held his hands up to the light. His hands were bluey-white like glass. The light passed through. The mountain shivered from afar. He felt the cold of nothing there. He heard the cold of no one here. No god, no gardens, just the wind. (193)

At his death Jesus dreams of returning to Galilee. "This was his final blasphemy." (193)

After Jesus dies, in the following chapter Musa prepares to engage in his most disturbing act, the violation of Marta. His self-justification is grotesque: "She wanted to return to Sawiya, transformed by miracles, made fertile by her quarantine. He would oblige. He'd do what the little Gally had refused to do. He'd throw his seed on to her fallow ground." (197) The rape confirms his worst qualities. Curiously, as if transformed by the wind itself, symbolizing the spiritually transcendent, this act offers her redemption through both the ensuing pregnancy and by confirming her common sisterhood with Miri, a bonding that challenges Musa. They are both repulsed by him. In Chapter 25, Musa returns to the site of his tent almost guiltless, contemplating the detail of her resistance and his violence. "She'd only quietened when he'd stunned her with his fists. But he had not enjoyed her stunned and unresponsive. He hadn't wanted sex alone, with no participant except himself. That had never been the plan." (202) Facing his actions, he sees Jesus for a second time, "walking in the mud, naked, thin and brittle as a thorn," (204) but Jesus seems unaware of Musa. The scene is related from the latter's uncomprehending perspective. "He could have sworn the man was glowing blue and yellow, like a coal." (206) According to Kazunari, "What has happened to Musa is a supernatural, spiritual experience. Musa is inwardly experiencing the 'resurrection' of his 'lesser twin', and envisioning it outwardly in the form of Gally."

In Chapter 27 led by the badu they recover Jesus' body and Miri searches the scrub for Marta as the badu seeks a bird to sacrifice for Christ's funeral. This landscape echoes the sorrows of the world. "The empty lands – these very caves, these paths, these desert pavements made of rock, these pebbled flats, these badlands, and these unwatered river beds – were siblings to the empty spaces in the heart . . .

At the end of their forty days, the scrub sent all of them away enriched and dryly irrigated. Even Aphas. Even Shim." (219) The personal transitions accelerate as others resist Musa's power of persuasion. In the following chapter Miri discovers Marta in the scrub and learns of her desecration. Musa's influence is diminished after the burial and the sacrifice when the badu disappears with Musa's goats, not having paid any tithes to him. In ritually burning the tent Musa destroys both his "fever devil" (230) and the past, his second rebirth or renewal. On the journey towards Jericho Shim and Aphas abandon Musa's goods and the women set off to Marta's home: "They walked until evening closed in. It did not matter where they spent the night. They were back in the world of the sane and would be safe. Only their faces ached, from smiling." (237) On arrival they will claim widowhood for Miri, fulfilling her dream at the beginning of the novel, for as Kenneth Arnold notes in 'Emptiness Is All,' (1997) "The community of women is born of the desert, from solitude." (140)

Musa's initial recovery from death and Jesus' demise are interconnected since both are visionary or spiritualized moments, and Musa renders both perversely as narratives of resurrection. Whatever his failings, Musa retrieves Christ as an intellectual possession, creating spiritual capital from 'Gally's' death, whereby ironically Musa becomes Jesus' prophet and disciple inspired primarily by profit and necessity. As Proctor says, "In Crace's version, the apocryphal Jesus character dies of hunger, and his miracles are more the stuff of coincidence, hallucination and interpretation than of scripture." (2) However, ambiguously, Musa's ministry is inspired by his sighting of Jesus in the scrub, Musa's second vision of Jesus after death. The meaning is equivocal. In Musa's vision and its effects, one can perceive perhaps elements of Benjamin's exposition of the relationship of finitude and narrative: "Death is the sanction of everything that the storyteller can tell. He has borrowed his authority from death. In other words, it is natural history to which his stories refer back." (93–4) For Musa, as he joins another caravan of travellers after being abandoned, his appropriation of Jesus' life and death authorizes him and provides him with a new voice beyond weaving stories as previously about his goods and their act of exchange. Transformed he speaks of more expansive tales, of transcending both the self and the material realm. He merchandises the storytelling possibilities of a belief system, each narrative device extending the literal:

Quarantine and Being Dead

> They were amazed at all the stories he could tell. He'd come from forty days of quarantine up in the wilderness. He hadn't drunk or eaten anything. He'd gone up thin and come back fat, thanks to god's good offices. He'd shared his cave with angels and messiahs; he'd met a healer and a man who could make bread from stones. His staff had come to him one night, a dangerous snake which wrapped itself around his arm and turned to wood. They could hold it, for a coin. One touch of his staff would protect them against all snakes. (240–1)

Such claims both mirror the rhythms and invert the logic of the proverbial and the parabolic. Musa remains a trader. However, his two roles are interconnected. He previously enhanced the object through the moment of exchange. There are traces of the miraculous in that system since his demand for belief elevates the act of exchange by a manipulation of the benefit (*goods*) anticipated. His deceit that underpins the trade of muddy water and caves he does not own, and further of the selling of unstable wool dyed with urine that deceives initially even the trader with its alchemical stench possesses a movement that is parallel to that which he perceives in Jesus' death; for in this act of ascetic finitude Jesus is separated from form and presence and can be made into something other than factuality. Although not tied to their material origins Musa redeems these events as a form of exchange. He both reinforces and yet defies the parabolic. He transforms the significance of the real, using the chimera of the word, requiring a transcendence of the mundane, the referential. He trades the equivocal nature of the miraculous in terms of its effecting belief, especially in its outcome in terms of enabling him to capitalize the aspirational in others. He exchanges hope. As Miller explains, parable is itself implicated in contradictions and paradox, stating, "Paradox: the economy of equivalence, of giving and receiving, of equable translation and measure, of the circulation of signs governed by the Logos as source of proportion and guarantee of substitution or analogy, is upset by the parables." (141) Jesus' appearance necessarily evokes culturally the parables, his ministry and the possibility of the miraculous. Musa's appropriation and vision of the dead man exhibit features of Bataille's critique of the interconnection of death and the miraculous. One perceives in Christ's fate and Musa's intended (parodic) ministry something that was already inherent in the latter's cajoling and cheating, a capacity to transform the nature of relations and the world. There is a similarity in such trade with Christ's finitude and absence. Bataille says in *The Accursed Share; Vol. III*:

> This *negative miraculous*, manifested in death, corresponds quite clearly to the principle ... according to which the miraculous moment is the moment when *anticipation dissolves into* NOTHING. It is the moment when we are relieved of anticipation, man's customary misery, of the anticipation that enslaves, that subordinates the present moment to some anticipated result. Precisely in the miracle, we are thrust from our anticipation of the future into the presence of the moment, of the moment illuminated by a miraculous light. (207)

There is appropriately something grotesque in Gally's death, in Musa himself and in his appropriation of the death's symbolic potential, for as Mikhail Bakhtin says in *Rabelais and His World* (1984), "The grotesque image reflects a phenomenon in transformation, an as yet unfinished metamorphosis, of death and birth, growth and becoming." (24) Musa offers a belief located in the moment of immediacy and being, but something beyond his apparent trickery haunts him and his mission, the vision of Jesus in the distance, "A thin halting figure tacking the scree, almost a mirage – ankleless, no arms, in the lifting light," (241) which figure seems barely human, but Musa is convinced of its identity. According to Musa, "'I am the living proof.' He'd travel to the markets of the world. He'd preach the good news ... 'He came into my tent,' he'd say. 'He touched me here, and here. "Be well," he told me. And I am well. And I have never been so well. Step forward. Touch me. Feel how well I am.' (242–3) Crace positions the miraculous appropriately as possibly elusive or mundane, but never banal. For Kazunari in Crace's account the gospel is "based not on Jesus Christ's heroic life, but on the smooth sales-talk of a windbag," and this is the accusation Friedrich Nietzsche levels against St Paul. Kazunari adds:

> Nietzsche is by no means a thorough denier of Christ. He sees the necessity to feel 'the poignant charm of such a compound of the sublime, the morbid and the childish' of the 'original traits and idiosyncrasies, often so painfully strange' which 'all great ... veneration ... tends to erase from the venerated objects' (48; ch. 31). Nietzsche emphasizes that 'the type of the Savior has reached us only in a greatly distorted form' (48; ch. 31), which implies that Nietzsche posits that there existed an original Christ and that he was a man of some value.

Crace admits that despite his own atheism textually he allows a space for the resurrection of Christ himself, an intriguing reading of the biblical, for as Kamiya reflects it is possible that:

Quarantine simply takes the ambiguity and controversy that has always surrounded Jesus' death and resurrection and moved it up: Instead of Jesus dying and possibly being reborn after the crucifixion, he dies and is possibly reborn after his ordeal in the wilderness. This is an ingenious idea. After all, it was only after the wilderness that Jesus began his public ministry, and so it might make sense that Jesus assumed his divinity after dying. (2)[22]

Crace confirms that the ending is "absolutely supposed to be ambiguous," and that in fiction one can "offer the possibility of alternative explanations."[23] Musa, rather than engage with transcendence or sacrifice, chooses his vision's exploitative potential, deciding to trade the word. "He would not wait, he persuaded himself, because it was not sensible to wait. There were practicalities to bear in mind ... The Galilean might be a healer and the lord of miracles, but he was not a cart." (242) For Irwin, "*Quarantine* is a beautifully crafted enigmatic parable which is about nothing except itself." (21) Perhaps finally what links it with the subsequent novel is their serious metaphysical issues, and Crace's neo-Darwinistic convictions reflected in his explanation in 'Crace on *Quarantine*: An Introduction for American Readers', which conjures the kind of forces relevant both to the Judean desert and the cliffside path that features so strongly in *Being Dead*: "A universe which is an outside job, inflicted on us by a Creator in seven days, is a lesser marvel than a universe which is an inside job, the slow, painstaking product of natural forces. Evolution is a greater wonder than all the gods. The Blind Watchmaker is more inspiring than Blind Faith."

Being Dead

In another littoral setting, *Being Dead* opens with the aftermath of a nostalgic weekday trip to the coast. With few preliminaries it announces the death of Joseph and Celice, the Director of the Tidal Institute and his wife, a part-time tutor at an unnamed university at Baritone Bay. Given they are seemingly a reserved middle-aged couple, Crace offers an ironic commentary.

> Hardly any of their colleagues had ever seen them together, or visited them at home, let alone witnessed them touch. How unexpected, then, that these two, of all couples, should be found like this, without their underclothes, their heads caved in, unlikely victims of unlikely passions. Who would have thought that unattractive people of that age and learning would encounter sex and murder in the open air? (1)

The intimacy of detail of the deaths is juxtaposed with their reserve. Such contrasts are the driving forces of the novel. Gradually, the reader learns how they die so intimately. As Phil Whitaker says in 'The Absolute End,' (1999) "It is powerful writing, both in its remorseless detail and in the mordant irony of the two zoologists becoming substrates for the food chain they once studied." (57) Culturally and historically, death is not an incongruous narrative subject matter. *Being Dead* extends Crace's concern with the continuities of narrative and its archetypal trans-historical possibilities, which is precisely where it is situated by its central subject matter, for as Phillipe Ariès points out at the beginning of *Images of Man and Death* (1985), "Death loves to be represented. That not only was true of the long periods before the invention of writing but remained so thereafter." (1) Garrett Stewart reminds one in *Death Sentences: Styles of Dying in British Fiction* (1984) that death is a mainstay of prose fiction, and Crace accentuates an aspect observed by Stewart: "A novel, without seeking an unmediated knowledge of death, or any extraordinary wisdom on the subject, must nevertheless arrange to be informed by mortal boundaries, not just constrained by them." (6) Hence Crace's inversion of the couple's last day, and the evocation of various other deaths both recent and distant, as discussed below. Certainly the novel insists on the realities of death, and as Miranda France comments in 'Supping Full on Horrors,' (1999) "It's powerful, innovative and philosophical. You don't come away liking Crace for it, but then it isn't the writer's business to be liked." (46)

Being Dead is perhaps Crace's most celebrated book; after being short-listed for the Whitbread Novel of the Year, *Being Dead* won the American National Book Critics Circle Award for Fiction published in 2000. The novel was inspired in part from the memory of his father's death, and shaped by the experience of writing the previous novel, and as Crace admitted when interviewed by Ron Hogan in *Beatrice Magazine* (2000).

> The impulse of this book came when I was writing *Quarantine*. At the end of writing that book, I was no less of an atheist than I was before, yet it did make me think about my atheism. Thinking about the bleakness of my own atheism, and the inadequacy of the old fashioned kind of atheism when the big events of life – especially death – came along, made me want to see whether I could come up with a narrative of comfort, a false narrative of comfort, but one that could match the narratives of comfort religions come up with to get you through death and bereavement.

Quarantine and Being Dead

In 1979, I had buried my own father, who was also an atheist, a really good old fashioned political atheist, and he had asked for an appropriate funeral for him, which was no funeral at all. No guests. No announcement. No flowers. No eulogy. No hymns, God's sake, no hymns. And no collecting of the ashes. We carried out his wishes, and it was a huge mistake. The memory of how we failed to bury my father properly and pay attention to his unique life was with me as I wrote this novel.

People are often inarticulate when faced with death, so when confronting such an absence according to Stewart perhaps "the verbal artifice of fiction [may] help to redeem our speechlessness in the face of such vacancy," (3) especially given his observation that "Despite its brutal factuality as the close of life, dying is by nature the one inevitably fictional matter in prose fiction." (4) As Proctor says, "Crace continues in his role as the secular grand inquisitor of the big metaphysical questions." (2) In contrast to what Crace regards as the spiritually bankrupt and fantastical narratives of salvation offered by religious beliefs, it is from the quotidian, the observable, the prosaic and relentless mechanisms of nature that Crace establishes his neo-Darwinistic and yet curiously optimistic view of finitude. Drawing upon the grotesquely observable and tangible, and from the incorrigible and provisional, Crace weaves diffuse and stubborn interconnections that render a world far from the prosaic. Some critics are sceptical. Jonathan Levi observes in 'Origin of Species,' (2000) "Not even their chance return on a sunny day to the site of their first love provides a satisfying evolutionary link to the necessary chain of their lives. Their lives, it seems, are as simple and inexplicable than their deaths." (19) Eric Miles Williamson in 'Beyond Postmodernism' (2001) perceives an over-insistence redeemed by Crace's stylistic virtuosity (174).

The central event derives partly from a television reconstruction of an unsolved murder of a middle-aged couple shot while walking along the coast of Pembrokeshire, Wales, their bodies undiscovered for almost a week.[24] The intimacy of their relationship inspired and intrigued Crace.

> I knew the landscape where those people died, the great big, high striated cliffs in the west of Pembrokeshire, where I'd walked many times, starting as a kid. What you had was an image of a couple in their fifties, with grown-up children, and who were still doing this intimate business of a long hike along the coast with each other. That's a very tender and fond thing to do. Such a holiday cannot survive with somebody you

don't get on with. They had been married for decades. You could infer, probably wrongly – I don't know and I shouldn't infer things about people I've never met – that here is one of those relationships which is as solid as granite.²⁵

Crace transcends this provenance, focusing on the possibility of an image of "enduring fondness" something he admits to Proctor he developed sentimentally. "I imagined, though it didn't turn out to be true, that as they were lying in this beautiful landscape, their bodies were touching. It was as if somehow, even though they were dead, this fondness was allowed to survive for the days in which their bodies laid unfound." (12) Crace's response to the original crime is aesthetic rather than spiritual, reflecting his own notion of eternity and immortality.

> Here was going to be a book which denied the narratives of comfort you find in religions. It was always about denying those, but it needed to come up with its own version, its own narrative of comfort, one which was worldly and ungodly, but which also allowed that although death is absolutely final, nevertheless something does survive and that there is a certain immortality of a kind. The story of the couple up on the cliff delivered that perfectly, because they weren't discovered straightaway, and I could see in metaphorical terms that definitely their love survived.²⁶

Crace attempts to synthesize two unlikely elements, a discourse of mature love with the challenges of the meaning and impact of violent deaths, in which he seeks a transcendent meaning. The detail of the decomposition of the two bodies recurs, which Crace uses as a further opportunity for his creative deceptions, ones taken literally by interviewer, Ron Hogan. Crace takes delight in revealing, "I wanted the bodies to just rot away and I could have gone and done some real research, but being the kind of writer I am, I made things up. None of the animals that you encounter going into their bodies are real animals. They don't exist. The detail is actually invented because this whole book is a narrative rather than a work of natural history. They [the insects] don't exist. I've invented them."

Critics have noted the symmetrical structural pattern. Crace uses this to juxtapose life and death, diffusing the latter's negativity. Carol Birch in 'Quivering' (1999) describes the opening scenes detailing the murder as an "episode [which] is interwoven with accounts of the couple's last day on earth, of their hard-nosed daughter's slow experience of their disappearance and the discovery of the bodies, and the long detailed accounts of the biological reality of death, maggots and all. From bloody violence to the morgue, we are spared nothing of these deaths and thereby see our own. The book is a modern *memento mori*." (10) For Begley in 'A Quiet Brit's Loud Talent: Jim Crace's Corpse Comedy' (2001) the novel consists of various strands "at once macabre and lighthearted, violent and tender, witty and profound, irreverent and moving – and perfectly calibrated, so that all these crosscurrents seem to ebb and flow in harmony." (27) After the opening episode Begley perceives three contexts in which the disappearance of personal time and the inevitably of our mortality are thus emphasized. "One is a kind of necrometer: It runs forward from the instant of death to the discovery of the bodies by police dogs six days later; it charts decay and the necrophagous activity of beetles, birds, crabs and rodents; and it monitors, also, the half-hearted search conducted by the dead couple's disaffected daughter." (27) The other two chronicle first the day of the murder in reverse until the couple are safely in bed on the dawn of their demise, and second the meeting thirty years previously of the couple, which results in their marriage, but only after the death of another student, Festa, in a fire over which Celice suffers pangs of guilt and remorse.

Although Begley is broadly correct, according to my analysis below, the novel is more complex and each division is less discrete than implied in Begley's schema. There are labyrinthine interelationships and overlapping chronologies. Thematically the secular and scared are juxtaposed, and hence the novel cannot be comprehended or apprehended conventionally, by expounding its main occurences teleologically. Rather it is best understood variously through revealing recurrent themes and motifs, by juxtaposing interconnected repeated settings and time periods analytically, as I will do. As Hogan notes, "the narrative structure . . . not only peels back from the moment of death, it also goes forward, even before their bodies are discovered, to continually isolate what is happening to their bodies as they lie there." As Gary Krist comments in *Salon.com* (2003) the novel adopts an "eccentric course, swerving backward and forward in time in order to put these two deaths in context."

Various chapters share certain affinities as part of the interrelated narrative clusters, which principle structures my analysis. However, certain chapters can be seen as straddling several strands. Crace says:

Consider a plan of how all these elements fit together, and how the strands leapfrog each other. Every jump taken advances each of the strands towards the most optimistic point. All of these optimisms – the orgasms, the couple placed in bed, the reconciliation with the daughter even though they're dead – happen or cluster at the end. This is an example of narrative form itself delivering the thesis for the book. To state your thesis, of course you can do that in a book, through the author's intention, but actually structure itself can state the purpose of the book, simply by changing time frames.[27]

This process embeds the reader, who shares as close to an affinitive sense of the fate of the dead as possible. The dominant strand of the novel features a series of chapters which are variously and differently concerned with death and decomposition, of being dead. The initial chapters describing the murder and decomposition, Chapters 1, 3 and 5, unfold in reverse order in terms of a traditional plot (although each chapter moves forward conventionally in a chronological sense within its own bounds) moving backward from the fact of the couple's bodies initially after an attack, to the details of the prelimiaries, to the fact of the murder by a drifter with a rock of granite – curiously Krist perceives "a mentally deficient miscreant" without much textual basis – with Celice caught completely unawares. In the *New York Times Book Review* Jim Shepard (2000) notes:

> The imagery surrounding the murder weapon, for example, returns with uncanny frequency: the insect Joseph studies is 'granite gray' and the housing development that is planned for the dunes involves granite fill and a granite esplanade – at other times those coincidences, or ironies, feel didactic. Celice lectures her students that anyone who studies nature must get used to violence, that you'll see more death at a beach than anywhere else. The zoologists' mantra is that change is the only constant; decay and growth are synonyms. (10)

The novel's juxtaposition of images and commentary is deliberative, and hence in narrative terms there emerges both a pathos and negation of all suspense with the reversal of events, as when in contrast to his partner the unfit Joseph attempts to protect himself:

> Joseph brought his hands up to his chest to shield himself against the granite . . . Unlike his wife – who, though still bucking from the blows, could feel no pain – he was loudly conscious. There was the taste of vomit in his throat; an orchestra was tuning up between his ears. His gut was punctured by a broken rib. He understood the danger he was in. He must have known that there was worse to come. (33)

There is a numbing poignancy in such details, which reasserts the tension between the 'physical' and the 'spiritual' that informs the grotesque possibilities of representing human form.

Such grotesqueries are further heightened in the graphic detail of Chapters 6, 8, 9, 12 and 13, which together relate the natural processes of decomposition of the body, hence taking the reader forward chronologically from the novel's opening.[28] There is a highly uncomfortable quality for the reader, whose gaze becomes as times potentially voyeuristic, only balanced by the complementary nature of the narrative strands being juxtaposed and interrelated thematically. The very un-beatific form of the couples scavenged flesh interrogates and subverts the body's spiritual potential, exemplifying a literary process that Greg Metcalf describes as centring upon the "profanation of the human form . . . The shift in emphasis to the literal deconstruction of the human body." (161) Crace also emphasizes the distortion of the grotesque as a natural process that transforms not only the literal, but also the contextual world affected by that change. Hence this cluster of chapters demonstrates affinities with Chapter 20, where the daughter, Syl, is shown by the police a glimpse of the bodies in a tent set up by the forensic team; Chapter 24 with the lifting and removal of the bodies to reveal the marking of their resting; and Chapter 26 which returns to this site where Crace hypothesizes, as the grass recovers from being shielded from the sun, how if undiscovered the corpses would have returned to nature, a neo-Darwinist view of the rolling process of integration. "By final light on the ninth day since the murder all traces of any life and love that had been spilt had disappeared." (209) The progression through this second phase is chronologically conventional. Another related perspective is found in Chapter 2, which considers the tradition of 'quivering,' a funereal practice popular a hundred years before. The narrator hypothesizes the active role of such mourners.

> The greater the racket the deeper the grief. A hundred years ago no one was silent or tongue-tied, as we are now, when death was in the room. They had not yet muzzled grief or banished it from daily life. Death was cultivated, watered like a plant. There was no need for whispering or mime. Let the hubbub drive the devil's out, they'd tell themselves. Let's make a row. Let's shout. There were even quiver sticks to buy and shake, made out of metal rods with clacking wooden rings. The children would compete for those; their squabbling and their snatching would only benefit the din. (2–3)

This contrasts with modern western cultural mores, as Ariès indicates in *The Hour of Our Death* (1983 [1981]): "The hidden death in hospital, which began very discreetly in the 1930s and '40s and became widespread after 1950." (570) The hypothetical cacophony of the quivering exemplifies the social aspects of Crace's desire to signify and mark the passing of the dead even without belief. Other elements permeate these accounts, such as in Chapter 9 a description of others the couple has known who have suffered early or apparently undeserved deaths, including the suicide of Celice's Academic Mentor of the Natural Science Faculty, a man to whom she found herself attracted.

> A better death she'd thought, despite her desperation, than the one she was hoping for: a death doled out in microscopic installments by senility, her tent repitched each day, a footstep nearer home. His suicide had saved him from old age ... He'd died with all his futures still in place. His *will*. His *might*. His *could*. There were still concert tickets on his mantelpiece. His winter holiday was booked. He still had debts. The Mentor's suicide, she could persuade herself, was neo-Darwinist. (63)

Another intersecting element in Chapter 6 is a fragment of Celice's lecture on "Senescence" and "Thanatology," that reveals the shared knowledge of science and religion of the "inextricably entwined" (40) nature of life and death, where the alternative indicated by Celice would be a single-cellular eternity. This scene also allows Crace to interrelate this vignette with another strand of the novel, interconnected by the couple's first youthful encounters, consisting of Chapters 4, 7, 10, 14, 17 and 19, and finally 22, which tells of a group of young students on a field trip at Baritone Bay. This first meeting concludes with their first lovemaking in the dunes. At the heart of these episodes is Festa's death.

There are two further strands. The first in Chapters 12, 15, 16, 18, 20 and 23 concerns the reactions to her parent's disappearance and death of the couple's daughter, Syl. The last strand considered consists of another reversal of chronological narrative of the couple's last day in successive chapters where the times of the last day are given: Chapter 8: 2.20 p.m.; Chapter 11: 1.20 p.m.; Chapter 19: Noon; Chapter 21: 7.05 a.m.; and Chapter 25: 6.10 a.m. Each variously and successively describes the day leading to the attack, moving back from the event, vignette by vignette: from their lovemaking in the dunes to rising for breakfast; leaving the site of the burnt-out study house and the land overlooking the bay; exploring the site of the study house where Festa dies in a fire, and Celice re-inhabiting her sense of guilt; Joseph taking breakfast as he waits for Celice to awake for their sentimental journey; and finally the couple in bed together, Joseph dreaming ironically of his old age on a geriatric ward. Crace thus memorializes these moment, and the inversion of time, perhaps finally only a very self-conscious consolatory narrative device, adds a peculiarly elegiac poignancy given that the outcome of events is known.

> So this has been a quivering of sorts for Joseph and Celice. A day lived forwards has retrieved itself by fleeing from the future to the past. The dead are resurrected and they lie in bed at backward-running dawn, with first light of a perfect summer's day ducking and then dropping from the sky into the east, into the morning light. Ahead of them, the almost thirty years of married life, the more than twenty years before they met. The shrinking and retreating universe has left their deaths behind. They are not mortal any more. (204)

The movement echoes Mikhail Bakhtin's sense of renewal from death: "The essence of the grotesque is precisely to present a contradictory and double-faced fullness of life. Negation and destruction (death of the old) are included as an essential phase, inseparable from affirmation, from the birth of something new and better." (62)

Of course, additional to the neo-Darwinian theme, Crace's reversal includes detailed and often curiously poetic scenes of the bodies being consumed by insects, and its logic ends with the moment of creation. And yet, Crace resists religiosity, rather insisting upon the power and necessity of narrative, foregrounding especially its capacity to re-invoke or 'resurrect' in secular terms the experience of the past. The complex and interrelated aspects of the novel can be overdetermined. Lane ponders:

> Death, in *Being Dead*, interrupts life in multiple ways, making a mockery of all human systems, all human desires and deeds; the protagonists of the novel are murdered *in flagrante delicto*, doubly exposed to the elements, through sex and violence, they appear ridiculous, absurd and messy. Their leaking bodies are a continuation of Joseph's premature ejaculation in a play on the notion of *premature death*: the latter is almost always so, for human beings. In life, young people often discuss the 'best way to die'; *Being Dead* suggests the hierarchy and choice implicit in the question may not be quite so readily available. Systems making sense of death proliferate even in a secular world; genetics replaces

spiritual destiny, but both suggest a lack of control, even if there is a fantasy that one day death may be endlessly deferred. (36)

It would seem, however, that for Crace human systems actually adapt and proceed relatively uninterrupted even in the face of death, hence the natural and evolutionary instincts of Syl. In truth if one considers *Being Dead* closely, death would hardly seem to interrupt any lives, apart from the deceased. At the start their lives have already been abruptly ended, allowing them to be celebrated as if at one with nature, however temporarily, and in the lacunary space before their discovery Crace can evoke their past as if addressing their wake.

There are changes in Baritone Bay on the couple's sentimental return. "Yet, even without the intercession of architects and builders, they would not have expected the foreshore and its hinterland to remain exactly as it had been. Zoologists have mantras of their own: change is the only constant; nothing in the universe is stable or inert; decay and growth are synonyms; a grain of sand is stronger and more durable than rock." (87) The depiction of their "leaking" bodies represents an ongoing series of grotesque, vivid images. For Wolfgang Kayser in *The Grotesque in Art and Literature* (1981), the grotesque represents a comprehensive structural principle (29–47) and he comments, "The art of our day shows a greater affinity to the grotesque than that of any other epoch." (11) The Cracean grotesque is congruent with an underlying quality found in much recent British fiction. As Tew says in *The Contemporary British Novel* (2004), "an evolving British aesthetic is concerned variously with a familiarity of location, a disrupted conventionality, and a sense of otherworldliness." (29) Death is the ultimate otherworldliness; as Stewart says, "Death is the phenomenon absolutely distinct from others, the ultimate difference, antithesis taken to the limit." (4) Crace describes the decomposing flesh both as humanizing the dead and revealing nature's continuing process of decay (108–9). The multiplicity of images means no single one dominates. The textual regenerative process is similar to Bakhtin's notion of the carnival grotesque, a cycle in which the couple are variously reincarnated and returned to their death, at times even within the same paragraph. Physically they decay. Crace's text insists that "death does not discriminate. All flesh is flesh. And Joseph and Celice were sullied everywhere." (109)[29] And yet, despite glimpses of an apparent inchoate universe beyond human constructs in this graphic morbidity, its depiction remains curiously affirmative.

Crace's redemptive view of the detail of death and decomposition derives in part from the subject matter of Joseph and Celice's professional careers, echoing the informing principles of the field trip where they first met. After the details of their murder, in Chapter 6 the bodies are abandoned to nature, the first scavengers being a single beetle and a gull. The gull is drawn to feeding on the approaching crabs. "More violent death. The sudden downward beating of a beak." (38) Subsequently the reader learns of crabs and swag flies on the wounds. The description is in part scientific, but its forensic detail is supplemented by metaphoric descriptiveness.

> Her hair was matted with wet blood and the syrup of her brain. One cheek was flattened by the pounding imact of the granite. Two teeth were cracked, longways. Her facial artery, that superficial lifeline from the carotid, which climbed over her lower jaw to supply the colour to her cheek and feed the brain with oxygen, had been torn in two. Blood had spread across her throat and shoulders and soaked invisibly into her summer jacket. There were dark patches on the grass and sand. Blood does not keep its livery for long. Celice was blackening. It looked and felt as if she'd been pelted with molasses. Her body made good pickings for the glucose-hungry flies. (38)

Such minutiae typify these scenes and as Bakhtin says, the grotesque involves "a great wealth and fullness of meaning, worked out to the smallest detail. It has at the same time a universal character." (309) According to Kayser, this follows a tradition of the grotesque found in the art of Bosch and Bruegel, with its depictions of limbs and torsos as infernal (32) and the deformation and disproportion of the habitual aspects of the body (32–3). For Kayser the ambiguity in such visions is central to the grotesque and a similar ambivalence structures Crace's novel. "It does not constitute a fantastic realm of its own (for there is none such). The grotesque world is – and is not – our own world. The ambiguous way in which we are affected by it results from our awareness that the familiar and apparently harmonious world is alienated under the impact of abysmal forces, which break it up and shatter its coherence." (37) In Crace, normal expectations are disrupted with the bodies left unattended. Ironically, the professional world of Celice and the putrefaction threatening her are specifically interrelated:

> Here in the dunes – with Celice's spread body, her rustling hair, her husband hanging from her leg, as centrepiece – was a fine display to

illustrate the annual fieldwork lecture that she gave, normally with slides of putrefying seals or tide-abandoned fish, to the faculty's new and squeamish students: 'Anyone who studies nature must get used to violence. You'll have to make yourselves companionable with death if any of you want to flourish as zoologists.' She meant that fear of death is fear of life, a cliché amongst scientists, and preachers too. Both know that life and death are inextricably entwined, the double helix of existence. Both want to give life meaning only because it clearly has none, other than to replicate and decompose. Hard truths. (40)

Celice's lecture conveys the tedious limitations of the only eternity in science, of splitting, single cellular organisms. Bakhtin insists that "The grotesque body is cosmic and universal . . . This body can merge with various natural phenomena, with mountains, rivers, seas, islands, and continents. It can fill the entire universe," (318) and in the vernacular world the grotesque includes bodies that die and are diseased (319).

In Chapter 9 the crabs disperse in darkness and the rodents drawn to the corpses are driven back by the chill wind and rain, the bodies cleansed by the storm, and a day later with discoloured piebald skin they begin to lose their habitual forms, sinking into the sand until the crabs and rodents return, "flippantly browsing Joseph and Celice, frisking them for moisture and for food, delving into their pits and caverns for their treats, and paying them as scant regard as cows might pay a turnip head." (69) In Chapter 12 the ringing of Joseph's mobile dislodges momentarily a feeding gull, a mordant image. "By the fourth trill of the phone the gull had dropped again on to Celice's abdomen and was tugging at the lace of skin it had already picked and loosened. Her skin was tough. In two days she had lost her moisture and her elasticity." (97) The world beyond continues, the secretary disturbed by Joseph's change of routine, indicated by his tardiness, so much so that later that evening she rings Syl six hundred kilometres distant, who is stirred reluctantly into action. In a Bakhtinian sense, that the parental disappearance leads to Syl is suggestive symbolically, for "In the grotesque body, on the contrary, death brings nothing to an end, for it does not concern the ancestral body, which is renewed in the next generation." (322) This ringing of the phone in an unfamiliar and macabre scene evokes a structural aspect of grotesque, for according to Kayser, "It is our world that has to be transformed. Suddenness and surprise are essential elements of the grotesque. In literature the grotesque appears in a scene or an animated tableau."

(184) In Chapter 13 the torrential rain reminds the narrator of Mondazy – a writer who recurs in Craceland – and his account of folklore where 'Fish' leave the sea and cause death, evidence of which superstition might be seen in the silvering of their skin. By the fourth day of putrefaction Joseph and Celice were themselves silvering and "They had both dissolved and stiffened. They were becoming partly semi-fluid mass and partly salted drift; sea things. They even smelt marine, as spermy and rotting as bladderwreck or fish manure." (108) Once again Crace invokes certain elements and characteristics of the grotesque, for as Kayser's explains familiar elements become strange and ominous, since "The grotesque is a structure. Its nature could be summed up in a phrase that has repeatedly suggested itself to us: THE GROTESQUE IS THE ESTRANGED WORLD." (184) In Chapter 20 Syl is finally confronted with an instantaneous view of the bodies under sheets. Chapter 24 describes the removal of the bodies: "The four young policemen, too close now to the pungent details of mortality to concentrate on anything but horrors of the flesh, were nauseous as they prepared to lift Celice and Joseph from the dunes." (201) They leave a smudge of faded, lighter grass which by the following chapter has recovered, with the waves and tides removing all the remains of the creatures that make up the ecosystem with which the zoologists were briefly conjoined.

The chapters concerned with the field trip in the 1970s both extend the contexts of the couple's characterization, and introduce an element of suspense and some mystery concerning Festa's death. At the beginning of Chapter 4 the narrator reflects on the beauty of Joseph's voice, which contrasts with his otherwise unprepossessing figure, a quality that had helped cement the couple's affair. However, at their initial meeting, the tall and inelegant Celice is not drawn to the short and awkward figure; she "judged him to be cold, spoiled and snobbish." (16) Knowing their subsequent marriage and later deaths creates a poignant irony which resides in the outcome of this unpropitious meeting. This sense permeates and structures the reading of the events of this youthful episode. The narrator's reflections make this evident. "In these, her most disquieted and unhappy months, Celice could find no time for innocents like Joseph. She wanted to be courted by loud and tall and handsome men. She had the choice of three." (16) Joseph avoids the first night trip to a local bar where Celice hopes she can use her recently discovered skills as a flirt to her advantage on her fellow male students, Victor, Hanny and Birdie, but

"Festa was more demure than Celice, cherry-faced and warmly brimming, with thick loose hair and an enraging voice, low-pitched and deferential to men." (18) The narrative explains Celice's own recent changing sense of her attractiveness, with successful encounters with strangers. A man sharing her train and taxi has seduced her, and two men have been drawn to her as if biologically at the National Aquarium. However, her newly acquired forwardness is random, and returning from the bar she reflects on the men's preference for the local truck-girls "whose usual customers, the produce drivers coming to the town and the few surviving 'fish chauffeurs' with that day's catch, would not arrive till evening. Whatever seduction tricks Celice had tried in the past ten months were timid compared to those of these young, stalwart girls. They were all fingernails and heels." (25)

Crace charts the minutiae of the growing attraction between Joseph and Celice, drawn together because of the group dynamics. In Chapter 7 Joseph is wakened by the returning drinkers. Guilty about paying for the truck-girls in the shanties on the airport road, the other boys mock Joseph, who earlier has returned from the dunes after searching for nocturnal wildlife. In response he sings, much to Celice's initial annoyance and subsequent pleasure. In Chapter 10, Joseph departs for his field study early, sensing Celice might be an ally, an object for his desire, having watched her the previous day. "Her heavy, shapely thighs were centimeters from his waist. She wasn't beautiful. She was provoking, though. She was, he knew instinctively, his only chance." (72) He passes the women smoking in their room, waving at Celice who ignores him, but nevertheless is still amused by his singing. One senses the change in her mood as she follows him to the dunes, but too embarrassed, agitated and unfit to catch him. She continues her work on bladder flies in the sea, its transient and almost unreal qualities highlighted. "The milky morning light, which had been curdled by an unconvincing sun, diffused by mist and cloud, was turning purple grey. The once-blank sea was beryl green. The colours were unearthly, did not last, and within five minutes had been blown away." (79) Finally they meet on the shoreline, where he blows on a sprayhopper, the subject of his thesis, so it disappears. Unable to capitalize on her responses, Joseph does not initially share her fanciful sense of the place, which is ironic given their ultimate fate.

> 'It's lovely here. It's beautiful,' Celice replied. She'd never found a place more beautiful. She'd never been obsessed like this before.

Joseph shook his head. He'd always shake his head when she was fanciful. He'd shake his head at her for almost thirty years. 'It's beautiful for us. Zoologists have all the fun. They've no idea, these little guys. They only eat and hop and die. Even after dark. Whenever it's high tide. Most of them only last a day or two. Kaput! The gulls and jetfish get them, if they escape the waves." (83)

Whimsically, Joseph ponders whether the point of the evolution of the sprayhoppers is to keep zoologists happy, calling her Cecile, part of their family history that later would delight their daughter.

Chapter 14 begins dramatically with the fire, although dissipating any suspense apart from the cause. Festa's fate contrasts with Mondazy's folkloric account featured in the previous chapter. "It was Fire not Fish that put an end to Festa. Some water might have saved her life." (111) After a visit of a generally approving thesis tutor, on the fifth day in mist the study house appears almost symbolically to merge with nature. The students celebrate with a meal. Joseph and Celice's intimacy grows. Festa kisses Birdie, the ornithologist. "It must have been one of those two, Joseph thought, who'd placed the kerosene lamp underneath the table and turned the flame down to its lowest setting for a more romantic light, perhaps, then left it burning through the night." (112) Leaving Festa to sleep off a hangover, Celice pursues Joseph in the dunes, her cigarette abandoned on the sink, a saucepan on a lit hob and the lamp only vaguely noticed by the departing pair. The narrator hypothesizes as to the cause of the fire – although "The dead don't speak. It could have started in a thousand ways" (115) – and describes the inconsequence of Festa's death, the men able to escape, assuming she is safe. Chapter 17 describes the aftermath. While his two roommates go for the authorities, Birdie seeks the others on the dunes, curiously aroused by the incident.

> He was pumped up by all the thrilling chemicals of shock. The effort brought it home to him. Death had been near; he had been fortunate. He'd never been so fast or spirited, so oddly close to nausea and joy. How glorious he would appear too Festa as he called to her, half naked and half Hollywood, an envoy bearing messages and running from the fire toward the sea. (133)

In Chapter 19 two strands integrate, the retrospective last day of the couple as they visit the sight of the fire and Celice's reluctant recollection of the facts. She finally confronts her guilt, allowing herself to resurrect the past. She recalls calling out and vainly searching for

Festa, and her confession to the police and the girl's parents concerning her own negligent culpability. She blames the passion between herself and Joseph, but as Crace indicates this expresses part of an evolutionary progression.

> Passion such as theirs, brief as it was, was strong enough to shake the balance of the natural world, and test its synchronicity. Where there is sex, then there is death. They are the dark co-ordinates of one straight line. Grief is death eroticized. And sex is only shuffling off this mortal coil before its time to plummet to the post-coital afterlife. (149)

Perversely it is appropriate that a murderous intent overtakes them, a balancing of nature and their lives, at least according to Celice's scientific instincts. Of course these events ironically negate Celice's apparently whimsical claim in Chapter 6 in her introductory lecture to have never been the cause of a student's death. Her underlying feelings of culpability are clear. Chapter 22 describes the area with its inhospitable winds and encroaching airport, much changed. Crace identifies the forewarning sound of the wind. "This was the baritone of mourning and of saxhorns, sepulchral, pessimistic, deep. If they'd had any sense, if they had been less scientific and self-occupied, they would have run, as any small child would." (183) Oblivious of such portents of the future the couple explore each other for the first time. Death haunts this environment, almost as a warning, as if echoing Festa's death. This strand ends with them passionately discovering each other, oblivious to another's death, the landscape encompassing them much as it will at their own deaths.

The third strand details Syl's responses to the disappearance and death, offering a renewal or rebirth for Syl herself, as she moves towards not only an acceptance of her parents, from whom she had been estranged, but a realization that she has superseded them biologically. In Chapter 12, notified of her parents' disappearance while waitressing at the Metro Gnome next to the concert hall, a metropolitan environment contrasting with her home, Syl's initial response is irritation. Later, drunkenly, after failing to communicate with her parents she resigns her job over the telephone. She dreams of their deaths and travels home by train the following day, taking a taxi with Geo who seems unhurried and drawn to her. Almost paradoxically in emotional terms, but logically in a neo-Darwinistic sense, the possibility of the deaths allows Syl's metamorphosis, symbolized in her uncanny sense of overwhelming familiarity at the entrance to the house.

Now she felt as if her skin was too tight, that she could split and burst at any moment. This was a familiar sensation. She'd often trembled in this porch, and at this door . . . To cross this threshold was to cross the Styx. Sins were discovered there, and questions asked. She would be judged. Now, no longer adolescent, in this brief shelter from the rain, the image of the Styx was doubly relevant and chilling. Something ancient and intuitive was telling her that she was entering the chambers of the dead. This was the gate to the underworld. Geo was her ferryman. She'd have to call him Charon from now on. (120–1)

Crace's classical allusion is oblique. Charon would accept only those buried with the proper rites, and those living or dead who paid appropriately for their passage, hardly the case with Joseph and Celice, although Syl repays her driver with sex to obtain passage. Explicitly she eroticizes and associates death with their sexual encounter. As Ariès says in *The Hour of Our Death*, "In the modern era, death, by its very remoteness, has become fascinating; has aroused the same strange curiosity, the same fantasies, the same perverse deviations and eroticism." (608) And equally for Georges Bataille in *Eroticism* (2001) death is ambiguous in terms of simultaneous repulsion and attraction (45).

In Chapter 16, after checking with a neighbour Syl reads her father's last words in the soaked day book she has retrieved the previous day from the garden: "'Tuesday. Far too fine to work.' And then, '(In search of sprayhoppers!)'" (131) Geo suggests she trawl the clinics and hospitals and finally Syl visits the police to report her parents missing. Chapter 18 details her visit to the morgue, with its smell of chemicals and of the dead, its over-attentive clerk high on barbiturates and beer. These contrasts draw comically upon the gothic and grotesque, but Syl is untroubled while a possibility of survival remains. Finally she receives a call concerning the parents' stolen car, a parking ticket issued in Baritone Bay. In Chapter 20 after news of two bodies found, she travels there, and before seeing the corpses she imagines the likely causes of her parent's demise, resurrecting them by reliving childhood visits to other beaches, reflecting ironically that "Her mother had not liked that stretch." (159) Recalling an episode where her father might have drowned, death and its presentiments haunt her.

Viewing the corpses, Syl is moved by the intimacy of her father touching her mother. She escapes Geo and implicitly rejects her parent's by seeking solace in a service at the nearby Mission Church. She pictures her murdered parents.

She tried to let the hymning voices pick up the bodies from the dunes and take them to the kingdom of their verses, amongst the heavens and eternities, into the everlasting peace. But it was obvious that these were voices and these were verses that had not got the muscle to displace a single leaf, let alone pass sinners into paradise. Her father's songs, for all their mawkish sentiment, were far more powerful. Love songs transcend, transport, because there's such a thing as love. (170)

Syl faces a godless and expanding universe, the inevitability of death, and in this she embraces new realities of life, since "Their deaths were her beginning." (171) She senses this after she walks moneyless back to town through the Sunday carnival, and Deliverance Park through which she walks at night-time, thereby disdaining the warnings of her parents. She rejects the clichés of the condolence cards, deciding to travel, ignoring the hammering of Geo, the ferryman, and on awakening she discovers a symbol of transformation, her own milk teeth, apart from one she lost at school, stored by her parents, who "had preserved the rest, this first sign of their daughter's growing old." (196) As a new week approaches she imagines the sense of love interfused with death, commingling yet again Eros and Thanatos.

The final strand reverses the couple's last day. Chapter 5 conveys the thoughts and preparations of the attacker. He searches for half an hour for a victim before discovering the couple making love and it is his disgust at their nakedness that creates the rage motivating his attack. Perversely their continued passion contributes to their end. Each movement is detailed dispassionately as are their stolen possessions, indicating his psychopathology. In Chapter 11, two hours earlier Joseph and Celice are at the remains of the study house, reached by passing though the preliminary phase of the new building development. Joseph seeks in the Baritone Bay sprayhoppers, a symbol of the couple's earliest passion, in what has become an inhospitable environment. They make their way to the beach, ignoring the portents of change. "Death likes blue skies. Fine weather loves a funeral. Wise, non-scientific folk stay indoors on days like that, not walk along the coast, beyond the shelter even of a tree. The doctors of zoology were ill-informed. They didn't understand the rigours of the natural world. If spray-hoppers could not survive the changes on the coast, then how and why should they?" (95-6) Chapter 19 retraces the walk at noon to the ruins of the study house, overrun with vegetation, where Celice imagines the stages of the thirty years of life Festa might have enjoyed had she lived, from the uncompleted doctorate to "The man not

found, the children she'd not have, the house, the undemanding life
... All murdered by a coffee pan or by a toppling cigarette." (149)
Celice's negative creativity fuelled by her culpability mirrors the backward narrative, in that its reversal unravels the progressive aspect of life, removes its logical consequences. In Chapter 21 at 7.05 a.m. Joseph eats his breakfast outside in the same spot where his father had died of a stroke. Inspired by the sunshine, he determines they should visit the coast before waking his reluctant wife. There is a poignant irony in Celice's refusal to return on a thousand previous occasions until plans for the Salt Pines development threaten to remove her choice. Hence she agrees with her husband's wishes and thereby condemns them by her desire to offer penance for Festa's death. "He knew she only meant that they ought to see the burnt remains of the study house, to put Festa's ghost to rest before the bulldozers erased the place where she'd died. A resurrection in the dunes was not part of her plan." (178)

Chapter 25 ends the phase, although not the novel itself, with its image of the two sleeping at 6 a.m. in their separate rooms, which allows Crace to incorporate an earlier enigmatic cultural image of death as an essence that persists, as Ariès makes evident in *Images of Man and Death*, "Through this ambiguity surrounding sleep and death, we are brought back to the spirit if not the literal representation of the recumbent figure in a state of bliss – a figure neither dead nor alive." (56) It is the bravura with which Crace uses death as a narrative motif that leads Brooke Allen in "Meditations, Good and Bad,' (2000) to conclude that there is a unique quality to this novel (63), and induces F. González-Crussi in 'Approaching the Unknowable,' (2000) to consider that by its conclusion "we shall perceive absolutely nothing of death itself, but our vision of life – that other mystery – will be wondrously enhanced." (27)[30] *Being Dead* ends enigmatically, although continuing its elegiac impulse, with a symbol of renewal and iteration, in a scene that signifies more littoral possibilities, its atmosphere evoked as if some mediation of the scientific and illusory might be achieved through narrative reflecting the universalizing forms of nature:

> All along the shores of Baritone Bay and all the coast beyond, tide after tide, time after time, the corpses and the broken, thinned remains of fish and birds, of barnacles and rats, of mollusks, mammals, mussels, crabs are lifted, washed and sorted by the waves. And Joseph and Celice enjoy a loving and unconscious end, beyond experience.
> These are the everending days of being dead. (210)

Notes

1. Telephone conversation between Jim Crace and Dr Philip Tew, 9 December 2004, 15:40 onward, hereafter referred to as 'Crace–Tew: Telephone Interview 5.'
2. Ibid.
3. Ibid. Crace explains part of the genesis of the setting: "I received a postcard from two friends of mine, who visited Jericho, and the postcard that they sent me was a picture of Quruntal Gebel, which means Hill of the Forty Days, or the Hill of Temptation as it's called in English, which is the cliff above Jericho where Jesus was reputedly supposed to have spent his forty days. It is full of caves, and it wasn't just one cave, it was many caves. I thought, he only wanted one, and what were the other caves there for, but clearly there were other people living out there, undergoing their own crises at the same time that Christ was there."
4. Ibid.
5. Ibid.
6. Ibid.
7. See J. Hillis Miller (139); as quoted in Chapter 2 with reference to *The Gift of Stones*.
8. 'Crace–Tew: Telephone Interview 5.' Crace confirmed my suspicions as to the ironic nature of many of the biblical references. There is a further dimension to his critique, since he admits, "If you're Christian and a religious person, you believe in death and resurrection, so if there was another death and resurrection of the son of God at the beginning, before his scripture, that doesn't undermine Christianity at all. If Christ dies up there with Musa, and then is raised from the dead again and goes and does his ministry, and then dies and is resurrected again as in the Bible story, then neither of those things undermine each other, because you already believe in death and resurrection."
9. Ibid.
10. Moreover, as Kazunari specifies, "The first time Musa ever sees Jesus, Musa recognizes his own lesser twin in Jesus (38), and indeed Musa's lesser twin is 'briefly resurrected by the water' (29) Jesus tenderheartedly tips on Musa's feverish lips. The resurrection of Musa's tender twin is brief, but he re-resurrects after Jesus dies. Musa seems 'transformed' and 'a stoic, almost' (208) to his wife and the quarantiners." This intriguing article is replete with allusions to aspects of the Bible that Kazunari identifies as having parallels in Crace's retelling of the Christ narrative.
11. 'Crace–Tew: Telephone Interview 5.'
12. Ibid.
13. Kazunari cites Crace's narrative comment that Shim seeks a god immanent in everything, to conclude that "Shim may be playing the part of Philo Judaeus, Paul's contemporary, and other Christian Platonists, who

stressed the immanence of God." I remain unconvinced by such precise analogies. He also elaborates the possible origins of the term 'badu,' seeing a similarity to 'Buddhism.' When questioned by myself, Crace responded in an e-mail, "Badu is a diminutive form in Arabic for 'desert man' or Bedouin. Simple. No subtext, certainly not a Buddhist one. Ugh, the very thought!" (1) E-mail Jim Crace to Dr Philip Tew, Saturday 18 December 2004, 16:58.
14 'Crace–Tew: Telephone Interview 5.'
15 Ibid.
16 Nevertheless, Irwin does question drawing upon his own experience of the Sahara, the Empty Quarter and Judea the whole procedure of the badu's hunting techniques (21).
17 'Crace–Tew: Telephone Interview 5.'
18 Ibid.
19 These followers of "Achim the psalmist" (130) negate and reverse the offerings of the world, seeking peace in wretchedness. This is a Cracean invention.
20 'Crace–Tew: Telephone Interview 5.'
21 Again this is ironically reminiscent of the spirit of God, which descends like a dove in Matthew, Mark and Luke in the Bible.
22 Kamiya adds in mediation of this possibility, "Jesus can only die once – otherwise he would not be fully human. To entertain the idea that Jesus died in the wilderness and was reborn is heretical, because it makes Christianity's central event, the crucifixion, a mere rerun." (2)
23 'Crace–Tew: Telephone Interview 5.'
24 Arguably the reality turns out to be stranger than even Crace's fiction. "Police discovered the bodies of Mr Dixon and his wife, who lived in Moorland Road, hidden in undergrowth after they were reported missing in July 1989. Mr Dixon's hands had been tied behind his back. A scruffy cyclist dubbed the Wildman was seen using Mr Dixon's card at three cashpoint machines shortly afterwards but extensive Dyfed-Powys Police inquiries drew a blank. Several months later police arrested two suspected IRA members and discovered a cache of explosives near the scene of the killing." To date no one has been charged with the crime. See 'Gun Clue to Dixon Deaths.' (1998)
25 'Crace–Tew: Telephone Interview 5.'
26 Ibid.
27 Ibid.
28 This idea of the juxtaposition of these elements was suggested by the exploration of the grotesque in popular fiction by Greg Metcalf, in 'The Soul in the Meatsuit: Ivan Albright, Hannibal Lecter and the Body Grotesque.' (1995)
29 The possibility of applying the Bakhtinian grotesque was suggested by

the work of one of my PhD research students, Nicola Allen. Hers were most useful observations which initiated a train of thought at just the right moment.

30 In 'Maximalist Fiction' (2000) Susan Balée goes so far as to conclude that "He will probably be the writer who defines this era for a future generation." (513)

5

Excess, passion and the uncanny: The Devil's Larder (2001) and Six [Genesis] (2003)

The Devil's Larder

As Crace explains, the choice of food as the interlinking theme and subject matter for *The Devil's Larder* is not simply gastronomic, but reflects a series of cultural and personal changes, often quite radical ones, which have taken place during his lifetime. He recalls the dreariness of the food in the immediate postwar period and the significance of the transitions that followed:

> During my lifetime, this is one of the major changes in the United Kingdom. Our relationship with food has become so laden with complication, and at times beset with danger. That is something very much present in the book, but playfully so, going against the grain, and hence undermining our relationships with food. Not only has this concept of a relationship with food developed in my lifetime, but so also has the whole idea of personal politics. The importance of boycotting South African goods, of opposing war, and of supporting strikes was my kind of politics. As the ideas of the 1960s and 1970s developed, politics started to be about the body, vegetarianism, feminism, all about your own personal status within life. To some extent as an old-fashioned Stalinist I'm very ambiguous about the rise of personal politics and I think there's a subtext in the whole of *The Devil's Larder* where personal politics is critiqued.[1]

The book concerns the turbulence and inventiveness associated with a radical notion of food and culture and the social negotiations expressed through the medium of food, especially its role in mediating social etiquette, familial interactions, commercial relations and certain visceral social exchanges such as desire and romance. In the *Austin Chronicle* (2001) Rachel Feit says, "Crace's treatment of his subject matter goes well past its previously prescribed limits, past the mouth and stomach, into the lower depths somewhere between Rabelais and Freud." (31) For Bee Wilson in 'Not in the Very Best of Taste,' (2001) "There is much cleverness here, and many of the fragments are darkly memorable," (12) although she objects to over-readiness to utilize sexual metaphors in describing food. Essentially Crace's stories conceive of the inner mind, particularly the erotic and the disruptive, as being released by certain relations with food. They are both structurally and thematically heterogeneous, and as Francis Gilbert in the *New Statesman* (2001) says, "Crace constructs modern riddles, fables, fantasies, jokes, tragedies and comedies out of food." (41) According to D. J. Taylor in 'A Light Collation,' (2001) there is no overarching community, but rather a metaphorical notion of consumption (39–40). The setting is roughly contemporary, as indicated in the fifteenth story which refers to the narrator's mother's recipes for blind pie (one with birthday surprises) written over forty years previously in a woman's diary for 1961.

The collection received very mixed reviews, many reviewers questioning whether the sections are sufficiently coherent as a unified project, although as Crace comments, "the collection proved immensely popular amongst readers," and furthermore it inspired various adaptations in other forms and genres.[2] Perhaps the book remains too enigmatic, exactly the quality that inspired the hostility of Dale Peck in *Hatchet Jobs* (2004):

> Its sum is if anything less than its parts, such that one emerges from the text with little to add to the jacket description. There are sixty-four pieces; they are short (ranging from two words to ten pages); they are to the best of my knowledge fiction; and they all feature food. They are also linked by the fact that they seem to be set in the same place – the coastal village where the protagonists of *Being Dead* were murdered, perhaps, or one of the towns of his unnamed *Continent*? It's impossible to say, just as it's unclear what to make of repeated references to 'Mondazy,' the fictitious – and terrible – poet who is also featured in *Being Dead*. Frankly, the stories in *The Devil's Larder* defy paraphraxis. (134)[3]

Certainly, few of the various segments or vignettes appear to have any well-developed plot, and are at times brief and unresolved. Because of the number of stories, this section will analyse and use illustratively some representative examples selected on the basis of common themes and subject rather than attempt any complete paraphraxis.

Interviewed by Laura Miller for *Salon.com* (2001), Crace details the change of emphasis in his writing for this project:

> I felt instinctively that I wanted to do something playful and something made up of small ingredients that I could just enjoy. I wasn't just doing that for me. For once, I was thinking of the reader. I figured if I needed a break, the readers needed a break. And what could be more inherently light-hearted and comic than food? Well, sex, of course, but that's my next topic. (1)

It seems unwise to attempt to reduce or conflate the self-evident variations of these stories, since as Crace says, "It's dangerous to tease out too many strands as unifying ones in *The Devil's Larder*, because there are sixty-four pieces in there, a number chosen because of the chess board."[4] The book was to be a series of political parables; its intended original title, *The King's Warehouse*, is drawn from a children's fairytale. In the original tale a king is challenged by a peasant because of the hunger of his people, and on being beaten by him at chess the king grants the peasant a wish, which is that the king should place a single grain on the first square, doubling the amount on each square to the sixty-fourth, by which time the amount has grown exponentially. Much of the meaning lies in what the reader can add as a supplement to the stated tale, the power in the possibilities of inference rather than the explicit topography of the tale. If, however, the intended overt political elements were soon to be subsumed into the text's playful and whimsical impulses, the inferential transmission of meaning remains an informing impulse.[5] Crace admits, "The prompting was politics, but as I progressed the book became more playful. Some political pieces remain, but essentially the work is about the table and the way food mediates relationships. Love, sexuality, family and nostalgia are involved. It's not simply about what's on the plate, but the setting of the table, and the sharing of a table."[6] The tales demand the reader's participation, perhaps exemplified by the cryptic, two word sixty-fourth tale, "oh honey," that attempts in its punning brevity to convey the metaphoric strength of food in its shaping of our most intimate experiences.

The social and personal cartography is essential, and even the thirtieth story, which was intended to be an anti-capital punishment polemic, turns into something more whimsical. A young baker, George, friend of the narrator in youth, formerly a hippie, according to rumour provided some of his hashish cakes for a prisoner's last meal. Thirty years later the bald baker cannot recall precisely. "'But I'll say this,' George added finally, 'if that guy had my cakes for breakfast, even though it might be thirty years ago, he's flying still. Those cakes of mine were savage stuff. I bet he hasn't realized he's dead yet. He's giggling up there . . . And boy, he's hungry. He could eat a horse.'" (94) A similar whimsical mood and tone, and suppositional humour, conjoin all of the pieces. The explicit and consistently comic intention changes the nature of Crace's perspective. Each story is primarily enigmatic, depending upon a whimsicality, upon suppressed laughter, and as Georges Bataille says in *The Unfinished System of Nonknowledge* (2001) laughter's dependence upon the unknown and disruptive – recurrent elements in this text – means it remains unresolved: "The joyousness of laughter remains. But in spite of everything, the joy that is given in laughter, and that it is paradoxical to see associated with the objects of laughter, which are not usually joyous, for me, this joy cannot be separated from a tragic feeling." (142)

Throughout this collection one can observe a certain poignancy in both the complexity and underlying contradictions of Crace's whimsical humour, and this involves the very tragic sense of laughter that attaches itself to the incongruity of objects, events and situations in the various stories. The tenth story is one such comic vignette concerning relationships and a subtle poisoning. The narrator observes that a neighbour's daughter is selling manac beans from a farmers' market to rich city women passing in their cars, initially a great surprise to the trader. This food, formerly for the poor and for livestock, enjoys a sudden vogue. A radio report has revealed that the consumption by stud animals of such foods leads to an enlarged penis and swollen testicles, but creates erection problems. "I think I've guessed the actual motive of these women, though. They're poisoning their husbands, in a way." (28) The irony is offered visually, for in the daytime the women arrive to buy more of the produce, and in the evening the men rush past for home with an appetite for this "marginally addictive" foodstuff. Curiously, the gender of the narrator is not revealed, the sympathies not fully articulated, remaining opaque. The laughter evoked is potentially bleak, and the myriad confusions of emotions beneath the formal surface unsettling, with a hint of tragic undertones. The abatement of their husband's sexual drive by such wealthy women also remains enigmatic, since the individual motivations remain obscure, unexplored, inscribed comically as if an amusing sociological occurrence. The characters are underdeveloped, the perspective oblique.

However, specific relationships can be equally enigmatic. The context of the thirteenth story is more particularized. It concerns a forty-year-old farmer's son trained at the conservatoire, on honeymoon with Rosa, his timid young bride, whom he tutored in playing the flute. It starts with their conflict, for they are "Bored by arguing." (36) Curiously her timidity defines the relationship, since they have agreed to become used to each other before sex. Isolated in a hired cottage by the coast, an hour's walk from the village, and finding themselves without sufficient provisions, they decide to consume what they can hunt, catch and garner. "He had his father's sporting rifle in the car, and in the cottage there were some fishing nets, a book on fungi, and a herbal, *Mrs Caraway's Guide to Medicinal, Culinary & Cosmetic Plants*." (37) This return to nature proves less than satisfactory, for although the collection of food and wood draws them together, she continues to resist the sexual side of their relationship. Soon the food obtains an erotic quality for her, but she is shy of him. As the nights progress, the husband's mood sours and becomes confrontational. Almost as an expression of his frustration, he strips naked to plunge into the sea for shrimps, but she will only join him fully clothed.

As in a traditional fairytale there is an item that transforms Rosa's condition, as if magically, but the humour of Crace's piece lies not in her arousal, but in her determination to keep this secret from her frustrated, fulminating husband, whose anger has been referred to proleptically at the start. They find a sea holly or *eringo* whose root is edible and purportedly, according to the guide, an aphrodisiac, but ironically its taste is bland and uneventful. She remains unmoved by his embraces and the explorations of her body, but later she is feverish, and transformed by a bodily hyper-sensitivity and eroticism, enjoying a solitary elevation of her sexual responses, which she repeats in the morning when he goes to a farm for provisions. Collecting roots to smuggle home, she plans further recipes, but remains ambivalent about sharing her knowledge, reflecting on the food they have caught, which neatly conveys her notion of her own vulnerability and desire not to be consumed by their relationship and his desires. "She'd have to share them with her husband, she supposed. She'd have to share with him what she had found out on her own. But not just yet. Marriage was for life, she reminded herself. There was no need for haste. It would be a joy to make him wait. She'd not be caught as easily as pigeons, pheasants, shrimps." (45)

In the twenty-seventh story desire subtends the relationship between the owner of a restaurant and the schoolteacher of the girls, all younger than twelve whom he employs to collect razor clams from the seashore, which she loves to eat. With a voyeuristic impulse, he watches the young girls through binoculars as variously they tease out the phallic pink and fleshy siphons in an act they call "prick-teasing," as they cavort and play instead of working, and as they urinate on the sand. The teacher teases him about his exploitation of their labour, and challenges his method: "I told the teacher how people from the coast had been catching and cooking clams for centuries, and they'd always used salt. It smuggled its flavour into the flesh. They can't all be wrong. 'Indeed they can,' she said." (84) Later she joins the girls, supposedly to test the traditional claim that only salt can be used to entice the clams, using various substances including vinegar, pop, and finally her own urine as she squats on the flats watched by the restaurateur. This elaborates the playfulness of desire, for by revealing herself she exposes both her own desire and his voyeuristic nature. As Bataille says in *The Accursed Share, Vol. II*, "Nudity is not always obscene and can appear without recalling the indecorousness of the sexual act. Possibly so, but as a general rule a woman stripping naked in front of a man exposes herself to his most unseemly desires. Nudity thus has the meaning, if not of outright obscenity, of a slipping toward it." (149) The restaurateur cooks a meal for the object of his desire that night. "They tasted just like prawns she said, but not as salty. She liked the satisfying chewiness and swore she could detect the jam, the cinnamon, the pop, and many things beside." (85) The tale is redolent of perversity, of unspoken attraction, and the suggested eroticism of food preparation and its consumption. The teacher's complicity in this curious eroticism is troubling, even potentially perverse.

The collection's voice is far from consistent, varying throughout; some sections are related in first person, and others in third person; there is a mixture of sexes and ages, which as a whole conveys a partial sense of the community of individual lives that are very loosely interconnected by their encounters with food, but finally certain aspects are contrasting. Consider two equally whimsical tales, where a suppositional context is explored in each, rather than a fundamentally naturalistic one. In the fifty-four story the narrative seems rooted in oral myths and folklore, relating the devil's propagation of mushrooms. "He feeds them disappointments, nightmares, fevers, indigestion, fear. He lets them breakfast on spite." (161) The narrator has followed a figure in the woods, tasting the blandness of the mushrooms that according to tradition the devil leaves, observing that the devil, rather than planting, must harvest the best.

> His greed is stronger than his spite. He thinks the mushrooms are too good for us. We'd appreciate the poisons or the tangs that they provide, their blasphemies. We are too dull and timid for the magic and the flesh. He roams the woods and meadows when it's dark to satisfy himself. He knows which mushrooms to pull up. The ones he leaves for us are flavourless. (163)

The implied themes and social commentary are interwoven, first suggesting that virtue is bland, and second revealing the utter provinciality and mundanity of this small town and its inhabitants. This is achieved in part by reworking into its structure the traditional saying that suggests that the devil retains the best tales, and therefore is tangentially reflexive since this serves to remind the reader of the narrative impulse, and its wayward inclinations. The mushrooms are related explicitly to afterbirth and death, stressing both the tale's implausibility and overtly symbolic dimensions.

Certainly the narrative does not represent any realist impulse on Crace's part, whereas the whimsical account in the seventh story of the merchant trader dining club, known subsequently as "the Whistling Chop," does retain certain naturalistic traits, a focus upon detail and specificity, although undermined both by its subject matter and comic mode. The tale combines recognizable human impulses with an observation of whimsical details that remain archetypal in that they are related to kinds of behaviour rather than any specificity. This results partly from the allegorical nature of the stories' mode, with their implicit moral structures and intentions. The resident manager is a type rather than an individual; he treats the establishment like a fiefdom, and on discovering one waiter has eaten meat from the dish he was to serve to members, the manager dismisses him and demands all waiters should henceforth whistle along the service corridor from the kitchen to the dining rooms. At first he is exultant at his ingenuity and the members are entertained by the musical diversity, which also enables him to identify his employees:

> He got to recognize the waiters from their whistling. There were the warblers, who merely offered a seamless trill without a melody. And then there were the songsters, addicts of the operetta and the music hall,

or country lads with harvest tunes. One waiter specialized in hymns. Another always piped the wedding march, a touch too fast. There were, as well, the irritating ones, who sounded either as if they'd lost their dogs, or as if they were impatient stationmasters. (17)

He is convinced he has prevented the stealing of food, and of course the reader anticipates that this hubristic pomposity must be undercut. Hence, on discovering that there is gravy on the stair-post, he realizes the waiters can leave food to be consumed on their tuneless return, so he institutes whistling both ways, much to the annoyance of members. The conflict of his desire to control their behaviour and the waiters' propensity for human ingenuity collide, reflecting a universal or archetypal human situation. There is a further irony when finally he decides that he will serve the meat dishes himself, and finds himself similarly tempted. "And, at those times, a colleague on the staff might catch him whistling as small boys do to help them cope with their remorse." (20) Overall this depends somewhat upon the reader's empathy and the possibility of self-recognition in the dynamics of the conceit. The whimsicality and comedy in this case must be situated in the realm of plausibility or the generally feasible. Both tales depend upon an elegance of style and the overall conceit, which as Bataille explains in *The Unfinished System of Nonknowledge* both undercuts the ethical significance, and limits the comedic mode. "Through elegance, we get away from heaviness, but lightness is paid for with insignificance. We avoid the excesses of the tragic. Above all, we avoid becoming comical." (7)

Peck appears frustrated by the paradoxical nature of such conceits, and he likens the contents of the collection to "prehistoric" cave drawings in that they "did not imitate life, they imitated art, and the same counterfeit status plagues the stories in *The Devil's Larder*. The short sentences masquerading as careful prose, the resonant observations which turn out to be nothing more than artless tricks of language, the use of enough irony to avoid appearing recherché." (137) In *January Magazine* (2001) David Dalgleish ponders over how the nature of these vignettes problematizes drawing and developing characters. "They are closer in spirit to fables or tall tales or parables or even Zen paradoxes. There is no shortage of people, but there are no 'characters' as we are accustomed to think of them. It is an entire cast of supporting players, each with little dialogue to speak and only a brief moment in the spotlight." This passing of successive individuals and moments, many of whom are focused upon the past, creates the nostalgic mood with its heavy sense of loss, often reflecting a literal loss, but of very different kinds. Story 39 commences, "Here is his name, written in our register the day before he died: Toby Erickson, in capitals, above his signature, his home address (illegible), his phone number, his fax." (166) The guest remains an individual passing through, his poisoning by botulism from his picnic lunch an embarrassment to the hotel, but a certain poignancy remains, the story ending with the indelible image of the dead man aboard his boat as staff prepare breakfast for the guests, unaware of his now rigid demise.

The unexpected qualities of this image of death highlight two conditions that animate many of Crace's narrative situations. As Bataille writes in *The Unfinished System of Nonknowledge*, "The domain of the known is, in one sense at least a stable domain, where one recognizes oneself, where one recovers oneself, whereas in the unknown there isn't necessarily any movement, things can even be quite immobile, but there is no guarantee of stability." (133) In the image of the guest the apparently known is transformed into an image of immobility and then becomes the unknowable. Story 62 relates the grief of an unnamed wife who eats a pinch of her husband's ashes to assuage her grief, her sleep subsequently disrupted by the return of her husband's awful singing voice. We learn little of her apart from her loss. There is comedy in this grotesque response, since as Bataille observes, "tears can be considered as linked, as well as laughter, to the invasion of the unknown, to the suppression of one part of the world that we consider as a world known in all its parts, that we consider as an ensemble. If someone dies, for example, the known order is profoundly altered." (145) Dalgleish fears the collection remains formally inchoate, but admits the stories are "ingenious" and comments:

> It is hard to discern a unifying intent. As the title might suggest, many of the stories echo the story of Eve partaking of the fruit of the tree of knowledge; our inability to resist the temptation of food becomes emblematic of our lesser qualities: greed, self-deception, malice and so on. But other stories are playful or celebratory, refuting the notion that our animal appetites are merely a reflection of our sins, of our fall from grace. Perhaps Crace means only to show that the variousness of food mirrors the variousness of human nature; if so, it is a credit to his talent that this short book manages to cover something like the entire spectrum of our emotions.

Temptation, fruitfulness and poisoned emotions are complex topics, and the formal limits of the stories narrow the possibilities of empathy. So too does the insistent whimsicality, for in the framing of elements through particular moments of activity that signify wider possibilities of meaning, the reader is left with an interpretative void. The protagonist of the thirteen-line Story 37 exercises daily, and eats natural foods selected to protect him from disease until the day he dies. The irony depends upon the universality of death, especially as the reader has no idea of his age, or any other detail concerning the man. The comic, often ironic narrative twist defines the nature of each vignette's reception, the reflective mode essential for even intuitively seeing the unconscious meanings, both cultural and personal, which is what Peck calls somewhat dismissively the "the a-ha! moment" of these tales (146). Peck objects to this tale, since he argues "The prose is detached, observational, objectifying its one-dimensional protagonist." (138)

In Story 18 a backward meal that the young narrator has organized as an amusement for his twenty-seventh birthday only becomes significant when the uninvited director of their company arrives at their private club room. He announces his own promotion to Director of Europe, and his need for an aide in Brussels when he takes up the post, before recalling that his own grandmother at eighty-three in a nursing home partook of a reverse meal. The narrator feels his prospects restored, echoing the old woman's words, "I am twenty-seven years of age today. Life is uncertain. Leave the soup till last." (56) Peck has a point about the one-dimensionality, but in some senses this is a result of the critique of a personalized politics very much centred upon food that Crace refers to above. The whimsicality can finally be situated as a means of undercutting such subjective or personal obsessions of the so-called postmodern individual, opposing what Herbert Marcuse in *One Dimensional Man* (1964) describes as "a pattern of *one-dimensional thought and behavior* in which the ideas, aspirations, and objectives that, by their content, transcend the established universe of discourse and action are either repelled or reduced to the terms of this universe." (12) Most of Crace's stories in this collection are predicated upon the contradictions inherent in the juxtapositions described by Marcuse, where public norms suppress inner meanings and interpretations, and the pressures of socially appropriated time and the external social realm diminish private space (10).

Social participation is often motivated by self-delusion or shaped by fashion, as is exemplified in the stories of restaurants drawing in various diners who appear to act collectively, their lives influenced by patterns of behaviour. In Story 3 a group of five potential diners contemplate wandering off into the jungle and across a river, drawn by its apparently unorthodox reputation to a wooden lodge, even risking cannibalism to taste the exotic. "We're wading, too, of course, into the dark side of ourselves, the hungry side that knows no boundaries. The atmosphere is sexual. We're in the brothel's waiting room." (5–6) Of course their desire is in large part commodified, postulated on the tastes of an elite for the apparently prohibited, the supposedly individualistic, which is the image of the group as they stumble back satiated on Curry No. 3, "strung out, five weary penitents, weighed down by our depravities, beset by sulphur clouds, and driven on by little more than stumbling gravity." (7) In Story 45 diners are drawn to a fashionable, yet modest restaurant in an unfashionable area, where the soup of fish, vegetables and occasionally beef or chicken constitutes the menu. The secret ingredients of the celebrated chef are revealed in the narrative of a regular habitué from the establishment's pre-fashionable days.

> Her secret is the sewer truffles that she ads to every pot of soup. She grows them in her cellar. Her secret is sea water: two parts of that to every three parts taken from the tap. Seaweed. Sea mist. The secret is the heavy pan she uses, made for her out of boiler iron by a ship's engineer as a token of devotion. Its metal is not stable, but leaks and seeps its unrequited love into the soup. Her secret is a special fish that's caught for her by an old man, at night. He rows out beyond the shipping lanes, anchors in the corridor of moonlight, and scoops them from the water in a kitchen colander. Or else the magic's in the vegetables. Or in some expensive, esoteric spice. (138)

The impulse for the mysterious is revealed as a trajectory towards one-dimensional individuation, which has guaranteed the restaurant its brief few months of fame, its fleeting popularity. Crace confirms this mood with Story 60, centring on the Air & Light restaurant which serves no food, based on a Japanese sect that denies itself sustenance, and was originally essentially a Situationist gesture of two lesser known artists and their friends. As its popularity rises, so too do its prices, and it attracts the rich and famous, even Al Pacino (star of the movie *Girder Man*, a reference that recurs in *Six*). Crace parodies the liberal, knowing cultural critique that attaches itself to such phenomena, a triumph of individual opinion over reality. This parodies both the populist versions of deconstructive personal politics, replete with polemicist gestures, and the New Age beliefs that have displaced traditional ones.

> It was, of course, a splendid comedy – but there were some who claimed that the restaurant, by formalizing diet and restraint, was servicing a greater cause than simply a desire to be amused. The Air & Light combated publicly, they claimed, the countless tyrannies of food. It opened up new channels from the body to the mind. It celebrated emptiness in an otherwise oversated world. (184–5)

The vacuity of the interpretation suggests a general failure to respond to concrete reality, where the manner and style of apparent radicalism becomes briefly chic, its antagonistic content assimilated. As Marcuse insists, "The alien and alienating oeuvres of intellectual culture become familiar goods and services." (61) Crace parodies the specificities of the liberal's radical ambitions and method of self-identification.

Each story depends upon a ubiquitous ironic twist and for Crace these endings represent a deliberate deflation, offering the obverse of his grandiloquent style in his novels, which revised technique he refers to as a "dying fall" required to conclude each moment, so that the elements are slightly loosened by the end of the tale, resulting in a cadence of "under-delivery." He adds, "To think of them as a series of tone poems is important."[7] However, the tone is consistently recursive and enigmatic. The plethora of ironic moments as endings and quasi-resolutions makes the overall direction of the narratives appears almost suspended and reiterative. The laughter evoked is dark and tinged with a propensity for the tragic, given the incongruous contexts and objects for such laughter. Hence, ironically given Crace's intentions, this collection demonstrates a curiously pessimistic mood concerning the outcome of lives and the minutiae of everyday interactions, and perhaps consequently reflects at times both a touch of bathos and a hint of what appears to be incompletion.

Food might appear fanciful, even jovial, but the intersections of lives and desires add numerous contexts so that the whimsicality, rather than remaining neutral and simply joyful, thus becomes located in a sombre and potentially conflictual realm. The farmer in the fifth story takes pleasure in seeing the children of the picnickers who intrude into his field attempt to eat the crab apples, only to discover their sourness. And yet, he reflects, there are certain moods when still like the child he once was, he cannot himself resist tasting the flesh of the fruit, without swallowing, symbolically tasting of temptation. "Even after all these years – misled, misled, misled again – I like to test the flavours of deceit. And I still find myself surprised by its malicious impact in my mouth. It's bitter-sweet and treacherous, the kiss of lovers from opposing villages." (13) The final hint is of personal, romantic disappointment. The laughter becomes caustic, provisional, uncertain. Feit concludes that "More like prose poems, these stories are simply too rich to digest in one sitting. Their proper enjoyment requires careful contemplation. Like the episodic experience of a human life, each story seems absurdly simple, but taken together they comprise an unruly tangle. *The Devil's Larder* is at once dark and sentimental, optimistically ambiguous, and sweetly deceptive." (31)

The twenty-third story allows a glimpse of Crace's father, the diseased arm transformed into a "gammy" leg, working miracles on an allotment, where wiping carrots on his leg is characteristic of Crace's memory of the paternal produce: "My father would pull carrots from the ground, wipe them on his trouser leg exactly as the guy does in that story, and they would taste wonderful."[8] Even this nostalgic moment is undercut by the fear the boy feels whenever he is offered items by the neighbour's husband, inspired by the malevolent tales of his sisters. "I never saw him walking to or from his home. My sisters said he slept in the angling hut, washed in the river, lived on what he grew, wee'd [sic] on his lettuces, crapped on his greens, and poisoned strangers with his crops." (68–9) Paradoxically, years later the narrator as an adult cannot grow anything approaching these carrots, his young son suggesting that the man's loneliness left its taste. The irony is that in fear he discarded so many other foodstuffs offered by his peculiar benefactor. There is an echoing sense of loss here, of an inability to comprehend or account for oneself. Feit senses the overall negativity of the collection, commenting that

> These stories are less about cuisine than about the little eruptions of life. Crace is admittedly not particularly interested in food, but the ways in which life's great dramas play themselves out on tiny stages. Painstaking, fastidious, Crace's prose traces out the well-trodden paths of everyday life. But somehow his lens is distorted, throwing an eerie light onto each of life's rituals. The stories in *The Devil's Larder* are slightly

macabre, disturbing even. Their unifying feature, food, is not something the writer celebrates, but rather a circumstantial feature of each disquieting episode. (31)

Laura Miller seems to agree, and comments when interviewing Crace that "I don't know why I should be, but I was surprised – when I expected the book to be sort of simple-mindedly celebratory and life-affirming – by how much rotten, poisoned and inedible food there is in it." (1) Crace's response to her is a partial admission concerning the negativity of the quotidian, but he maintains his own sense of its affirmative core:

> I think that the world has a lot of dark corners to it, a lot of sour noises, and yet despite that we can look in those places and listen to those noises and come up with an optimistic view of the universe. And that's what I've applied to this book as well as to all my other books. This book is full of sour noises, and full of poisons and toxins and bad meals and bad encounters. But for me the overall feeling is that this is a tender book. There are relationships that work. Mums do love their children. There are marriages that last. (1)

Interviewed by Robert Birnbaum for *identitytheory.com* (2001) Crace concedes something of the collection's tone. He says, "I have to admit it's dark, I can't stop my books being dark. I'm enjoying doing it, for once. I almost go to it eagerly. Maybe it's because I'm writing little short pieces."

Although more approving than other reviewers, Feit notes an almost paradoxical result of the author's style. "Told through Crace's nostalgic, placid prose, each of the stories seems equivocally benign. Yet their tidy facades mask all of the turbulence of life's endless struggles, culminating in a two-word story that captures the spirit of humanity – 'Oh honey.'" For Crace the stories even in their negativity relate to the natural world, which is both indifferent and potentially cruel from a human standpoint, as he clarifies for Laura Miller:

> Those strange encounters that you've mentioned, that seem to horrify you so much, are encounters with the natural world – the man who dies out fishing, killed by botulism. Botulism is a product of the natural world, and stands as an encapsulated metaphor for the load of difficulties we're all going to encounter in the natural world. None of us will come out of this unscathed. (3)

However, although nature must be in a Darwinist sense indifferent to man, in this place of jungles and of bush meat, a world where tubers retrieved from a dying man's body grow into plants, the grotesque and paradoxical elements derive more from the social nuances, and the meaning of food and its consumption in relationships. Nature lurks at times as an almost atavistic or primal force, which contends with the practices of humans, decay threatening our foodstuffs and the control of our environment. This is seen in microcosm in the forty-sixth story where a freezer left for ten days is disturbed by some unknown force and tumbles its food into the temporarily abandoned kitchen, as if animated by some unspecific force. The consequences are unpalatable and evident.

> When we returned, the smell was scandalous, a nauseous conspiracy of vegetables and meats and insect waste. The rats had defecated everywhere. The larder slugs had filigreed their trading routes. Someone had left a green-blue mohair sweater inside the freezer, knitted out of mould. The broken flecks of wool were maggot worms and wax-moth larvae. The sweater seemed to shrug and breathe with all the life it held. (140-1)

This surge of life signifies the always potential disruption of the domestic, and of the family routine, and of the apparently civilized, which naturally reasserts itself. Briefly, the scene offers an almost uncanny image, but the cleaning up is so perfunctory that the hint of the unknowable passes. In what he describes as "grappling with small things"[9] Crace's intention appears to be that the uncanny qualities of the world, its natural impulses that are out of our control, may appear to haunt the fringes of our existence, but through the medium of food they can penetrate into our bodies, our lives and our consciousness.

Six, or *Genesis*

Six shares features with *Arcadia*: its metropolitan setting, the gossip columnist narrator, and a riot, although in *Six* this occurs near the beginning of the novel, creating a turbulent, almost tumultuous mood throughout. Additionally, it shares a sense of the enclosure or diminishment of lives rather than the expansiveness that characterizes Crace's rural narratives. The possibilities of the city, so strong in *Arcadia*, are retrospective in *Six*, as if Lix's middle-age represents a crisis much like that of the environment. He has appeared in Hollywood films, despite the imperfection of a birthmark or naevus on his face, for in Craceland even stars are palpably imperfect. "Who'd fail to recognize that celebrated granite head, those expressively nervous beryl eyes, that cherry-sized, cherry-shaped and cherry-coloured birthmark on the ridge of bone below his left eye?" (5) For Crace his very imperfection is central to a world-view that is anti-romantic and opposes the illusory coercion of the self.

> There was the decision early on to represent someone who was successful sexually in Darwinist terms, but not sexually successful in any other terms. I thought it would be much more honest to the world to present someone who really wasn't very good sexually, and whose relationships were faulty. Most of our relationships are faulty, and most of us are useless in bed, and most of us don't have our best moments together simultaneously. This is very much part of my anti-romanticism, which is a romanticism of its own. My sense of romanticism is that the glory of human relationships is that they are immensely blemished, but nevertheless they are strong. The cynicism of the Hollywood version is that everyone is good-looking and has simultaneous orgasms – unlike most of us.[10]

Lix lives in the City of Kisses, its soubriquet derived from a photojournalistic assignment, and typically the city's actual name is unspecified. In 'Reproduction Values' (2003) Anthony Quinn comments, "the topography in Jim Crace's fiction has contrived to be both piercingly strange and naggingly familiar, an amalgam of the imaginary and the realistic." (8) D. J. Taylor says in 'Gone to Seed,' (2003) "this habitual topographical vagueness is highly appropriate for the elemental themes on display." (2) Crace creates a curiously familiar environment with an Eastern European topography combined with the underlying oppression one associates with either South America or the old Communist Bloc, making the events seem both anachronistic and yet ahistorical. Also, so typical of Craceland, there is a collective knowledge about this environment that the narrator assumes for himself and the reader, as if both were intimate with the community depicted, a mutuality and complicity.

Taylor claims that "However stoutly lashed to the engines of human desire and striving, the prevailing urge is always bleakly naturalistic." (2) Indeed the riots with nine dead evoke a sombre mood, but Taylor's response may be due also to a strong sense of Lix's lack of agency, and his inability to sustain any moral view of his world. According to Boyd Tonkin's review the mood of the narrative remains overall perhaps more optimistic than that of its predecessor, although this seems to hinge upon his viewing the novel as a romance form.

The optimism of *Six* gleams through the tender erotic comedy of Lix's affairs and marriages: his 'history of love rebutted and love devalued'. It shows in the memorable individuality of each woman who carries his seed – from patrician Alicja to bohemian Freda and unfathomable Mouetta, whose pregnancy brackets the plot. It climaxes in the joyful eruption at the close of the children that this likeable but deadbeat dad has half-ignored. (32)

Certainly there is a diversity of women, and importantly each of them is wilful enough to challenge Lix variously, but the strong ambivalence of Lix towards these women and his insensitivities make one interrogate the novel's resolution which is equivocal. In some senses an uncanniness of turmoil and inner turbulence is a recurrent undercurrent to each of the episodes. Crace's reflects on the book's composition:

> I thought *Being Dead* was a very optimistic book, but I was irritated when critics couldn't see that. I feel I was relatively successful in coming up with a comforting narrative, despite the horrible subject matter, so I was determined next to write my unambiguously optimistic story, given my life, my fortunate set of circumstances and long marriage, and answer my critics in *Genesis* or *Six*. My determination fails because several things stood in the way of that intention. First, fiction doesn't like un-ambiguity, trying to find instead ambiguity, so my intention was perhaps doomed. Secondly, fiction doesn't like love; it likes despair. Fiction doesn't like good fortune; it likes dismay, preferring pessimism to optimism. However, I wonder whether there wasn't an extra ingredient, given that when I was writing *Being Dead*, even though it was a grim subject, and my father's death was a prompt at my shoulder, I was a very happy, contented person. However, *Genesis* or *Six* was composed during a time of my life that was beset with dismay, and even though I claim not to be an autobiographical writer, the circumstances of my life were extremely dark with my mother's illness and death. Not only was my own mood very dark, but the overall circumstance for writing the book was impossible.[11]

The novel is further affected by grief and the demands of his publisher's deadline. Sub-textually it becomes the portrayal of a man under pressure, his emotions constantly in turmoil. He concedes the failure to produce an optimistic book and its flaws to Andrew Lawless in 'The Poet of Prose – Jim Crace in Interview,' (2005) explaining the context:

> My mum started going down with dementia and cancer, and during the last year of writing that book I was her sole carer, which meant in the

first instance 60–70 phone calls a day and lots of pressure, and in the end, the last couple of months, meant constant care, changing of nappies as if she were a baby, and finally she died . . . I couldn't concentrate fully on the book, due to the emotional strain of caring for a 91 year old dying mother. That was of course my priority. (3)

Rather than exploring his bereavement explicitly, Crace projects his pressures onto Lix, focusing upon the character's inner demons of sexual desire, on his nagging sense of displacement and his unconscious fear of the emergence of a new generation.

Lix's libido constantly fluctuates, reflecting his strong sexual imagination. After the night of rioting whose impression of crisis mirrors his inner, unconscious turmoil, in his wife's brief absence he ogles three women as part of an elaborate relationship game. The narrator ponders on the seductive potential of his career, and stresses almost polemically:

An actor's touring life is cut out for adultery, affairs, the weekend fling. What harm in that? And what – if he were truly someone who would cheat on his wife, other than inside his never-faithful, ever-scheming head – if he were to go up to the likeliest? If he were to step across and what? Invite her to abandon her workmates and come with him on to the long-imagined beach? What harm in that?

The harm in that was the misfortune – was it truly a misfortune? – that every kiss produced a child. Remember? Fertile Lix had never slept with anyone without – eventually – a pregnancy. There was always an aftermath for him. (41)

The text's moralizing tone, however ironic, and Lix's mental promiscuity evoke a palpable sense of distance from the protagonist. By charting his surprise at and ambivalence towards each of the couplings, each unexpected, each misunderstood, Crace makes evident Lix's surprise at both people and events, seemingly subject to external forces rather than in control. Lix remains curiously characterless. Cynical and bored there is something uncanny in the urgency of each spate of reproduction, a periodic repetition often coming after long periods of celibacy.

Lix only tangentially senses the possibilities of love. The primary focus on the procreative repetitions becomes so insistent and integral that it creates a recognizably uncanny context. In *The Uncanny* (2003) Nicholas Royle says of the uncanny:

It disturbs any sense of what is inside and what is outside. The uncanny has to do with a strangeness of framing and borders, an experience of liminality. It may be that the uncanny is a feeling that happens only to oneself, within oneself, but it is never one's 'own': its meaning or significance may have to do, most of all, with what is not oneself, with others, with the world 'itself' . . . It would appear to be indissociably bound up with a sense of repetition or 'coming back' – the return of the repressed, the constant or eternal recurrence of the same thing, a compulsion to repeat. (2)

Although romantically and often socially liminal despite his fame, Lix is ineluctably drawn to repeat himself, as if driven by a deeper instinct than the amatory or social. As Sigmund Freud says in *The Uncanny* (2003), "In the unconscious mind we can recognize the dominance of a *compulsion to repeat*, which proceeds from instinctual impulses." (145) Curiously, Lix seems hardly compelled by sexual or libidinous desire itself. Thus the allusive nature of his desires haunts the text as a supplementariness that exists beyond the capacity of ascription, outside of the narrative form, uncannily so. And the overarching unification of these couplings creates something excessive. According to Quinn, "It gradually becomes clear that Crace's priority is not so much to tell a story as to explore the psychopathology of a driven man. We learn perhaps more than we need to about the grapplings, gropings, swellings and spillings of the priapic Lix, whose sex life seems to have been busier than most but certainly not happier." (8)

In his later writing Crace appears increasingly to predicate his fiction on the obverse or reversal of earlier universalizing observations, where the particular and the formal conceit of the narrative creates a different type of synthesis and therefore particularizes the content. Characters previously have been essentially humanized by their struggles; Lix remains enigmatic. His fecundity sets him apart, producing what Janet Maslin in 'Books of the Times: A Hero's Surfeit of Fertility and the Poetic Use Thereof' (2003) describes as "This honeyed, sometimes overripe novel." (8) Lix embodies and articulates much of the marginality of the uncanny, the prose style its excess, for as Royle says with reference to Freud's text, "To write about the uncanny, as Freud's essay makes admirably clear, is to lose one's bearings, to find oneself immersed in the maddening logic of the supplement, to engage with a hydra." (8) Lix's offspring offer another supplementarity, of himself, and the contexts of his serial insemination conspire to leave him distant from all of these extensions of himself. At the end of the novel, Bel, the child of whom he has no knowledge, the product of his first sexual encounter, has her own child, Cade. "Bel knows exactly who her father is. Her version of his birthmark makes him unmistakable. She is twenty-six already and has not been greatly tempted to turn up at blood's front door to claim her heritage." (217–18) This mirroring of the self is an aspect of the uncanny, one that literature can exemplify, since as Freud says in his famous essay on the concept of the uncanny. "The uncanny that we find in fiction . . . actually deserves to be considered separately. It is above all much richer than what we know from experience; it embraces the whole of this and something else besides, something that is wanting in real life . . . *In literature there are many opportunities to achieve uncanny effects that are absent in real life.*" (155–6) Tim Adams in 'On Fecund Thoughts,' (2003) cannot concede and even excludes this necessary element that explains the tensions of the novel: "Lix and his lovers remain rooted in a world full of little jealousies and neuroses. Given the unlikeliness of the plotting, this insistence on a kind of realism makes the whole a little strained and uncomfortable." (15) This very "unlikeliness" is in part what creates an uncanny effect, an almost haunted quality of Lix, mirrored by his moral ambivalence and self-centredness. Freud identifies in literature "the factor of unintended repetition that transforms what would otherwise seem quite harmless into something uncanny and forces us to entertain the idea of the fateful and the inescapable, when we should normally speak of 'chance.'" (144)

Although there is an inescapability about Lix's fate, a space is created so that the reader may respond ambivalently to him, and equally he responds to his emotions and the fact of his offspring equally ambivalently, as if the possibility of the children might represent an unwelcome supplement of himself, an omission in the sense of self. There is something more than the neo-Darwinian about the novel, with its emphasis on the interrelated and overlapping lives of various women who encounter him. This intensification of a recurring pattern, and the almost paradoxically oblivious sense Lix has of his life, bring to mind Freud's observation concerning the uncanny effects in literature. "Whatever has an uncanny effect in real life has the same in literature. But the writer can intensify and multiply this effect far beyond what is feasible in normal experience; in his stories he can make things happen that one would never, or only rarely, experience in real life." (157) The most significant intensification and multiplication in terms of Lix is his ambiguity, and the proliferation of children, each one the culmination of what is initially a sexual fantasy, a reminder of Crace's comment that "Our imaginative lives do present themselves physically."[12]

The first insemination in 1979, narrated after the last, takes place during Lix's time as a drama student when he discovers sexuality late in his twenties, but from that point his progress is defined by his various sexual encounters. There are further uncanny elements in such acts, devoid of deep emotion, in the fact that simultaneously they are more a product of circumstance and happenstance, even though they are significant moments retrospectively. In *Critique of Everyday Life, Volume II* Lefebvre postulates a theory of the moment, which he describes as constituted by choice (344–5), as possessing duration so that "it stands out from the continuum of transitories within the amorphous realm of the psyche," (345) and also as possessing memory (345–6) and form (346); finally, "It can establish itself as absolute" (346) in its very impossibility, and thus is related to an alienating sense, with "the alienation which threatens every activity within the very process of its accomplishment." (347) Crace's novel creates a sense of such moments, attempted 'absolutes' that are marked paradoxically by transitoriness. For Lix a very similar sense of the momentary is focused, as if charged with a sense of form and memorability, in the curious libidinous repetition that is yet often barely erotic. Each sex act is haunted by each of the preceding acts, as if cumulatively, and by the prospect of an abundance of fertility, whose achievement is known to the reader and narrator. Lix, only gradually acquires even a partial overview of his biological legacy.

In the novel's brief initial scene Lix and Mouetta, at a draughty art house cinema, watch "young lovers on the screen, young actors making love, or seeming to." (1) Mouetta feels a sense of good fortune, viewing the event of her pregnancy, resisted by Lix, as a blessing and a miracle. In contrast, he continues to feel troubled by the news, even having tried to avoid such a conception. This disparity of Lix's worldview and that of the women in his life recurs throughout the narrative of his "beleaguered, complicated life." (2) Lix appears bemused by this pregnancy, as if it were an alien turn of events. He attempts unsuccessfully to remember or locate the possible occasion of the conception, which curiously becomes the conceit that structures the novel. However, he lacks the precision of science as the narration informs us, and it is for the narrative to guide the reader through the peregrinations of his conceptions. As for Lix, "He wants to say he feels besieged. Another child? He only has himself to blame. To be so fertile is a curse." (2)

In contrast the narrator places this insemination very precisely on 18 August, the night of the couple's second wedding anniversary; this conception is the subject of the first section, occurring against the backdrop of the Banking Riots leaving initially six dead in the City of Kisses, which was the night of the actor's thirty-eighth performance of "Molière's *Tartuffe*, updated as a New Age satire, with songs, dance and video." (3) Almost grotesquely what ensues is a detailed description of the night of conception, although "*Conception* suggests a meeting of like minds, dedication, diligence, technology, and not the rain-damp, springing seats in the front of Lix's grey Panache where no two minds and no two thoughts achieved on that occasion even the briefest instant of concord or shared a common cause. That's one of the reoccurring oddities of sex, where it falls short, again, again." (2)

As Lix finishes his performance, the mayhem of the riots causes a blockade of the streets. He retreats to the Debit Bar, where Mouetta is with her cousin Freda, Lix's former lover and mother of his son, George. During the evening performance, despite having to kiss his leading lady twice, he has fantasized about his new wife, and sex with her on their stairs at home. However, in the bar Lix's libido is stimulated by his wife's cousin, Freda, his long-necked former lover. Their affair dates from the same time as the emergence of the city's nickname. "It was a photojournalist with *Life* magazine who, in 1979, when Lix was in his first term at the theatre academy, came up with the phrase the City of Kisses to replace the more alluring, truer title given us by Rousseau, the City of Balconies." (7) The picture essay concentrated on the better-looking girls kissing, and Crace's choice of magazine title indicates that he is making direct allusion to the postwar photography of Robert Doisneau (1912–94) who undertook a *Life* assignment in 1950 on 'young love in Paris' by creating scenes with young acting students kissing in various locations around Paris, the most famous, *Le Baiser de l'Hôtel de Ville* (Kiss at the Town Hall), becoming a poster just like the one Crace describes as the "Lipstick poster" taken in the Debit Bar, which was also one of a series.[13]

> But, famously, the photograph that truly caught the spirit of the place, so *Life* would claim, the photograph that sold countless posters and, for several years, was responsible for packed hotels and the resurrection of

our red-light district, was taken at the Debit Bar. A woman in a Cuban beret applying lipstick to a glass of wine with her red mouth. Reflected in the glass, two men, their own mouths gaping and both encircled by the kiss . . . There was still a framed copy of the original Lipstick poster in the lobby of the Debit on the night of Lix and Mouetta's anniversary, the first evening of the riots when interest rates seemed so much more relevant than kissing. (7–8)

Crace's image is more erotically ambivalent than the young love verging on staged sentimentality celebrated by Doisneau, and it is set against a backdrop of protest, that also evokes the radicalism of Freda and Lix (his cultivated to satisfy her). It also obliquely and ironically refers to the cover of British edition of *The Devil's Larder*.

Freda dominates the evening, concerned to rescue a young male student activist, even younger than their son, who she fears may be beaten by the police if apprehended. He is hiding in her office at the Human Science Academy and she appeals for help from Lix, having during the performance obtained Mouetta's promise to offer sanctuary on their study couch. Lix is reluctant, in part because of his intended seduction of his wife, but he is both fearful and desirous of Freda. Crace, despite this description of his failings, nevertheless balances the view of his protagonist, as he traces his ruminations:

> A week or so she'd said. That meant three months minimum. A stranger in the frying-pan. His egg with theirs. The staircase always busy with the sound of running feet. The sound of running taps. Worse even than the alternate weekends when his acknowledged children came to stay, descended on his house and his routines, his two adolescent boys, Lech and Karol (the products of his first marriage) and four-year-old Rosa (the unplanned fruit of a short, bizarre and punishing liaison not quite before he'd met Mouetta). At least their running feet were known and loved. For, yes, despite the evidence so far, the selfishness, the sexual jealousy, the lack of courage, the peevishness on this night of their anniversary, theirs was a house of love. Lix, for all his faults, for all his fickleness, was capable of love. He had been thwarted, though, on this occasion, by the unforgiving first love, second conquest of his life. (13)

Crace's negation of the negative aspects of Lix is both uncannily reflexive, and yet remains unconvincing. The overlap of lovers, casually referred to as an ironic afterthought, is hardly designed to enamour us of him, though naturally it could be taken as emphasizing his human failings and tendency towards self-deception.

Significantly only after their departure – when Freda is arrested – does Lix notice how attractive his wife has made herself. The term Crace uses to explicitly compare the cousins is revealing. "Mouetta was a sort of beauty too, although a quieter sort, not theatrical but . . . well, *homely* was an unfair word. *Unaffected*, perhaps. *Contained*. She was the kind – and this was cruel – whose company was supportive rather than flattering. She'd only turn the heads of wiser men." (16) It is Lix's repetitious nature that adds a quality of the *unheimlich*, or the uncanny. Mouetta's homeliness is evident, partly in her eagerness at thirty-nine to have a child, to further domesticate their lives (20).

Unable to return home partly due to flooding, which mirrors an episode from Lix's previous first marriage, they decide to sleep in the car in Deliverance Park on Navigation Island. Lix's sexual impulse initially founders on the underlying tension of their marriage. "They had not had sex in the car for months, not since their Sunday drive down to the lakes that spring when Mouetta – mid-cycle and ovulating, according to her charts and her thermometer – had tried to stop him using any contraception and what had started out as love had ended up as argument. He would not take the risk of having one more mouth to feed (even on alternate weekends)." (23) Lix slips into one of his regular fantasies, of making love to his sleeping partner, which is a curious objectification of women. He ponders over her response, making her part of the mental titillation that makes up much of his sexual drive:

> Her body, almost naked underneath the rucked and pushed-up nightclothes, would wake before she did, as he imagined it. Or perhaps she'd wake only after he'd pushed into her, alarmed and shuddering and animated by the wet and warm conjunction of their limbs. She'd wake aroused. This would be arousal in both senses of the word for her. She had to wake aroused. That was the whole point of his dream.
> Or then again, she'd persevere with sleep despite his unignorable embraces, and he would have to penetrate *her* dreams, so that the husband would become a sleeper's chimera and only prove himself flesh again within her slumber and her reveries. Fat chance of that. Because, of course, that was the stuff and nonsense of a dream, his dreams, not hers. (Well, that's a sham. Not *dream*. This never was a dream. In men, these fantasies are conscious and contrived. They are the product of a concentrated mind, not slumber). (24)

There is a striking aspect to this passage, despite the final presumably authorial or narrative reservations in parenthesis, which again stresses the lack of empathy with Lix's psyche and the dream-like quality of desire. Moreover, it suggests something unconscious in Lix's notion of his wife and of women generally, since the violation of her dreams, of his sexual intrusion, is transformed uncannily from a penetrative act into a fear of his own dissolution, an image of the loss of his identity. This could be seen as comparable to the castration complex Freud perceives in uncanny elements of Hoffman's Sand-Man (140). Lix's desire for women is ambivalent. He reflects upon what ought perhaps to be another source of guilt, since he has betrayed Freda's boy to the authorities, an action he ascribes to his own cowardice, dismissing his lack of any ethical position. He knows his information will result in the boy's arrest. Nevertheless, Lix plans to use the spurious promise to retrieve him as a pretext to embrace his wife. As the narrator reflects, Lix is more comfortable with the world of acting, of a scripted, rehearsed, unhesitating and staged performance rather than the hesitations and uncontrollable aspects of real life. "He'd know no fear – although he'd have the tremors, possibly. That was the bitter joy of acting. It was the business of not being yourself, but knowing you could only be your best when you were being someone else." (25) Unnerved by the banking riots and her cousin's arrest, Mouetta accepts his advances, initially in a "motherly" fashion (28) and then emboldened sexually as she imitates her notion of Freda's sexual aggressiveness to risk the chance of pregnancy while reassuring Lix that this was not possible. "He took the risk. He gambled on the moon and her honesty." (28) Ironically the advances result in the very pregnancy and homeliness (motherliness) in Mouetta that he resists.

Their encounter is undignified, uncomfortable and finally disappointing for both, although, "The sperm do not require sincerity before they can proceed. The eggs are not judgmental. They do not even favour love." (29) The narrative juxtaposes their untroubled dreams with various elements that ought to have troubled them: with the activist boy about to be detained; with Freda and eleven others crowded in a cell (ironically Freda ruminates on Lix and her cousin having rescued her young lover); with the three fresh bodies in the city morgue; and with Lix's five current offspring. The child has won the 'lottery' of life; its unpropitious and turbulent conception represents a conjunction of chance elements. "Change anything and you change everything else. Another place, another time produces someone else." (31) Such contingencies are an underlying theme of the novel.

The next morning in the Palm and Orchid Coffee House at breakfast Mouetta and Lix engage in a relationship game, one that is often a postscript to their lovemaking, where Lix chooses another woman he would have sex with. The narrative implies calm before an ensuing storm by revealing proleptically that the ensuing night's riots will worsen, with nine dead, "And, dramatically, the fire-bombing of the Bursary Chambers Club where – wrongly – it was thought some bankers and some military were dining. The wounded victims were, in fact, two waitresses, a cloakroom clerk, a fireman, and fourteen members of an investment club who hadn't had the lungs or legs to get away from their third-storey dining suite." (32) This stresses the importance of appropriate judgment and the dangers of supposition, implying one might judge similarly Lix's choices both in the game and life. Learning from previous episodes he is wary of their game, choosing an old and grey waitress. The night has unsettled Mouetta, she has been discomforted by being second best to her cousin, "even on their wedding anniversary. The small rejections of the evening before, in the Debit Bar, which normally she'd shrug away as meaningless, now seemed insufferably huge, inflated by the disappointments of the night. She could not readily forget how Lix'd stared into Freda's lap – goddamit, yes, her cousin's magnetizing lap – when she'd approached their dining table after his performance." (39) Ironically Mouetta feels defeated by her childlessness, mystified by her husband's desire for Freda. Of the women in the bar, Mouetta is convinced he would be attracted by a red-haired woman in blue, and around whom – demonstrating his highly active eroticized imagination – Lix attempts to construct a scenario of seduction in a hotel room, but finding her too young, perfect and expressionless, he prefers her companion, a plump woman in her thirties in all-black "strip" whom he imagines seducing in a forest as she walks her dogs. In these elaborate daydreams Lix creates the equivalent of what Freud identifies as a doubling or *Doppelgänger* of both himself and his wife (141). Significantly, the second daydream is referred to as a "fairy-tale" (44), and the third a "fantasy." (46) Lix indulges in what Freud describes as a duplication, division and interchanging of desire (142), which conveys a shifting sense of the protagonist, a further uncanny element which indicates Lix's primordial narcissism, and as Freud notes, "The invention of such a doubling [serves] as a defence against annihilation," (142) the very thing Lix fears in individual women, with the fear of literally doubling himself through procreation. Finally Lix

The Devil's Larder and Six

is fascinated by an uglier, older woman in her fifties, whose appearance and implied character most resemble his wife. "She was what Frenchmen call *une jolie laide* but in this city is more cruelly known as a Prickly Pear." (45) Her description stresses the "unusually large" lips (45), cropped hair and both the disproportionateness and almost incongruity of elements.

> The too-large nose, the long, demanding jaw, the slightly protruding eyes too greedy for their sockets, the Apache cheekbones, the manly ears might all have benefited from some costly surgery. Everything about her, except her breasts, needed taming and reduction. (45)

There is something almost surreal in the description, which as Royle notes is interconnected with the uncanny (97–8). Her imagined seduction takes place on a beach among the rocks, clothes at their ankles. Mouetta's retreat to the toilet "was an opportunity, but not to contemplate his undermining shame at trading in the firebrand student for six minute's pleasure in the car. He had to bury that at once. Rather, it allowed him to concentrate unambiguously on all the women in the room. Lix could not help himself." (48) His compulsiveness emphasizes not only his lack of control, and the primeval nature of his desire, but an uncanniness in Royle's sense, who describes a Freudian notion of a "compulsion to repeat," part of the death drive (92). At Mouetta's return he re-engages the game, knowing he could only favour an older woman well beyond childbearing age, a denial of fertility and its impulse towards death. On the drive home Mouetta confronts him with his preference for Freda, denied by Lix, but as the narrator comments, "He'd always think of her as someone he desired. Mouetta was the woman he required. This is the nature of the beast." (53) This oblique reference to the atavistic fairytale element of the man reinforces the overall sense of the uncanny.

Chapter 1 opens in November 1979 when Lix, a twenty-one-year-old student of acting at the Arts Academy, has his first full sexual encounter. Lix appears politically active, but his radicalism has been subverted by the initial chapter's portrayal of his selfish cowardice, which knowledge undermines his beliefs and gestures. Lix's youthful notions are grandiose. "This was a time when Theatre, newly unleashed from the censors, was argumentative and powerful. Lix truly wanted to improve the world, believed that Art was Revolution's smarter twin, that Acting and Action were equal partners. Collaborators, in fact. He'd signed up with the Mime/Scream Community

Drama Collective in his first month as a student and was active, too, in Street Beat Renegades, Provocations & Co, and the Next Stage (as in Paul Roesenthaler's 'The next stage is the elimination of Captains, Chaplains and Kings')." (54–5) The narrative emphasizes the transitions not only in Lix, but in the city and this further emphasizes the text's own diachronic (if not multichronic) nature:

> Lix had a democratically modest fourth-floor room amongst the tenements down on the wharf, with not only skylight views across the newly named City of Kisses toward the river but also a narrow glimpsing view from his box kitchen into Cargo Street, where now there are boutiques and restaurants instead of groceries and bars and 'working folk.' (55)

The first scene opens with a woman wearing fashionably revolutionary clothes on his balcony. With the aid of binoculars Lix spies habitually on the people below including this woman, justifying his intrusions as a research on types and behaviour for his acting. The familiar distant figure becomes unfamiliar and is distorted by proximity. She is out of proportion, fascinated herself by the diminishment of the familiar world as she peers through his binoculars. In contrast Lix notices the transformation of the other into a living being.

> She, too, seemed large and detailed, in a way she'd never been through his binoculars. Her outfit was familiar, of course, her general shape . . . But mostly she was unfamiliar . . . Binoculars had shortened her. Binoculars diminish the world, reduce the senses to one. Precision optical instruments, no matter how finely ground, fogproof, waterproof, and vision-adjusted, could not hope to convey true proximity, the candid softness of the flesh, the spiciness of scent, the rustling, independent simpering of clothes, the clink of her bracelets, the perfect imperfections and the blemishes of someone close to thirty years of age. Until that night, he'd only seen this woman from afar. (56)

Lix has watched women from afar, especially his voice tutor, Freda, the daughter of his apartment house's concierge. Used only to fantasizing, Lix has been surprised by the woman, aware of his spying many times in previous weeks while waiting for her married lover in the bar opposite Lix's apartment. That evening proves uncanny for both of them.

First, abandoned at the bar when her lover called with his excuses, she is irritated at the wasted effort rushing to prepare and the blow to her confidence, a pattern that she recognizes. "The pattern was familiar. This was the third time in ten days that he had let her down in one way or another. This was the third cheating husband in the last two years who had disillusioned her. She took the hint. She felt the chill. Another cooling, flagging man was scuttling from her life." (59) She judges the humiliation, the insult on being "stood up," and orders from the menu before noticing Lix, familiar because of his birthmark, looking for a place to sit. Uncharacteristically she gestures him over and consciously reverses the familiar gender roles, introducing both an uncanny element into the encounter and a sense of threat. "She'd never seen such fear on anyone's face. It made her feel unusually powerful, to be able to bring on such involuntary discomfort in a man. The shoe should be on the other foot. Had always been before. So this was what it felt like to be male, a hunter, predatory, to have a blushing quarry within reach, the colour in his face the flag of his arousal." (63) Lix's theatricality, his adoption of other voices and personae fascinates her rather than his talk of activism and ideological issues, of the street performance called PolPottery he has organized to respond to the famine in Cambodia (63). She follows Lix to his apartment, returning to the moment of her peering through the binoculars with which the chapter begins, fantasizing about reversing the events of the evening to be still waiting for her lover in the bar, desirable, becoming the woman in the "Lipstick poster", something ephemeral almost. "The telephone could ring and be ignored. She'd not be caught. Four stories up the winking lenses could only catch the light." (65)

In this reversal and intimate knowledge of her thoughts and desires, especially given its intensity and the strangeness of the encounter, Crace foregrounds another implicit uncanniness of the literary. As Royle says, "There is uncanny knowledge. Someone is telling us what someone else is thinking, feeling or perceiving. That someone else may not even be aware of experiencing these thoughts, feelings or perceptions." (256) As Royle further elucidates, this allows a species of secretiveness in which the reader is complicit (266). Kissing Lix's naevus or birthmark transforms the encounter, especially since he has imagined it will always "unman" him, suggestive of his underlying fears (67). As she intuits the contrary is true, despite his boyhood nickname of Smudge, since "It lent to an otherwise inexpressive face a sardonic and whimsical note, a touch of innocence and beauty." (69) Despite initial tentativeness a physical passion seizes them in turn during two sexual moments, and despite her admission of the motivation for her precipitous actions, by the second occasion

Lix is changed from embarrassment to aggressiveness, stressing the theme of the transformational. "The sycophant became the psychopath in seven seconds flat." (73) She is unnerved by the loss of control, and as the narrative specifies in a stranger's room and a potentially dangerous place. Ironically his only previous physical contact with women has primarily been on stage, following stage directions, where although the actresses were real flesh, the experience was as if suspended, ghostly, almost not incarnate. They copulate, her forehead against the glass of the window through which he spies on the world, and again a disembodied quality overtakes her as she gazes at the empty street:

> Lix might be lost in her. But she had half forgotten him. She'd not delude herself. She was not passionate for this probationer. She was the subject and the object of her own desires. She lost herself, four storeys up, in only what was happening to her, a woman in so many places all at once, it seemed, the bar, the bed, the ABC, the gloomy street-lit room, the city's dark, conspiring boulevards, a woman who had only meant to reassure herself. (74)

Such lack of control marks many of the situations and characters in the different episodes, but here the significant outcome overall is the birth later of Bel, his first child, unknown to him, another dislocation, echoing that of her mother at her conception. These elements produce a multilayered set of co-ordinates not all open to the characters and almost an uncanny impression, as does the strong sense of coincidence caused in part by the narrative's overlapping and intersecting elements.

Chapter 2 concerns Lix's love affair with Freda in 1981, during the period of "The Big Melt or Laxity," (76) a period somewhat reminiscent of the Prague Spring in Czechoslovakia in 1968.[14] Crace describes the spirit of democracy pervading the city, the black-market stalls selling clothes redolent of 1970s rebellion, and the festival like Woodstock on Deliverance Island. The mood reinforces the sexual theme: "The city is simply drawn from my imagination, but I wanted it specifically to be in crisis. People's sex lives are more profligate, and they are more likely to stray in times of social tension. There is something very exciting about demonstrations and taking part in events, particularly political events like *les événements*, which I wanted to include."[15]

At a radical fringe meeting in November at the "Roesenthaler Comrades Co-operative (so named mostly to achieve the acronym

RoCoCo)" (78) rather than the clichéd suggestions of a picket or vigil to protest against the tainted donation of $7 million from Marin Scholla, mogul of MeisterCorps, "to pay for a new bar, a theatre, a concert hall, a gallery and cinema on campus, all in one custom built star-shaped complex. A pentacle of creativity," (79) Lix suggests that they undertake a situationist kidnapping of Scholla, who will visit the Arts Academy on Thursday 17 December to celebrate his endowment. The response is limited, most realizing the risks and the few volunteers are driven by desire and flirtation rather than ideology. These four include: "a glumly cute, gay woman from the Language School (who wanted more than anything to disappoint her lecturers and undermine her job prospects), two tall and overweight post-Maoist anarchists from Freda's science faculty, and Lix, all of whom it was soon apparent aspired to more than comradely contact with their dazzling colleague." (83) Naturally, Lix's plan is predicated on impressing Freda, so the details seem naive and simplistic. Their debates and planning allow Crace to reflect upon the curiously fervent dynamics of the left and its radical politics. Many of the other allusions are political: the "Seven Principles" that MeisterCorps has refused to sign is reminiscent of the Kyoto Protocol.

Freda's fantasies are fuelled by images of revolution, particularly the photograph she carries of a Czech student activist baring his chest to the barrel of the gun on a Russian tank, and "Freda always needed someone in her bed when the optimistic ghost of 1968 invaded her. Her body and spirit demanded company." (85)[16] She sees a passing resemblance in Lix, and impressed by Lix's radical fervour – as the reader knows later in life the loss of this is anathema to her – she decides that after the kidnapping she will sleep with him. They plan a posse with decoys, three of whom will crowd Scholla with their successive demands for signatures of his supposedly "inspirational" autobiography, after which *Fredalix* (as Crace repeatedly refers mockingly to the couple) will bundle him into a lift and down to the basement, claiming a student prank if the doors fail to close in time to escape. *Fredalix* stresses the temporary and uncanny nature of their relationship, since in Royle's terms, "The uncanny is a crisis of the proper: it entails a critical disturbance of what is proper (from the Latin *proprius*, 'own'), a disturbance of the very idea of personal or private property including the properness of proper names, one's so-called 'own' name, but also the proper names of others." (1) This merging is ironically appropriate for two weekend revolutionaries;

Lix's fears of commingling and disappearance may originate in this relationship. The pair plan to drive the abductee to an Arts laboratory on the wharf where a group will perform "*Mister Scholla's Dirty Dollars*, their hurriedly improvised morality play in the medieval style, based on the fable of the Fat Man and the Cat." (93) They exult over the rehearsals, the clandestine meetings and, for Freda, the use of Alicja Lesniak's name, the plump President of the student caucus whom she dislikes, for the communiqué of grievances they plan to release. They divorce themselves from reality, re-imagining Scholla as an almost willing guest. Lix abjures a safer relationship with Alicja, and loses his supply of courage in the turmoil of their activities.

Freda's underlying anxiety produces violence in her caresses, captivated "By his fear and reticence, which she mistook to be the saintly attributes of patriots and revolutionaries like Nyere, Cezar and Mandela, a kind of granite sweetness, which showed no malice and no alarm, which never raised its voice without good cause. He had what she would never have, she thought, the Gift of Sympathy." (95) To celebrate their impending anniversary of a month, her longest relationship, he imagines himself dominant and her submissive, controlling his fear as they wait for Scholla. Ironically, Scholla cancels because of the demonstrations in Gdansk and instead of informing the waiting Arts Laboratory, *Fredalix* have sex, acting as if the kidnap had happened, with Freda in charge. During this afternoon of passion, Lix is absorbed into that moment, everything uncannily present and interfused. "So Lix and Freda might *imagine* that their day of lunacy and passion had let them off scot-free, no police, no blame, no aftermath. Except? Except that Freda had become some moments earlier the unexpecting mother of his child." (117)

Chapters 3 and 4 concern Lix's marriage relationship with Alicja Lesniak eight years later, initially in their river view apartment. Previously they inhabited a modest one away from the river. "Alicja and Lix had not been made of gold when they'd moved in together. His meager, irregular fees from the stage and, more frequently, from busking in the local restaurants, and her low wages as a consultant-volunteer on the night-shift at the Citizen's Commission were not enough to rent a river view." (127–8) To demonstrate their independence they refuse the largesse of the Lesniaks, both the imported furniture and river-view apartment, and Lix refuses the offer of a fashionable surgeon in the father's debt, and Alicja seeks the anonymity of her new identity, since Lix was not yet famous. Hence this is the obverse of Freda who satisfies herself with an image projected onto Lix; Alicja projects her own onto the impulsive marriage. Lix keeps George a secret from Alicja, and Freda despises him even further because of his wife. She had rejected Lix, claiming the pregnancy and child as her own. Three months into the marriage, with limited possessions, in early May nine days of rain brings floods and initiates a dramatic transformation of the city, watched by the couple through Lix's binoculars. They share this as an intimacy, for as the narrator stresses, Alicja is not Lix's type, and only gradually does his desire for her emerge, an unexpected seduction, as surprising as the weather. "The flooding was an unexpected wonder, too rare and beautiful to miss." (132) As the cellars fill, a holiday atmosphere permeates the disrupted city. The couple ignore the evacuation, despite the power of the river and her father's arrival in a motor boat. Lix caresses Alicja as she shouts down her refusal to move, resisting the sense of her parent, and allows Lix in his excitement to penetrate her. Aroused by a fessandra leaf (another Cracean invention) with which he scents her body, his instincts prevail:

> Let's not forget that Lix, indeed, was just an animal, compelled by base impulses to spread his seed in his selected mate so that his species could, in principle anyway, negotiate from eighty thousand genes an offspring more efficient than themselves. He was content to be 'just an animal' on these occasions in his married life, to be instinctive and unambiguous in ways he couldn't be when not aroused, to be unembarrassed by his irrational self, to be unselfconsciously brave, patient and cunning. (149)

Crace describes the physiological transformation in Alicja as during their coupling another conception occurs. Much later, they celebrate the confirmation of her pregnancy in the Palm and Orchid Coffee House, where Freda has previously arrived with George, and departs on seeing Lix, much to her son's annoyance: "He drags behind his mother's arm, afraid to make a fuss, and as he drags, he catches for an instant the eye of a man he cannot recognize but knows, a hypnotized and startled man who's staring at him with an open mouth." (153)

In Chapter 4 Alicja herself is transformed. "Mrs Lesniak-Dern was the new Director of the Citizens' Commission and also a District Senator, elected by the waitresses and office workers of the Anchorage quarter because three years before she'd done so much – without success – to fight for flood repairs and compensation for the neighbourhood. Her little kindnesses had paid big dividends for her, exactly as she'd thought they might." (155) Lix prepares to celebrate his first Hollywood contract with a supper or "Obligation Feast," for which "Lix had hired the Hesitation Room (as the windowless private cellar beneath the Debit's public areas was known)," (157) ironically marked by the high point of the flood of May 1989, which was the apex of his relationship with Alicja. Less intimate with Lix for months, she finds him negative and avoids his company. Even her dreams recall the past and the flood they had witnessed, and signify the failings of their marriage.

> Her husband sighed while he was sleeping, as if even his dreams were flat and saddening. To share a bed with Lix was to wrap yourself in sheets of woe. How had the man become so wounded by success? Alicja's dreams were livelier and full of hope and opportunity. She dreamed, just the night before his Obligation Feast, that he was in the flood-tossed houseboat, and lost downstream amongst the crocodiles and koi. She understood her dream to mean their marriage was, well, waterlogged, too swept away to save, and this was an opportunity for her to be an adult finally, liberated from the Lesniaks and Derns. (160)

The first image is suggestive of a shroud, and the central image of Lix swept along with cold-blooded creatures by the current conveys Alicja's unconscious sense of his inability to control either events or remediate his emotional weakness. The episodic interlinking adds poignancy, since it is as if the inevitability of the end of their relationship is inscribed in its beginning. As she dresses for the evening Lix is stimulated sexually, but avoids the risk of rejection with which he is familiar, leaving him "standing, swaying in a fug of vertigo, that familiar nausea and loss of balance," (161) an uncanny sense of the self. Alicja believes Lix has been absorbed by the theatrical and performative, and his instinct to manufacture closeness by adjusting the label on her blouse confirms the gestural emptiness of Lix's compulsion. At the celebration is Alicja's lover, Jupiter or Joop, whose presence signifies her opposition to her husband. The evening includes various games including "Never" suggested by Joop where "each diner at the table had to admit to something they'd never done that everybody else there most certainly would have done." (168) Lix lies, and embarrasses his wife by claiming never to have had sex standing up, which she trumps in her annoyance by claiming never to have had an orgasm. He is humiliated, the guests mocking his failings by pretending to order oysters. This is the end of their relationship. However, they return to find themselves the victims of a burglary that offers a sexual postscript, for in the aftermath and its visceral responses they have sex for a final time and conceive their second child, Karol. "Vasectomized Jupiter, the columnist, would speedily lose interest in the Senator when she discovered she was pregnant." (179) Lix departs for the theatre, his cowardice extending to his suspicions as to her faithfulness, drawn away from his problems into the lead role ironically of *Don Juan Amongst the Feminists*. Almost every night with "*incongruity*" (my italics) a tram passes at the same time, alarming the audience, and on this occasion Lix's words respond not only to their nervousness, but his predicament. "*Uncannily*, the answer came from off the stage. 'Of all edifices in our town,' Don Juan explained, as trams passed by, 'no one can doubt, not anyone who's lived at least, that love's the frailest tower of them all, meant to tumble, built to fall.'" (181, my italics)

Chapter 5 concerns both Lix's brief affair literally on stage with his co-star Anita Julius or An in a romantic comedy *The Devotee*, and Freda's revelation to her son of his father's identity. The theme is a variation on the uncanny, which Freud connects with repression and describes, summarizing Schelling's view, as "'something that should have remained hidden and has come into the open.'" (148) An, no longer a young woman, will satisfy a simply somatic desire, Lix's impulse stimulated by another form of repetition. In their nightly performance they simulate falling in love. At first "Lix has become wearied by his performance, its drudgery and duplication, and only truly involved in the closing moments of the play when finally An's body crossed the boards to hold her Devotee." (189) The now reclusive Lix, after his initial indifference, if not antipathy, has transformed the familiarity of the moment into a physical sexual response, pressing upon her an erection. This culminates on New Year's Day of the new millennium on "01/01/01," (183) when the city's celebration is a year behind the rest of the world, a night full of its own citizens rather than planned for tourists wooed by the city authorities. As if a supplement to the uncanny sense of revelation, a series of appearances, outcomes and expectations abut uncomfortably, almost abrasively. The incongruous and the unexpected recur as a subtext. At first the intimacy of the onstage kiss with An is faked, but as the stars become more familiar on the long run, and despite the disparities of their characters and

Lix's distaste for her breast implants, a curious physical intimacy ensues onstage. Lix's erection has been palpable but unconvincing. Ironically, Freda has brought George their son, along with Mouetta, to the theatre, fulfilling her promise four months earlier that on his eighteenth birthday she would reveal his father's long-suppressed identity, about which the boy has fantasized. Freda invokes the past. Her revelation to her son is clumsy, even if well-intentioned, and subsequently George is embarrassed by the onstage kiss, by the bodily impulses eroticizing the two actors. The audience is fascinated by the simulation appearing almost real. Ironically, George is unimpressed with the play, and he has expected someone else more modest and less shaming for a father, as if reality is both secondary and yet a surplus to his expectations, which has an uncanniness since as Freud says, "an uncanny effect often arises when the boundary between fantasy and reality is blurred, when we are faced with the reality of something that we have until now considered imaginary, when a symbol takes on the full function and significance of what it symbolizes." (150)

Meeting Freda's party after the performance, Lix himself feels old and displaced by the very maturity of George which disturbs Lix's self-image. Lix feels unlike himself and yet despite this self-negation Lix is attracted to Freda's companion, Mouetta, in spite of her unsettling and blatant stare, because finally she smiles at him. Lix tries to bridge the gap between himself and his son despite the boy's age by suggesting George might spend some time with him and the two younger step-brothers on New Year's Day at the zoo, but Freda sneers at what she regards as Lix's inappropriateness. There is a moment of concealment when unknown to Freda's party Lix follows them to a firework celebration. Curiously when recognized by Mouetta, An happens upon him with a gesture of intimacy, and Lix abandons the three for An. With our proleptic knowledge this juxtaposition seems incongruent, as if the choice might well be misjudged by Lix, incapable of bravery or appropriate choice.

Later after drinks the two actors return to the theatre inebriated and finally copulate onstage in costume, reducing their actions to a performativity, as if without consequences, which of course ironically is a misjudgment. As Lix attempts an unsuccessful reconciliation with a child he hardly knows, he creates another. Returning home alone, haunted by the mistakes of both that night and his entire life, an answerphone message from Freda agrees to George's presence chaperoned by Mouetta.

The final short Chapter 6 returns the narrative to Lix and the pregnant Mouetta at the art-house cinema, where the logic of the pregnancy, and its Darwinist imperative, has marginalized Lix. "Her husband's feelings do not really matter any more. His purpose has been served, she thinks. Biology has overtaken him." (211) Freda is still imprisoned to Mouetta's relief, so she accedes to dining at the Debit Bar. Lix is fearful of being a witness for Freda who is accused of various charges including assaulting a militiaman. Lix reasons that his own betrayal of Freda's young student might emerge. The past haunts him, as does the spectrality of his relationship with his children. As the couple dines, the narrative becomes panoramic, omnisciently illustrating in successive separate vignettes of simultaneous moments the fate of Lix's existing children. Rosa plays with dolls watching a mouse on the balcony until a bird swoops to kill it. Lech and Karol are at tennis coaching unable to play on the sodden courts. The less sporty Lech finds his *forte* sharing cigarettes and kisses with a girl. George is departing for a trip home from America with his pregnant girlfriend. Finally we see the undiscovered child, Bel, with her own child, Cade, deciding that with her mother's imminent death Lix will have to play another part. Once more Lix is to be surprised and out of control of events, more acted upon than acting. Finally the particular is diminished and the perspective transcends the earthbound. Above Bel's tram on her journey home, a helicopter takes a new series of panoramic pictures for *Geo* magazine, another photojournalistic project uncannily varying the past. Rather than images of corporeal kissing, it reflects the pattern of lives from afar, seen as interfused in an "aerial depiction, the City of a Million lights." (219) The novel ends with an image of the detail of lives being absorbed into their generality, a socio-historical pattern that conveys a sense of collective being, for "The streaks and pricks of light are eloquent. They tell of people going home. They tell of love and lovemaking, of children, marriages and lives. You think, But this could happen anywhere. It does." (220)

Notes

1. 'Crace–Tew: Telephone Interview 6A.'
2. Ibid. Crace indicates there have been two film shorts and there are several more in the making at this time. An adaptation of 'The Whistling Chop,' story seven, was directed by BAFTA winning director Michael Baig-

Clifford and adapted by writer-actor Alex Jones (currently Clive Horobin in the BBC Radio 4 series, *The Archers*). There has been a public jazz performance inspired by the stories, and the Scottish Theatre group Grid Iron performed *The Devil's Larder* at the Edinburgh Festival in 2005.
3 Peck's review originally appeared as 'The Devil You Know,' *The New Republic*, 31 December 2001: 38.
4 'Crace–Tew: Telephone Interview 6A.'
5 'Crace–Tew: Telephone Interview 6A.'
6 Ibid.
7 Ibid.
8 Ibid.
9 Ibid.
10 Telephone Conversation between Jim Crace and Prof. Philip Tew 21 March 2005 part B 15:10–15:55; hereafter referred to as 'Crace–Tew: Telephone Interview 6B.'
11 Ibid.
12 Ibid.
13 Peter Hamilton, *Robert Doisneau: A Photographer's Life* (1995); also see www.postershop.com/Doisneau-Robert/Doisneau-Robert-Le-Baiser-De-lHotel-De-Ville-Paris-1950-7800031.html.
14 During this period western-influenced 'big beat' Czech popular music symbolized youthful rebellion and the country's communist leader, Alexander Dubcek, liberalized the country and press censorship was ended in an attempt to create 'human socialism.' On 20 August Dubcek was arrested and the next day 200,000 Soviet Bloc troops invaded. Dubcek was forced to end the liberalization before his resignation in 1969.
15 'Crace–Tew: Telephone Interview 6B.'
16 Such a photograph of a man baring his chest to a tank can be seen at a website dedicated to the Prague Spring: *Prague Spring 1968*: http://library.thinkquest.org/C001155/index1.htm.

Addendum: *The Pesthouse* (2007)

The Pesthouse opens dramatically as the population of Raft dies.[1] The natural forces concerned are trans-historical, but Crace's perspective is localized, the event momentous and yet stealthy. This conflicted and contradictory environment is hostile and indifferent to human existence.

> Everybody died at night. Most were sleeping at the time, the lucky ones who were too tired or drunk or deaf or wrapped too tightly in their spreads to hear the hillside, destabilized by rain, collapse and slip beneath the waters of the lake. So these sleepers (six or seven hundred, at a guess; no-one ever came to count or claim the dead) breathed their last in passive company, unwarned and unexpectedly, without experiencing the fear.
> Their final moments, dormant in America. (2)

The visiting travellers in a Cracean reversal are returning eastward to emigrate to Europe. Human vulnerability is a constant in this post-apocalyptic America where no one retrieves or counts the dead. Boyd Tonkin reports the author's intentions: "'Optimism is only worth having if you visit the dark corners of the universe,' he counters. His next novel, entitled *The Pest House* [sic], sounds especially dark. In this dystopian vision of America, begun well before 11 September, 'the machine stops' and the planet's beacon of hi-tech modernity sinks into 'a medieval future'." (32) The mudslide disturbs sediments in the lake, and releases gases which roll silently down the hill, unheard by the unsuspecting sleeping inhabitants and their animals. The corpses appear uncannily untouched. The vocabulary describing Nash's fate, a young boy who tends the tethered animals, offers a paradigm of the state of the people's beliefs,

He was the victim of magic, possibly, or fever – there was already fever in the town, he had heard – or a curse, the sort that storytellers knew about – or else some dead air from the grave, encouraged by the rain, had come to press its clammy lips on his. He'd tasted it. His lungs were rigid, suddenly. (7)

Theirs is a superstitious knowledge, of a familiar medieval kind, suggesting rational scientific judgment has been abandoned. Those suffering from disease are quarantined in a pesthouse to save the wider community from the vapours and vagaries of infection. The power of the landscape and geological, historical forces dwarfs both the individual and the community. In *Three Monkeys Online* he clarifies his impulses to Lawless:

> 'What I'm interested in is to learn the nature of our 21st century existence by taking it away. By taking away those things that define the 21st century: science, technology, the abandonment of belief, etc. So, where would be a better place to set this than America, because if you're going to return humankind, or western humanity at least, to a medieval existence, how mischievous would it be to give it to America which has never had a medieval past. [. . .] Of course there is a medieval history in the persons of the native Americans, but to a large extent that history has been removed' – he adds, – 'so I wanted to set this book in the hot seat of technological, and business development, which is America, and return it to a medieval past, although it never had one, to give it a medieval future, to examine something about ourselves. To see what human kind has become, now that we're not huddled around fires with hot faces and cold backs'. (1)

Crace researched variously for the novel, including details of the medieval world in Europe, of the Way West and pioneer journeys, and both Francis Parkman's *The Oregon Train* (1849) and accounts of the Lewis and Clark expedition westward of 1804–6, which was commissioned in June 1803 by President Thomas Jefferson who had remarked at his first inaugural address, "Let us, then, with courage and confidence pursue our own Federal and Republican principles, our attachment to union and representative government. Kindly separated by nature and a wide ocean from the exterminating havoc of one quarter of the globe; too high-minded to endure the degradations of the others; possessing a chosen country, with room enough for our descendants, to the thousandth and thousandth generation."[2] The Lewis-Clark expedition helped confirm such an expansionary and idealized notions of America. Responding to ecological, ideological and other uncertainties, Crace uses a futuristic context to refute such notions of manifest destiny by reversing modernity's myth of irreversible progress, by contracting both those future generations and their horizons as imagined by Jefferson, although much of the novel's apparently ephemeral details, its world of carts and pack mules, seems to be derived from accounts of the Lewis and Clark expedition.

The provenance of this novel draws upon direct experience. Its central notions of disease and of a pesthouse housing the sick away from the community derive from Crace's yearly visit to the Isles of Scilly. Crace explains to Begley in *The Paris Review*, "I discovered the ruin of the pesthouse, a building where anyone with an illness who was passing through the western passages into the British Isles in the eighteenth and nineteenth centuries would be quarantined and left to die." (207) This refers to St Helens, an uninhabited island, where sick emigrants and travellers were left to their fate to prevent the spread of disease. Clearly the starting point for his imagination was fuelled by physically helping to reveal its presence, allowing sight of a building that is the residue and echo of past cultural behaviour and of a world in its own almost pre-modern and yet constant state of transition. Crace adds in this interview: "It struck me as being an immensely interesting conceit – the shared abandonment of people with nothing in common except illness. It offered the irresistible title for a book, too." (207) From his travels in America Crace draws upon the topography of the east side of a chain of hills and mountains running through North Carolina and Virginia for his setting, as the novel's emigrants retreat towards the coast, which was ironically the first area to be colonized. The same dynamics apply, since the tug of what is outside remains greater than the magnetism of home.

These specific ideas occasioned the novel, but they were supplemented by retrieving notions of social formality found in more traditional cultures, reinstating a system of barter where money has been abandoned, and conceiving of the positive re-evaluation of woman's virginity: "The phrase 'The virgin pulls the plough,' did not mean that in Raft the young unmarried women were put to work in the fields, but that a pure girl would be worth a pair of horses or a team of oxen in a marriage contract. You wouldn't get a brace of conies for a girl who'd drifted." (75) All such details form part of a critical and ethical scheme. Such conceits of difference from the contemporary world allow Crace to identify the moral freedoms and bountiful quality of current existence, and yet demonstrate the deficiencies of the present.

An implied schema underpins the narrative. This is demonstrated when the novel's protagonists, Margaret and Franklin, encounter the Dreaming Highway, something inconceivable to them, a relic thought to be mythical or exaggerated: "This was no escarpment provided by nature, unless Nature had on this one occasion broken its own rules and failed to twist and bend, but had instead hurtled forward, all symmetry and parallels. But soon their bafflement was overcome by astonishment (149). *The Pesthouse* promises to be the most political of Crace's novels, for in an oblique fashion this future can be regarded as an allegory for past failings.

As part of this ecological disaster, Crace conceives the disappearance of the great population centres, with humanity suffering in a Darwinistic sense the same fate as large mammals whose population plummeted from lack of resources. The reader is left to imagine the specifics of such an erosion of plenitude; commodification itself now a myth. He hints at the poisoning of the landscape and a final crisis of unrestricted industrialism, of which there remain signs. In Raft, swarf in the ground, literally the discards of manufacturing, represents one of the few residues of the lost technological age, allowing Crace to ironize the concept of a post-industrial age as not conventionally futuristic but apparently regressive after a cataclysmic reversal of globalization. Interviewed by Romana Koval (2004), Crace describes an object he keeps on his desk while composing the novel:

> I have a piece of metal which is rotting away as I write every day. It's amazing [. . .] I found it on the beach in the Isles of Scilly and it's the part of a boat, and when I took it out of the sea it was relatively tough and compact and it wasn't flaking, but within a week of putting it in the atmosphere it started to fall apart, and it's sitting on my desk at this very moment, collapsing. And that stands for the book that I'm writing at the moment, so there's always something like that which is my kind of talisman I guess.

The decay of the residue of industrial products, and their fragility, feature in the novel, reminding his readers of their own utter dependence on the very fruits of a global economy that he posits as having disappeared. The world is hence familiar, given that it is so redolent of the past, and yet ominously and profoundly atavistically estranged from contemporary co-ordinates. In Raft, all else that remains are "the stone footings of the one-time shoe factory and leather tanning works." (4) Subsequently he describes the doubling of a journey across Middle America whose landscape is haunted by the past, the detritus of the industrial in debris fields in badlands where gangs led by the equivalent of robber barons roam. People's perspectives may be localized, but ironically of course in this detail Crace satirizes the populist notion of ordinary Americans' insularity. Perhaps there is a similar irony in the fact that people's knowledge of science and the world has regressed to a superstitious state of affairs.

Crace situates the initial catastrophe by its very suddenness as one moment among the greater processes of time and nature. "In the time that it would take to draw a breath and yawn, there was a muted stony splash accompanied by a barometric pop, a lesser set of sounds than thunder, but low and devious, nevertheless, and worrying – for how could anyone not know by now how mischievous the world could be?" (2) Thereby Crace sets the relentlessness of nature against the ambitions of man, offering an implied critique of America's new imperium with its hubristic sense of power and authority. The novel by reversing American culture deconstructs its essence. The future is anachronistic, redolent of an earlier pre-industrial age, but Crace situates its consequences among his characters where their values and culture are implicit, as is indicated by the responsibilities of one victim, a young boy dressed in his coat of farm goat skins and hair traded earlier for food: "Nash whose job that night was to protect the animals from cougars, wolves or thieves." (4) This is an age of superstition, magic and storytelling, of the fear of fever, of ferrymen taking travellers across the river, and a constant migration eastward. America is in full reversal. The plethora of details conveys an early modern, almost quasi-medieval mixture of superstition and naivety. In the town in a guesthouse, where men and women are normally quartered separately behind locked doors, a "beauty boy" and his slightly older wife are making love against the customs of both the lodging house and their society's puritanical culture, as the gas snuffs out their minor rebellions as it kills them with all the inhabitants of Raft. "This used to be America, this river crossing in the ten month stretch of land, this sea-to-sea. It used to be the safest place on earth." (11)

In the first chapter Franklin Lopez and his older brother, Jackson, are two months into their trek eastward across the prairie, as inhospitable as the prairies crossed by Lewis and Clark, with Jackson fearful of the coming winter delaying their anticipated voyage to Europe. The land is unforgiving, both in natural and human terms, some scavenging from each other:

> The emigrants who'd been rash enough to travel in the company of carts and animals or had packed a year's supply of food and their prize possessions – best pots, their jewelry, good cloth, good tools – paid a price for their comfort. The more they had, the more cruelly they were robbed, not by the other travelers but by the ones who wouldn't emigrate until they'd picked the carcass of America quite clean. (18)

As Jackson reminds Franklin, "Only the crazy make it to the coast." (16) As Franklin's injured knee worsens they reach the Butter Hills above Raft, tantalizingly close, and have to decide that Jackson should proceed alone to the riverside settlement, leaving Franklin to fend for himself until his brother's return.

It is clear in Chapter 2 that knowledge of medicine has regressed so far that most imagine disease to be like a spirit and that clothes themselves harbour pestilence. In Raft Margaret is feverish with the "flux," an affliction from which her father died and from which few survive. As a sign her family shaves off her hair. "She'd have to go up to the little boulder Pesthouse above the valley for ten days or so – unattended and unvisited – to see if she recovered or was lost." (29) Like most women from her community, this is her first time beyond the palisades, and on the journey her grandpa makes her hide her condition from the travellers on whom they depend. Comforted by talismans she sleeps, awakening to ponder the old coins which represent for her the mysteries of the lost past of late industrial America. Fingering these artefacts from the past, she ponders on their significance: "Was that the One Cent palace with the twelve great columns at the front? She dragged her nail across the disc to count every column and tried to find the tiny seated floating man within, the floating man who story tellers said was Abraham and would come back to help America one day with his enormous promises?" (38)

Left alone Franklin retreats from the torrential rain and stumbling fearfully on the pesthouse, recognizes the signs of Margaret's illness: "Only a fool would socialize with death just to stay warm and dry for the night." (44) In the fourth chapter the reader senses Jackson's inevitable fate as he tussles with his conscience, tempted to travel on without his brother. Nash trades provisions for the giant traveller's coat. Jackson dines with other travellers, some optimistic that in crossing the river,

> Something of the old America would be discovered, the places their grandpas and grandmas had talked about, a land of profusion, safe from

human predators, snake-free, and welcoming beyond the hog and hominy of this raw place, a place described by so many of their grandparents in words they learned from *their* grandparents, where the encouragements held out to strangers were a good climate, fertile soil, wholesome air and water, plenty of provisions, good pay for labour, kind neighbours, good laws, a free government and hearty welcome. (57)

Of course, this represents the American Dream, the myth that sustained it historically. Crace contrasts the present of the novel with the plenitude of its barely remembered past. Other travellers tell tales of cannibals and the Dreaming Freeway, a land of half-truths and ignorance. In Chapter 5 Franklin is drawn to the pesthouse by the promise of warmth and company. He too talks of the vision of a land beyond the river, where there is abundance and the people "*Are* all fat. Like barn hogs." (71) Crace ironizes contemporary America in the deployment of these misconstrued, surviving details, ironic understandings of a lost world.

In Chapter 6 Margaret thinks Franklin has saved her by massaging her feet and revels in his touch, since women are not allowed such contact if they are to retain their "value" and potential for marriage. "She was, at thirty-three, she had admitted to herself, a woman who might be a daughter and a sister and an aunt, but never a wife or mother. Her body would retain its value and remain untouched." (75) Eroticized by the intimacy, Margaret feels recovered and imperceptibly is drawn to him, but on leaving the pesthouse she notices a profound change. "Margaret could see at once that something odd had happened in Raft. There was hardly any hearth smoke for a start. And at that time of day – too early in the town for the sun to make a difference, except to the sky itself – she would have expected to see the flames of braziers and courtyard lanterns, not yet doused in households lucky enough not to have an early start." (79) She insists that a reluctant Franklin accompany her, carrying her tied to his back by tarps, to Raft, which they find lifeless and abandoned. Franklin discovers his brother's abandoned coat beside a dead mule, from which the body of Nash emerges. The absence of flies leads to both a superstitious conclusion and guilt on Margaret's part:

> So Margaret's premonition had been correct: here was pestilence, or flux of some new sort, that did not care if you were man or fly or horse or mule or (now that they were hurrying into Raft and discovering more beastly cadavers at every step) chicken, pig or dog or coney. The ground outside the stockades was scattered with animals. Even before they

found the second human victim, Margaret had begun to blame herself. Who else? She'd been the first to host this current flux – so maybe she had passed it on to her grandpa and he'd brought it back into the town once he had left her safely in the Pesthouse. (93)

In Chapter 7 the pair flees the valley and its intimations of death as quickly as they can. They have discovered more bodies including Margaret's family and other villagers; ironically she has been saved by the flux. By the river they encounter "A group of lucky latecomers to Raft – fewer than forty adults – [who] had gathered at the river's edge, uncertain what to do." (103) They shy away from the shaven-headed Margaret, who is then ironically unable to help them with her local knowledge. Driven away by stones and threats, she rests while Franklin loads a barrow, salvaging various items from the village, including foodstuffs and valuables, and taking "a hunting bow and a wrap of as yet unbloodied arrows." (105) As Crace indicated this image is adapted from the wheelbarrow of the indomitable survivor found in Bertolt Brecht's *Mother Courage*, and Franklin's openness resonates with the naive innocence that is central to Fyodor Dostoevsky's *The Idiot*. At Margaret's request Franklin burns her family's house and then the remainder of Raft, a symbolic act of renewal and the cleansing of the past. He returns to her, passing the putative emigrants, despite common sense indicating that he should progress alone towards the coast without Margaret. She reveals the secret of a bridge hidden by undergrowth. "The light was weakening when they reached the bluffs where the falling torrent from the lake had etched a deep, unclimbable gulch into the hillside." (121) Afraid of heights and the potential fall from the wooden bridge Franklin reminds himself of his brother's admonition, "Only the crazy make it to the coast." (123) After crossing, he destroys the bridge so the others cannot follow, but this phase of the novel ends with his premonition: "What troubled Franklin from the moment he reached the east side of the bridge was the fear that he had made a big mistake, that where he truly should be traveling was westwards, back to the family hearth, back to mother waiting at the center of abandoned fields." (122) A similar presentiment recurs later with Margaret, when they are separated by events, linking the characters as if empathically for the reader and indicating their eventual reunion.

In Chapter 8 as they climb to the lake and beyond, the barrow becomes burdensome, pushing a furrow through the landscape, through the forest; Franklin is sorrowful for the loss of his brother, although he nurtures a residue of hope. His overwhelming grief reveals his vulnerability to Margaret, allowing him to differentiate himself from his brother: "Jackson would have been appalled, especially as this display of weakness and emotion was partly in his name. His death or disappearance had occasioned some of the tears. No, Jackson would have said that weeping was undignified and cowardly. It showed a lack of self-respect." (130) Eventually together the two travellers settle down for the night, their bodies set as an image of innocence amid the turbulence of the world: "And there they slept, back to back, the pale-faced shaven woman and the younger man, in their great wooden wheeled bed, between the canopies of trees, like children in a fairy tale, almost floating, almost out to sea. So, finally, some happiness." (136–7) In the morning she renames him "Pigeon," after one of their cultural symbols of healing, and they return to nature itself by breakfasting on quail, nuts and mushrooms from the forest.

In Chapter 9 they discover beyond the forest, the unimaginably straight road, the Dreaming Freeway that will take them to the ships for emigration. "What at first they might have mistaken as cattle, turned out to be a horse-drawn carriage traveling at an unusual speed along the center of the valley surface as if its route had been designed specifically for wheels and hooves." (149) This is one of the few remnants of America's former power and in a world of lawlessness and uncertainty, Margaret is fearful of its openness, referring to the knowledge in Raft of the dangers on this side of the river and the hidden knowledge of returning, fearful emigrants to whom they refused passage. As in Raft where the residue of "a great workshop where shoes were produced in enormous numbers," (159) over the road lies the residue of past, rock, stone and steel, the abandoned remnants of modernity. They camp with two other families, eight travellers together, only to be trapped by metal scavengers, who smash or steal their possessions, and take the healthy adults captive. "They made nooses for their necks and wrists, so that the Joeys, young Acton Bose, Margaret and Franklin could be joined and led away like the mules in one long train." (167) Drawing attention to her potential infection, Franklin pulls off Margaret's scarf so that she is abandoned by the gang, taking the rest as slaves.

Chapters 10 and 11 chart Margaret's journey with the Bose parents and their grandchild, Bella. Initially Melody and Andrew are suspicious of her, fearing her apparent social signs of illness, but gradually they accept her intercession, allowing her to carry and nurture the child as her health becomes more self-evident. Heading southward they encounter more cultivated land, where in an echo of Em and Victor in *Arcadia*, Margaret uses Bella to help her beg food from homesteads that they pass. On her final attempt, she has to flee the attentions of several men of the house who mistake her intentions: "the pulling down of her blue scarf together with her smiling offer of doing 'anything at all' in return for milk and food, had been taken by this man to be an invitation to advance and put his hands on her." (205) In the ensuing chase she escapes, parts from the Boses and travels onwards alone with the child to the nearby settlement where the saltwater reaches the river from the sea, giving an opportunity to adopt this daughter as her own.

> Margaret, though, – could she ever admit it to herself? – was not inclined to hurry after Bella's grandparents. To catch them up was to relinquish the child – and that was something she was not impatient to do. It might have crossed her mind during the previous few days how joyful it would be to have a child of her own – this child. The thought of stealing Bella away might have stained her daydreams briefly. But Margaret would never actually have done it. It would have been wicked. She would have felt guilty to her grave. (232)

The Boses' theft of her possessions allows her to feel justified in her adoption of Bella, and in Chapter 12 the two travel onwards on an increasingly busy road to reach the embarkation point too late for the boats as winter has halted all departures. There they encounter Baptist pilgrims and reach their destination:

> Tidewater, a town which had to be passed by anyone hoping to escape America from those flat quarters of the coast. Beyond Tidewater's buildings and beyond its double set of defensive walls, the ground sloped gently to the scrub covered shores of the river estuary, so much slower and broader than the river at Raft, browner too, and turbid with silt. (237)

Seeking a safe sanctuary after the sexual attentions and abductions, Margaret winters at the Blessed Ark, a cultish, monastic enclave where the Finger Baptists take in travellers who have no residue of the metallic products of the industrial past, such as buckles and knives, rejecting one family as Margaret queues because of their resistance. Crace seems to have refocused his original intentions as outlined to Begley in *The Paris Review*: "I'm going to set a novel four hundred years from now in America's medieval future, then vocabulary

The Pesthouse (2007)

matters immensely. In this community, everything metal is hated. Metal is the enemy of good fortune – so anything metal is avoided. It's bad luck. So the dangerous places to avoid would be metal-contaminated, surviving parts of the old American empire. I've called it 'the junkle.'" (208) The chronology may be significant, since the imagined future is separated by a similar timescale from the present as the contemporary world is from the founding of America. Outside the palisades of the Blessed Ark the trenches are filled with metallic objects, mirroring and defamiliarizing those in the contemporary world confiscated at airports and buried *en masse*, un-recycled, as if tainted or cursed. Margaret passes their inspections:

> 'These two are untarnished,' he said finally.
> Margaret, then, had nothing to declare, not even a brass button. She was, they let her understand, the perfect applicant for entry to the Ark. She and 'her son, Jackson' registered their names and birthplace (Raft), and were allocated lodgings in the Kindred Barn for Women and given a wooden token to exchange for food. (250)

Over the next few months Margaret becomes the mother of the child, renamed first Jackson and then Jackie to suit her sex. The Finger Baptists have twenty bearded "Helpless Gentlemen" who are administered to by the temporary residents, never using their arms or hands, which were withered, emaciated and lifeless; a creed simplistically extending and reworking a familiar maxim as a fellow diner explains to Margaret, "'The hands do devil's work.'" (256) The Baptists are having a tower constructed for them, its growth mirroring that of Jackie. With the first intimations of spring, Margaret is the first to notice the arrival of the gang that abducted Franklin. It has now begun killing the Baptists and has put its captives to work digging up the valuable metal buried outside the Ark.

Crace's typescript ends at this point, but as he explains, anticipating the shape of his plot, in his absence from Margaret, the enslaved Franklin has encountered a destroyed city landscape and a fortress-like medieval castle made out of the residue of the industrial era. Crace's projected ending has Margaret helping Franklin to escape and make the sea journey eastward. But they quickly discover that the emigrant boats will only take healthy or skilled men. For Margaret, at least, the promise of emigration proves an illusion. Franklin, though, chooses to stay with Margaret and her *adopted* – or *stolen?* – daughter, rather than leave America. Where else can they go but back to Raft, back to the pesthouse, retracing the mythical westward impulse of America. But first Margaret protects Franklin from the dangers of the road by shaving him, as she herself had been shaved during her journey eastward. He will seem diseased and untouchable, an invisible pariah, and therefore safe.

Back at the pesthouse, this perfect nuclear, though totally unbiological family of three warn travellers against fleeing east. On their return Margaret retrieves her three good luck charms, which they find under the pillow, and in them she senses something of the promise of the past, feeling coins of old America and the image of Abraham Lincoln. Setting up home as an ersatz family, the journey has been one of discovery, concerning not only rites of passage, but also a different kind of providence, and drawing from adversity. They finally recover something of the pioneering and trading spirit that established America.

This will not be Crace's swansong, despite his original notion of retiring at around sixty, since as he says to Lawless of his plans after *The Pesthouse*, "Then there's a book called *Archipelago*, which is about someone visiting an archipelago of islands and gradually getting to the more and more remote islands, discovering his remoter, remoter self. It's very much a metaphorical book – meeting dead parents and all that kind of stuff." (3) Craceland continues to expand and thrive. Crace appears willing to continue exploring his inner imagination and the external world to great literary effect.

Notes

1. The quotations taken from *The Pesthouse* are from the latest version of several incomplete typescripts sent to me as Word files.
2. President Jefferson's first Inaugural Address, 4 March 1801, Merrill D. Peterson, ed., *Thomas Jefferson: Writings* (1984): 493-4.

Bibliography

For certain reviews, articles, interviews and other sources, internet versions, additional to the original hard copies, are cited to aid the reader. Others may originate on the web, and together with certain other sources they may not be paginated; this is indicated first by the absence of pagination in my text when sections are quoted and further it is appropriately indicated in entries below. Where it may prove useful, I cite the details of the original publication of a work later translated and reprinted in English or add the original publication date in square brackets.

Primary sources

Shorter unpublished and uncollected fiction, prose and poetry

'Nile Marshes/Green Moon.' Unpub. poem appended with the note 'The Koit-Juba Ferry, The Sudan, May 1969.' N. pag.
'The Theory and Practice of Non-Violent Resistance.' Unpub. N.d. Crace archive. N. pag.
'Annie, California Plates.' *New Review*, 1. 3 (June 1974): 30–3.
'Helter Skelter, Hang Sorrow, Care'll Kill a Cat.' *New Review*, 2. 21 (December 1975): 45–9.
'Cross-Country.' *New Review*, 3. 25 (1976): 47–52.
'Annie, California Plates.' *Introduction 6: Stories by New Writers*, London: Faber and Faber, 1977: 79–89.
'Helter Skelter, Hang Sorrow, Care'll Kill a Cat.' *Introduction 6: Stories by New Writers*. London: Faber and Faber, 1977: 90–102.
'Seven Ages.' *Quarto*, 7 (June 1980): 3.
'The Sixth Continent: Talking Skull.' *Quarto*, 20 (August 1981): 10–11.
'Hearts of Oak.' *21: 21 Picador Authors Celebrate 21 Years of International Writing*, London: Picador, 1993: 71–9.
'Crace on *Quarantine*: An Introduction for American Readers.' (1998). www.jim-crace.com/Crace_Q_intro.htm. Retrieved 19:30, 4 August 2005. N. pag.

'THE PEST HOUSE (working title only) – to be delivered summer 2004 (?).' www.jim-crace.com/Forthcoming.htm. N. d. Retrieved 16:38, 12 August 2005. N. pag.
'Wrath.' *Eight Little Greats*, Ed. Dominic Gray, Leeds: Opera North, 2004: 18.
'Untitled.' E-mail from Jim Crace to Dr Philip Tew, 16:58, 18 December 2004. N. pag.
'Too Young for Funerals.' *Harvard Review*, 28 (Spring 2005): 6.
'Blood Strangers.' BBC Radio 4 [read by Jeremy Swift], 7 September 2005.

Novels and short story collections
Continent. London: Heinemann, 1986.
The Gift of Stones. London: Secker & Warburg, 1988.
Arcadia. London: Jonathan Cape, 1992.
Signals of Distress. London: Viking, 1994.
The Slow Digestions of the Night. London and New York: Penguin, 1995.
Quarantine. London: Viking, 1997.
Being Dead. London: Viking, 1999.
The Devil's Larder. London: Viking, 2001.
Six. London: Viking, 2003; *Genesis*, New York: Farrar Straus Giroux, 2003.
The Pesthouse. Unpub. m/s Word file, forthcoming, London: Penguin, 2007.

Radio plays
The Bird Has Flown. BBC Radio 4, 28 October 1976.
A Coat of Many Colours. BBC Radio 4, 26 March 1979.
Seven Ages, Quarto. Broadcast as *Middling*, BBC Radio 3, June 1980.

Literary awards including nominations

1977
Socialist Challenge Short Story Competition, 'Refugees' (winner) – judges: John Fowles, Fay Weldon, Terry Eagleton.

1986
David Higham Prize for Fiction *Continent*.
Guardian Fiction Prize *Continent*.
Whitbread Book Award *Continent* (first novel).

1988
Premio Antico Fattore *Continent*.

1989
GAP International Prize for Literature (USA) *The Gift of Stones*.

1992
American Academy of Arts and Letters E. M. Forster Award.
Society of Authors' Travelling Scholarship.

1994
Royal Society of Literature's Winifred Holtby Memorial Prize *Signals of Distress*.

1997
Booker Prize for Fiction *Quarantine* (shortlisted).
Whitbread Book Awards *Being Dead* (novel).
Writers' Guild Best Fiction Book.
Elected Member of the Management Committee of the Society of Authors.

1999
Whitbread Prize for Fiction *Being Dead* (shortlisted).
International IMPAC Dublin Literary Award *Being Dead* (shortlisted).

2001
National Book Critics Circle Fiction Award (USA) *Being Dead* (first in fiction category).

2004
Premio Napoli Festiva (September) Prizewinner for Fiction *Being Dead* (Italian translation).

Interviews of Jim Crace by Philip Tew
Note that the extracts from the interviews cited below are quoted extensively in this critical study of Jim Crace's work. They were drawn from the various interviews below for the draft versions of this book. However, subsequently all of them have been further edited by Crace before final inclusion in the final draft version. The originals are all recordings (type/medium indicated below) in Tew's possession.

'Westminster 1998 Interview.' Unpub. interview Jim Crace and Dr Philip Tew. School of Languages, University of Westminster. Cassette tape-recording, 2 June 1998. N. pag.

'UCE 2003 Interview.' Unpub. interview Jim Crace and Dr Philip Tew. University of Central England in Birmingham (UCE). CD, 12 February 2003. N. pag.

'Crace–Tew: Telephone Interview 1.' Unpub. interview Jim Crace and Dr Philip Tew. MP3 file, approx. 15:30, 13 October 2004. N. pag.

'Crace–Tew: Telephone Interview 3.' Unpub. interview Jim Crace and Dr

Philip Tew. MP3 file, 12:15, 8 November 2004. N. pag.
'Crace–Tew: Telephone Interview 4.' Unpub. interview Jim Crace and Dr Philip Tew. MP3 file, 15:00, 25 November 2004. N. pag.
'Crace–Tew: Telephone Interview 5.' Unpub. interview Jim Crace and Dr Philip Tew. MP3 file, 15:40, 9 December 2004. N. pag.
'Crace–Tew: Telephone Interview 6A.' Unpub. interview Jim Crace and Prof. Philip Tew. MP3 file, 14:30–15:10, 21 March 2005. N. pag.
'Crace–Tew: Telephone Interview 6B.' Unpub. interview Jim Crace and Prof. Philip Tew. MP3 file, 15:10–15:55, 21 March 2005. N. pag.

Other interviews

Anon. 'Jim Crace: E-mail Interview Conducted on January 27, 2000.' www.jim-crace.com. Retrieved 19:35, 4 August 2005. N. pag.
Begley, Adam. 'Jim Crace: The Art of Fiction CLXXIX.' *The Paris Review*, 167 (Fall 2003): 183–214.
Birnbaum, Robert. 'Interview: Jim Crace.' *identitytheory.com* (2001). Retrieved 10:37, 18 October 2004. www.identitytheory.com/people/birnbaum14.html.
Field, Michele. 'Jim Crace: Moral Activist, Conservative Romantic.' *Publisher's Weekly* (2 October 1995): 49.
Hogan, Ron. 'Beatrice Interview: Jim Crace.' *Beatrice Online Magazine* (2000). www.beatrice.com/interviews/crace. Retrieved 13:22, 17 August 2004. N. pag.
Koval, Ramona. 'Edinburgh 2004 – The Writer's Life – Helen Dunmore & Jim Crace.' *Books and Writing* (19 September 2004). Transcript of Radio National, Australian Broadcast. *ABC online*. www.abc.net.au/rn/arts/bwriting/stories/s1201285.htm. Retrieved 17:36, 12 August 2005. N. pag.
Lawless, Andrew. 'The Poet of Prose – Jim Crace in Interview.' *Three Monkeys Online*. English language version. Issue 11 (February 2005): 1–4. www.threemonkeysonline.com/threemon_article_jim_crace_interview.htm. Retrieved 10:01, 22 September 2005.
Miller, Laura. 'Chowing Down.' *Salon.com: Online Journal* (29 October 2001): 1–5. http://dir.salon.com/books/int/2001/10/29/crace/index.html. Retrieved 14:13, 3 January 2005.
Proctor, Minna. 'Jim Crace.' *Bomb Magazine*, 71 (Spring 2000): 1–17. www.bombsite.com/crace/crace.html . Retrieved 13:14, 17 August 2004.

Secondary sources

Adams, Tim. 'On Fecund Thoughts.' *The Observer, Review Section* (7 September 2003): 15. http://books.guardian.co.uk/reviews/generalfiction/0,6121,1036890,00.html. Retrieved 13:40 EST, 25 March 2005.
Allen, Brooke. 'Meditations, Good and Bad.' *New Criterion*, 18. 9 (May 2000): 63.

Bibliography

Anon. 'Gun Clue to Dixon Deaths.' *Oxford Mail* (30 January 1998). www.thisisoxfordshire.co.uk/oxfordshire/archive/1998/01/30/NEWS4VQ.html. Retrieved 17:05, 31 July 2005.
Ariès, Phillipe. *The Hour of Our Death.* Trans. Helen Weaver. New York: Knoph, 1983 [1981].
—— *Images of Man and Death.* Trans. Janet Lloyd. Cambridge, MA: Harvard University Press, 1985.
Arnold, Kenneth. 'Emptiness Is All.' *Cross Currents*, 49. 1 (Spring 1999): 140.
Bakhtin, Mikhail. *Rabelais and His World.* Trans. Helene Iswolsky. Bloomington: Indiana University Press, 1984 [1965].
Balée, Susan. 'Maximalist Fiction.' *Hudson Review*, 53. 3 (Autumn 2000): 513.
Bataille, Georges. *The Accursed Share: An Essay on General Economy, Consumption* Vol. I. Trans. Robert Hurley. New York: Zone Books, 1988. *La Part Maudite.* Paris: Editions de Minuit, 1967.
—— *The Accursed Share: An Essay on General Economy, The History of Eroticism* Vol. II and *Sovereignty* Vol. III. Trans. Robert Hurley. New York: Zone Books, 1991. *L'Histoire de l'érotisme* and *La Souveraineté* in *Ouevres Complètes.* Vol. 8. Paris: Editions Gallimard, 1976.
—— *Eroticism.* Trans. Mary Dalwood. London and New York: Penguin, 2001 [1957].
—— *The Unfinished System of Nonknowledge.* Trans. Michelle Kendall and Stuart Kendall. London and Minneapolis: University of Minnesota Press, 2001.
Bawer, Bruce, 'Quarantine.' *Washington Post* (3 May 1998): X05. www.washingtonpost.com/wp-srv/style/books/reviews/quarantine.htm. Retrieved 23:54, 17 December 2004.
Begley, Adam. 'A Quiet Brit's Loud Talent: Jim Crace's Corpse Comedy.' *New York Observer* (12 February 2001): 27. www.findarticles.com/p/articles/mi_moICQ/is_2001_Feb_12/ai_81473984. Retrieved 12:43, 22 December 2004.
—— 'A Pilgrim in Craceland.' *Southwest Review*, 87. 2 & 3 (2002): 227–40.
Benjamin, Walter. *Illuminations.* Trans. Harry Zohn. London: Fontana Press, 1992.
Birch, Carol. 'Quivering.' *The Guardian, Saturday Review Section* (18 September 1999): 10. http://books.guardian.co.uk/specialreports/whitbread/story/0,6194,101771,00.html. Retrieved 00:00, 12 August 2005.
Bradfield, Scott. 'He's Dirty, He Slouches and He's Lousy at Woodwork. Still, He Does a Good Miracle.' *The Observer, Review Section* (15 June 1997): 16.
Brown, Helen. 'A Writer's Life: Jim Crace.' *Sunday Telegraph, Books Section* (31 August 2003): 2. www.telegraph.co.uk/arts/main.jhtml?xml=/arts/2003/08/31/bocrace.xml. Retrieved 20:48, 8 August 2004.
Burnett, Paula. 'Ocean Views.' *New Statesman & Society* (2 September 1994): 36.

Calvino, Italo. *Invisible Cities*. London: Picador, 1979.
Charyn, Jerome. *Metropolis: New York as Myth, Marketplace, and Magical Land*. New York: Putnam, 1986.
Constable, John and Hideaki Aoyama. 'Testing for Mathematical Lineation in Jim Crace's *Quarantine* and T. S. Eliot's *Four Quartets*.' *Belgian Journal of Linguistics: Linguistic Approaches to Poetry*. Eds. Christine Michaux and Marc Dominic. 15 (2001): 35–51.
Cooke, Judy. *Jim Crace*. Contemporary Writers Pamphlet. London: Book Trust (in conjunction with the British Council), 1992. N. pag.
Crossan, John Dominic. *Raid on the Articulate: Comic Eschatology in Jesus and Borges*, New York: Harper & Row, 1976.
Dalgleish, David. 'Mind Food.' *January Magazine: Online Journal* (October 2001). www.janmag.com/fiction/devilslarder.html. Retrieved 00:44, 8 October 2004. N. pag.
Damiani, Bruno and Barbara Mujica. *Et in Arcadia Ego: Essays on Death in the Pastoral Novel*. Lanham, MD: University Press of America, 1990.
Dubrow, Helen. *Genre*. London and New York: Methuen, 1982.
Dufrenne, Mikel. *In the Presence of the Sensuous: Essays in Aesthetics*. New York: Humanities Books, 1987.
Dyer, Geoff. 'Word Salad.' *New Statesman & Society* (20 March 1992): 45.
Eder, Richard. 'The Phantom of the Market.' *Los Angeles Times Book Review* (4 October 1992): 3, 12.
—— 'Cavedweller.' *Los Angeles Times Book Review* (12 April 1998): 2.
Empson, William. *Some Versions of Pastoral*. London: Chatto & Windus, 1935.
Ettin, Andrew V. *Literature and the Pastoral*. New Haven: Yale University Press, 1984
Feit, Rachel. 'The Tastes of Taste.' *Austin Chronicle*, 17 (28 December 2001–3 January 2002): 31. Retrieved 11:20, 5 August 2005.
France, Miranda. 'Supping Full on Horrors.' *The Spectator* (2 October 1999): 46.
Freud, Sigmund. *The Uncanny*. New York and London: Penguin, 2003 [1919].
Gilbert, Francis. 'The Devil's Larder.' *New Statesman* (3 September 2001): 41.
Glasser, Perry. 'A Stone Age Storyteller Speaks from the Dawn of Narrative Art.' *Chicago Tribune Books* (16 April 1989): 6.
González-Crussí, F. 'Approaching the Unknowable.' *Commonweal* (14 July 2000): 27.
Greenwood, Gillian. 'The Geography of Bleak New Worlds.' *The Times* (16 October 1986): 19.
Gutzwiller, Kathryn J. *Theocritus' Pastoral Analogies: The Formation of a Genre*. Madison, Wisconsin and London: University of Wisconsin Press, 1991.
Hamilton, Peter. *Robert Doisneau: A Photographer's Life*. New York, London and Paris: Abbeville Press, 1995.
Hamilton-Pearson, James. 'Voyages Out.' *New Republic* (6 May 1996): 38.

Bibliography

Harrison, Bernard. *Inconvenient Fictions: Literature and the Limits of Theory.* New Haven and London: Yale University Press, 1991.
Irwin, Robert. 'Hiveward-Winging.' *London Review of Books,* 19, 13 (3 July 1997): 21–22.
Jacobs, Jane. *The Economy of Cities.* Penguin: Harmondsworth, 1972.
—— *Cities and the Wealth of Nations: Principles of Economic Life.* New York: Random House, 1984.
—— *The Death and Life of Great American Cities.* New York: The Modern Library, 1993.
Johnson, B. S. *See the Old Lady Decently.* London: Hutchison, 1975.
Johnson Luke, Timothy. 'Jesus in the Desert.' *Commonweal* (8 May 1998): 18.
Jones, Tobias. 'A Voice Crying in the Wilderness.' *The Spectator* (14 June 1997): 39.
Kamine, Mark. 'A Prehistoric Tale.' *New Leader* (20 March 1989): 20.
Kamiya, Gary. 'Quarantine.' *Salon.com: Online Journal* (April 1998). N. pag. http://archive.salon.com/books/sneaks/1998/04/cov_10sneaks.html. Retrieved 23:56, 18 December 2004.
Kayser, Wolfgang. *The Grotesque in Art and Literature.* Trans. Ulrich Weisstein. New York: Columbia University Press, 1981 [1957].
Kazunari, Miyahara. '*Quarantine*: Jim Crace's Anti-Christ.' *English and English-American Literature* (Yamaguchi University), 35 (December 2000): 105–27. www.jim-crace.com/miyahara.htm. Retrieved 11:40, 5 August 2005.
Kearns, George. 'Post-Colonial Fiction: Our Custom Is Different.' *Hudson Review,* 40. 3 (Autumn 1987): 487.
Kegel-Brinkgreve, E. *The Echoing Woods: Bucolic and Pastoral from Theocritus to Wordsworth.* Amsterdam: J. C. Gieben, 1990.
Kermode, Frank. 'Into the Wilderness: Review of *Quarantine.*' *New York Times,* Late Edition (12 April 1998): 8. *New York Times Online.* http://query.nytimes.com/gst/fullpage.html?res=9801E3DD173AF931A25757C0 A96E958260. Retrieved 11 August 2005.
King, Francis. 'Nostalgia for the Mud.' *The Spectator* (21 March 1992): 34.
Kittay, Eva Feder. *Metaphor: Its Cognitive Force and Linguistic Structure.* Oxford: Clarendon Press, 1987.
Krist, Gary. 'Serendipity.' *Hudson Review,* 42. 4 (Winter 1990): 659.
—— '*Being Dead* by Jim Crace.' *Salon.com: Online Journal* (30 March 2003). N. pag. http://dir.salon.com/books/review/2000/03/30/crace/index.html. Retrieved 11:55, 22 December 2004.
Lane, Richard J. 'The Fiction of Jim Crace: Narrative and Recovery.' *Contemporary British Fiction.* Eds. Richard J. Lane, Rod Mengham and Philip Tew. Cambridge and Malden, MA: Polity, 2003: 27–39.
Lefebvre, Henri. *The Critique of Everyday Life, Volume I: Introduction.* Trans. John Moore. London and New York: Verso, 1992 [1947].

—— *Critique of Everyday Life, Volume II: Foundations for a Sociology of the Everyday*. London and New York: Verso, 2002 [1961].
Leithauser, Brad. 'Not Written in Stone.' *Washington Post Book World* (21 May 1989): x3.
Levi, Jonathan. 'Origin of Species.' *Los Angeles Times Book Review* (16 April 2000): 19.
Levinas, Emmanuel. *On Thinking-of-the-Other: entre nous*. London: Athlone Press, 1998 [1991].
Levy, Primo. *The Periodic Table*. Trans. Raymond Rosenthal. New York: Schocken Books, 1984.
Lewis, Norman. *Jackdaw Cake*, London: Hamish Hamilton, 1985.
—— 'Namek and the Smoked Ancestor.' *21: 21 Picador Authors Celebrate 21 Years of International Writing*. London: Picador, 1993: 205–14.
—— *The Happy Ant-Heap and Other Pieces*. London: Jonathan Cape, 1998.
Livingstone, David B. 'The Devil Inside.' *Spike Magazine* (March 1998). N. pag. www.spikemagazine.com/0498quar.htm. Retrieved 13:43, 17 August 2004.
Lynch, Kevin. 'A Process of Community Visual Survey.' *City Sense and City Design: Writings and Projects of Kevin Lynch*. Eds. Tridib Banerjee and Michael Southworth. London, and Cambridge MA: MIT Press, 1990: 263–86.
Mac Cormac, Earl R. *A Cognitive Theory of Metaphor*. Cambridge, MA and London: MIT Press, 1985.
Marcuse, Herbert. *One Dimensional Man: Studies in the Ideology of Advanced Industrial Society*. London: Routledge & Kegan Paul, 1964.
Mars-Jones, Adam. 'Hurrying Back to Nature.' *Times Literary Supplement* (13 March 1992): 22.
Maslin, Janet. 'Books of the Times: A Hero's Surfeit of Fertility and the Poetic Use Thereof.' *New York Times*, Late Edition (13 November 2003): 8. http://query.nytimes.com/gst/fullpage.html?res=9C01EED61638F930A2 5752C1A9659C8B63. Retrieved 01:43, 3 January 2005.
Matthews, Sean. 'Jim Crace.' *British Council Contemporary Writers Website*. www.contemporarywriters.com/authors/?p=auth24. Retrieved 00:52, 11 August 2005. N. pag.
Meletinsky, Eleazar M. *The Poetics of Myth*. Trans. Guy Lanoue and Alexandre Sadetsky. New York and London: Routledge, 2000 [1998].
Merleau-Ponty, Maurice. *The Visible and the Invisible*. Trans. Alphonso Lingis. Evanston: Northwestern University Press, 1968 [1948].
Merrill D. Peterson, ed. *Thomas Jefferson: Writings*. New York: Literary Classics of the United States, Inc., 1984.
Metcalf, Greg. 'The Soul in the Meatsuit: Ivan Albright, Hannibal Lecter and the Body Grotesque.' *Literature and the Grotesque*. Ed. Michael J. Meyer. Amsterdam and Atlanta, GA: Rodopi, 1995: 153–70.

Miller, J. Hillis. *Tropes, Parables, Performatives: Essays on Twentieth-Century Literature*. New York and London: Harvester Wheatsheaf, 1990.
Mumford, Lewis. *Art and Technics*. New York: Columbia University Press, 1952.
—— *The Highway and the City*, London: Secker & Warburg, 1964.
—— *The City in History*. Harmondsworth and New York: Penguin, 1984.
Olshan, Joseph. 'Meet a Despotic Octogenarian and his Utopian Marketplace.' *Chicago Tribune Books* (15 November 1992): 3.
Over, Luke. *The Kelping Industry in Scilly*. Pamphlet Series No. 14. St. Mary's, Isles of Scilly: Isles of Scilly Museum Association, 1987.
Parks, Tim. 'On the Rocks.' *The Spectator* (3 September 1994): 36.
Peck, Dale. 'The Devil You Know.' *New Republic* (31 December 2001): 38.
—— *Hatchet Jobs*. New York and London: The New Press, 2004.
Pei, Lowry. Untitled review of *Continent*. *Boston Review*, 12. 4 (August 1987): 30.
—— Untitled review of *The Gift of Stones*. *Boston Review*, 14. 4 (August 1989): 23.
Poggioli, Renato. *The Oaten Flute: Essays on Pastoral Poetry and the Pastoral Ideal*. Cambridge MA: Harvard University Press, 1975.
Quinion, Michael. 'World Wide Words.' www.worldwidewords.org/weirdwords/ww-har1.htm. Retrieved 12:30, 25 May 2005. N. pag.
Quinn, Anthony. 'Reproduction Values.' *New York Times*, Late Edition (23 November 2003): 8. http://query.nytimes.com/gst/fullpage.html?res=9804E6DD1438F930A15752C1A9659C8B63. Retrieved 16:34, 3 January 2005.
Ricoeur, Paul. *The Symbolism of Evil*. Boston: Beacon Press, 1969 [1967].
—— *Figuring the Sacred: Religion, Narrative and Imagination*. Trans. David Pellauer. Minneapolis: Fortress Press, 1995.
Royle, Nicholas. *The Uncanny*, New York: Routledge, 2003
Sackville-West, Sophia. 'Write and Proper.' *Observer Magazine* (22 March 1992): 30.
Sansom, Ian. 'Smorgasbits.' *London Review of Books*, 23. 22 (15 November 2001): 13–14. www.lrb.co.uk/v23/n22/sanso1_.html. Retrieved 19:07, 22 December 2004.
Scarborough, Milton. *Myth and Modernity: Postcritical Reflections*. Albany, NY: State University of New York Press, 1994.
Schopenhauer, Arthur. *Parerga and Paralipomena, Short Philosophical Essays: Volume Two*. Oxford: Clarendon Press, 2000.
Shepard, Jim. 'Dune.' *New York Times Book Review* (23 April 2000): 10.
Shillington, V. George. 'Engaging with Parables.' *Jesus and His Parables: Interpreting the Parables of Jesus Today*. Ed. V. George Shillington. Edinburgh: T & BT Clark, 1997: 1– 20
Squires, Michael. *The Pastoral Novel: Studies in George Eliot, Thomas Hardy,*

and D. H. Lawrence. Charlottesville: University Press of Virginia, 1974.

Stemporowski, Jakub. *The City and the Country, the Myth and the Reality in Jim Crace's Novel 'Arcadia.'* Unpub. masters thesis. Nicolas Copernicus University, Toruń, Poland. www.jim-crace.com/stemporowski%20thesis.htm. Retrieved 19:30, 22 December 2004.

Stern, J. P. *On Realism*. London and Boston: Routledge & Kegan Paul, 1973.

Stewart, Garrett. *Death Sentences: Styles of Dying in British Fiction*. Cambridge MA and London: Harvard University Press, 1984.

Stonehill, Brian. Untitled review of *Continent*. *Los Angeles Times Book Review* (12 April 1987): 4.

Taylor, D. J. 'A Light Collation.' *The Spectator*, 287. 9032 (15 September 2001): 39–40.

—— 'Gone to Seed.' *The Guardian, Saturday Review* (6 September 2003): 6. http://books.guardian.co.uk/reviews/generalfiction/0,6121,1036366,00.html. Retrieved 13:20 EST, 25 March 2005.

Teske, Doris. 'Jim Crace's *Arcadia*: Public Culture in the Postmodern City.' *London in Literature: Visionary Mappings of the Metropolis*. Eds. Susana Onega and John A. Stotesbury. Heidelberg: Universitätsverlag C. Winter, 2002: 165–82.

Tew, Philip. *The Contemporary British Novel*. New York and London: Continuum, 2004.

Thewlis, Paul. 'Death Warmed Up.' *Redbrick* [Birmingham University Student Newspaper] (13–19 May 2000): 20.

Tilley, Christopher. *Metaphor and Material Culture*. Oxford and Malden, MA: Blackwell, 1999.

Tonkin, Boyd. 'Jim Crace: Reasons to be Cheerful.' *The Independent, Magazine Section* (6 September 2003): 32–3. http://enjoyment.independent.co.uk/books/interviews/article85636.ece. Retrieved 13:56, 17 August 2004.

Vincent, Sally. 'Death and the Optimist.' *The Guardian, Weekend Magazine* (25 August 2001): 39–40, 42, 44.

Wheeler, Edward T. Untitled review of *Arcadia*. *Commonweal* (18 June 1993): 26.

Whitaker, Phil. 'The Absolute End.' *New Statesman* (20 September 1999): 57–8.

Wild, Peter. 'Interview.' *Bookmunch.co.uk: Online Journal*. www.bookmunch.co.uk/view.php?id=1140. Retrieved 13:48, 17 August 2004. N. pag.

Williams, Raymond. *The Country and the City*. London: Hogarth Press, 1985 [1973].

Williamson, Eric Miles. 'Beyond Postmodernism.' *Southern Review*, 37. 1 (Winter 2001): 174.

Wilson, Bee. 'Not in the Very Best of Taste.' *The Times* (22 August 2001): 12.

Wilson, Elizabeth. *The Sphinx in the City: Urban Life, the Control of Disorder,*

and Women. London: Virago, 1991.
Wilson, Robert. 'History on the Rocks.' *Washington Post, Book World* (4 February 1996): X9.
Woodward, Gerard. 'His Curse Is to Impregnate Every Woman He Sleeps With: Review of *Six* by Jim Crace.' *Sunday Telegraph, Review Section* (21 September 2003): 13. www.telegraph.co.uk/arts/main.jhtml?xml=/arts/2003/09/21/bocra21.x ml. Retrieved 16:40, 16 June 2005.
Wroe, Nicholas. 'The Reluctant Storyteller.' *The Guardian, Saturday Review Section* (8 July 2000): 13. http://books.guardian.co.uk/departments/generalfiction/story/0,,340878,00.html. Retrieved 13:53, 17 August 2004.

Internet websites/web-pages

Gibsons of Scilly. www.gibsonsofscilly.co.uk. Retrieved 18:30, 3 December 2004. N. pag.
Jim Crace Website. www.jim-crace.com. Retrieved 19:35, 4 August 2005. N. pag.
Prague Spring 1968. http://library.thinkquest.org/C0011155/index1.htm. Retrieved 17:26, 27 April 2005.
Untitled Website. www.postershop.com/Doisneau-Robert/Doisneau-Robert-Le-Baiser-De-lHotel-De-Ville-Paris-1950–7800031.html. Retrieved 13:03, 19 April 2005. N. pag.
Untitled Website. http://world.floonetwork.org/cgibin/ikonboard.cgi?act=ST&f=144&t=67. Retrieved 11:56, 25 May 2005.

Index

Note: 'n.' after a page reference indicates the number of a note on that page.

Abbas, 10
Allegory, x, 3–4, 18, 24, 28–9, 32, 45, 61–2, 161–2, 196
Anstey, John, 17, 23
Aoyama, Hideaki, see Constable, John
Arcadian, The, 4–5, 6, 89
   literature, 4
Ariès, Phillipe
   The Hour of Our Death 140, 149
   Images of Man and Death, 134, 151
Arnoldian–Leavisite axis, vii

Bakhtin, Mikhail, *Rabelais and His World*, 144
Ballard, J. G., 24
Bataille, Georges
   The Accursed Share: An Essay on General Economy, The History of Eroticism Vol. II and *Sovereignty Vol. III*, xiv, 28, 62–3, 67, 72, 128–9, 131–2, 160
   Eroticism, 149
   The Unfinished System of Nonknowledge, 158, 162, 163
BBC, the, 13, 191–2n.2, 206
Begley, Adam
   'Jim Crace: The Art of Fiction CLXXIX', ix, xi, xii, 195, 202–3
   'A Pilgrim in Craceland', ix, 1, 3, 5, 9, 25, 35, 62, 94, 97
   'A Quiet Brit's Loud Talent: Jim Crace's Corpse Comedy', 137

Benjamin, Walter, *Illuminations*, 64, 66, 71, 130
Booker Prize, 24–5, 207
Bourdieu, Pierre, viii
Bragg, Melvyn, 16
Brecht, Bertolt, *Mother Courage*, 200
Broadwater Farm Riots, 20–1, 33–4n.27
Brown, Helen, 'A Writer's Life: Jim Crace', 18, 25–6
Burn, Gordon, 10

Charyn, Jerome, *Metropolis*, 112n.2
Cobbing, Bob, 32n.8
Constable, John and Hideaki Aoyama, 'Testing for Mathematical Lineation in Jim Crace's *Quarantine* and T. S. Eliot's *Four Quartets*', 29
Cooke, Judy, *Jim Crace*, 42, 71, 76
Crace, Charley (father), 2–3, 7–8, 33n.12, 9–10, 64, 167
   atheism, 67–8
   auto-didacticism, 9
   death of, 18, 134–5, 171
   planting oaks, 2, 7
   withered arm, 9, 64, 167
Crace, Jim
   Africa, 11–13, 33n.16, 35, 36–7, 42, 53–4, 107, 111
   Birmingham, 10, 13, 18, 20, 21, 25, 32n.1, 61–2, 71–2, 91, 122

Index

Birmingham College of Commerce, 10–11
birth of, 2
childhood, certainties of, 2
ecological concerns, 7, 194–6
Enfield Grammar School, 8, 32–3n.8, 33n.11
English Literature degree, 10–11
France
  French girlfriend, 13, 14
  travelling in, 10
John Channon, self-portrait, 12–13
journalist, career as, ix, 13–14, 16–18, 20–1, 23, 25, 26, 36
Pilgrim Estate, upbringing and location, 5
radicalism, 7–8, 9–11, 26, 30
secretiveness, 1
self-narration, unreliable, 1–2, 22, 25, 136
style, ix–x, xii, 3–4, 6–7, 14–15, 18–19, 20–2, 22–3, 26–32, 31–2, 42–5, 60–1, 69–70, 71, 76, 82–3, 94, 95, 117, 156–8, 162–4, 166, 168, 173, 174–5
working-class culture, 5, 8, 9, 25, 32–3n.8, 33n.11
Zapata moustache, 13
Crace, Jim – cited works
'Annie, California Plates', 14–15
Arcadia, ix, xi, 3, 4, 6, 9, 18, 24, 27–8, 75–93, 94, 112–13, 169, 202, 206
Being Dead, ix, xii, 3, 6, 7, 34, 133–51, 153–4, 156, 171, 206, 207
Continent, ix–x, 3, 11–12, 18, 20, 21–2, 23, 29, 31, 35–60, 64, 94, 156, 206
in *Continent*, 53–4
'Crace on *Quarantine*', 133
'Cross-Country', 11, 12–13, 20, 205
The Devil's Larder, ix, x, xiii, xv, 155–69, 177, 191–2, 206
The Gift of Stone, ix, x, xiv, 9, 18, 28, 29, 60–74, 95, 152n.7, 206
'Hearts of Oak', 2, 7, 17–18, 32n.7, 33n.12, 205
'Helter Skelter, Hang Sorrow, Care'll Kill a Cat', 15–16

'Nile Marshes/Green Moon', 11–12
Quarantine, ix, xii, 26, 28, 29, 34n, 115–33, 134, 152–3, 205, 206, 207
'Seven Ages', 18
Signals of Distress, ix, xi, 7, 9, 24, 28, 29, 30–1, 93–114, 128, 206, 207
Six [Genesis], ix, xiii, xv, 42, 165, 169–92, 206
'THE PEST HOUSE (working title only) – to be delivered summer 2004 (?)', xiv
The Pesthouse, ix, xiii–xiv, 193–204, 206
The Slow Digestions of the Night, ix, xiii, 206
'Theory and Practice of Non-Violent Resistance', 19–20, 205
'Untitled', e-mail from Jim Crace to Dr Philip Tew, 152–3 n.13
Crace, Pamela, née Turton, 10, 13, 77–8
Craceland, ix–x, 1–34, 35, 42, 62, 67, 70, 83, 145, 169–70, 204
Crossan, John Dominic, *Raid on the Articulate: Comic Eschatology in Jesus and Borges*, 45–6, 55

Damiani, Bruno and Barbara Mujica, *Et in Arcadia Ego: Essays on Death in the Pastoral Novel*, 57
death, ix, xii, xiv, 18, 21, 27–8, 33–4n.27, 43, 50, 51, 54–8, 59, 65, 72–3, 75, 86, 89, 96, 106, 107, 111, 112, 116, 119, 120, 122, 127, 128–34, 134–51, 152n.8, 152n.10, 153n.24, 161, 163–4, 171–2, 181, 188, 191, 193, 195, 198, 200–1
disillusionment, late 1970s, 19–20
Doisneau, Robert, 176–7, 192n.13
Dovstoevsky, Fyodor, *The Idiot*, 200
Dufrenne, Mikel, *In the Presence of the Sensuous: Essays in Aesthetics*, 6–7

Empson, William, *Some Versions of Pastoral*, 4

Enfield, 2, 7, 8, 10, 22
erotic, the, x, 148–9, 156, 159, 160–1, 169–91, 199
Ettin, Andrew V. *Literature and the Pastoral*, 4

Field, Michele, 'Jim Crace: Moral Activist, Conservative Romantic', 22, 33n.27, 93
Forty Hall, 5, 7
Forty Hill, 2–3, 7
Freud, Sigmund, *The Uncanny*, 179, 180, 186, 189, 190

Ginsberg, Allen, 11
Greenwood, Gillian, 'The Geography of Bleak New Worlds', 21–2, 23
groteque, the, 44, 120, 129, 132, 135, 138–9, 141, 142–5, 149–50, 153n.28, 153–4n.29, 163, 168–9
Gutzwiller, Kathryn J., *Theocritus' Pastoral Analogies: The Formation of a Genre*, 4

Hamilton, Ian, 13–14, 16
Harrison, Bernard, *Inconvenient Fictions: Literature and the Limits of Theory*, 31–2, 82
Harry, Debbie, 17
Hill, Susan, 14
Hogan, Ron, 'Beatrice Interview: Jim Crace', 134–5, 136, 137

Irwin, Robert, 'Hiveward-Winging', 116, 122, 133, 153n.16
Islam, 36

Jacobs, Jane, xi, 76–7, 78, 79, 80, 81, 85, 86, 87, 92, 93, 112n.2, 113n.7
 Cities and the Wealth of Nations: Principles of Economic Life, 78
 Death and Life of Great American Cities, The, 77, 80, 81, 85, 86, 87, 92, 93
 The Economy of Cities, 77, 78, 113n.7
Jefferson, Thomas, 194–5, 204n.2
Jethro Tull, 17
Johnson, B. S., 24
 See the Old Lady Decently, 113n.10

Johnson, Samuel, *Rasselas*, 18, 20

Kamiya, Gary, 'Quarantine', 115, 119–20, 132–3, 153n.22
Karloff, Boris, otherwise Eric Pratt, 32–3n.8
Kayser, Wolfgang, *The Grotesque in Art and Literature*, 142–3, 144–5
Kazunari, Miyahara, '*Quarantine*: Jim Crace's Anti-Christ', 119–20, 121, 123, 129, 132, 152n.10, 152–3n.13
Keats, John, 2, 8
Kegel-Brinkgreve, E., *The Echoing Woods: Bucolic and Pastoral from Theocritus to Wordsworth*, 3–4, 40–1, 57
Kermode, Frank, 'Into the Wilderness', 24, 26, 29, 34n.5, 115–16, 117
Kerouac, Jack, 8, 14
Kyoto Protocol, the, 185

Labour Party, the, 2, 7
landscape, xi, xii, 3, 5–8, 11–12, 17, 24, 26–7, 29, 31–2, 34n.33, 58–60, 64–5, 67–8, 77, 86, 90, 92–3, 94–6, 97, 101, 106, 107–8, 115–16, 118–19, 121–2, 123, 129–30, 135–6, 141, 142, 146–8, 150–1, 194–6, 197–8, 200, 203
Lane, Richard J., 'The Fiction of Jim Crace: Narrative and Recovery', 26, 29–30, 34n.35, 62, 64, 66, 94, 117, 126, 141
Lawless, Andrew, 'Poet of Prose – Jim Crace in Interview', 171–2, 194, 204
Lefebvre, Henri
 The Critique of Everyday Life, Volume I: Introduction, 81
 The Critique of Everyday Life, Volume II: Foundations for a Sociology of the Everyday, 77, 78, 84, 175
Leithauser, Brad, 'Not Written in Stone', 60–1, 63
Levinas, Emmanuel, *On Thinking-of-the-Other: entre nous*, 94, 98, 104

Index

Lewis, Norman
  The Happy Ant-Heap and Other Pieces, 7
  Jackdaw Cake, 7
  'Namek and the Smoked Ancestor', 32n.7
Lewis and Clark expedition, 194–5, 197
Littlewood, Joan, Theatre Workshop, 9
loss of youth, fears of, 14–16, 20
Lynch, Kevin, 'A Process of Community Visual Survey', 91–2, 93

Mac Cormac, Earl R., *A Cognitive Theory of Metaphor*, 69–70
Magnum Photos, 10
Marcuse, Herbert, *One Dimensional Man: Studies in the Ideology of Advanced Industrial Society*, 164, 166
Mars-Jones, Adam, 'Hurrying Back to Nature', 27
Martin, George, 17
Matthews, Sean, 'Jim Crace', 19, 23–4
Meletinsky, Eleazar M., *The Poetics of Myth*, x, 50, 56, 58–60, 95–6
Merleau-Ponty, Maurice, *The Visible and the Invisible*, 66
Metcalf, Greg, 'The Soul in the Meatsuit', 139, 153n.28
Miller, J. Hillis, *Tropes, Parables, Performatives: Essays on Twentieth-Century Literature*, 42, 152n.7
Miller, Laura, 'Chowing Down', 157, 168
modernity, x, 24, 35, 36–7, 62–3, 76–7, 79, 193
  myth and, 28–9, 37–8, 40, 55
  remnants of, 201
Mujica, Barbara, *see* Damiani, Bruno
Mumford, Lewis, 82
  Art and Technics, 90
  The City in History, 112n.2
  The Highway and the City, 88
myth, or mythic, or mythopoeic, ix–x, xi, 3, 4, 5, 22, 24, 28–9, 31, 35–6, 37, 38–40, 42, 50, 53–6, 58–60, 76–7, 79–87, 92, 95–6, 110, 118, 160–1, 195, 196, 199, 204

National Book Critics Circle (USA) twenty-sixth annual award, 24, 207
Neill, Andrew, 20–1
neo-Darwinianism, 135, 139, 140, 141, 148, 174
neo-Darwinian narrative impulse, viii
New River, the, 8
Nose Flutes, the, 10

Over, Luke, *The Kelping Industry in Scilly*, 113n.20

parable, ix, x, 3, 22, 24, 31–2, 37–42, 45–6, 55–6, 64, 66–7, 82–3, 109, 117, 127–8, 130–1, 133, 157, 162
pastoral, the, ix, x, xi, 2–7, 8, 18, 26–7, 29, 40–1, 44, 57, 76, 77–9, 86, 89
Peck, Dale
  'The Devil You Know', 192n.3
  Hatchet Jobs, 156, 162, 164
Plath, Sylvia, 19
Poggioli, Renato, *The Oaten Flute: Essays on Pastoral Poetry and the Pastoral Ideal*, xi, 86, 89
Pollock, Jackson, first UK event, 9
Prague Spring, the, 184, 192n.16
Proctor, Minna, 'Jim Crace', 117–18, 123, 130, 135, 136

quarantine
  biblical account of Christ's, 115
  St Helens pest-house, Scilly Isles, 195
Quinn, Anthony, 'Reproduction Values', 170, 173

Raban, Jonathan, 16
radicalism, or radicality, 2, 95, 98, 99, 102, 166, 177, 181, 184–5
Radio Times, 16
Raine, Craig, 18
realism, imaginary, xi, 24, 36–41, 39–42, 161–3, 170

Ricoeur, Paul
  Figuring the Sacred: Religion, Narrative and Imagination, 37, 54–5
  The Symbolism of Evil, 94, 98–9
Robeson, Paul, 9
Rothko, Mark, 1961 exhibition, 9
Royle, Nicolas, *The Uncanny*, 172–3, 181
Rushdie, Salman, 24

Salinger, J. D., 14
Sansom, Ian, 'Smorgasbits', 5, 13
Scarborough, Milton, *Myth and Modernity: Postcritical Reflections*, 28–9
Schopenhauer, Arthur, *Parerga and Paralipomena, Short Philosophical Essays: Volume Two*, 49, 52
Shepard, Jim, 'Dune', 138
Shillington, V. George, 'Engaging with Parables,' 45
Silcott, Winston, 33–4n.27
Spurs, or Tottenham Hostspur Football Club, 15, 33n.20
Squires, Michael, *The Pastoral Novel: Studies in George Eliot, Thomas Hardy, and D. H. Lawrence*, 113n.12
Stemporowski, Jakub, *The City and the Country, the Myth and the Reality in Jim Crace's Novel 'Arcadia'*, 77, 79, 80–1, 86, 90
Stern, J. P., *On Realism*, 39–40
Stewart, Garrett, *Death Sentences: Styles of Dying in British Fiction*, 134–5, 142
Sudan, the, 11–12, 36–7
Swinging Sixties, the, 11

Taylor, D. J.
  'Gone to Seed', 170
  'A Light Collation', 156

Teske, Doris, 'Jim Crace's Arcadia: Public Culture in the Postmodern City', 4–5, 75, 76, 82, 85, 90, 91, 92, 93
Tew, Philip, xv, 25–6, 32n.1, 32n.2, 32–3n.8, 33n.13, 112n.1, 152n.1, 152–3n.13, 192n.10
  The Contemporary British Novel, 142
Thatcher, Margaret, 2, 18, 61, 116
Tilley, Christopher, *Metaphor and Material Culture*, 69, 70, 71
Tonkin, Boyd, 'Jim Crace: Reasons to be Cheerful', 1, 22, 170–1, 193
Tottenham, 15, 20–1, 33n.20
transformative, the, 37–9, 66–7, 68–70, 72–3, 75–6, 128–9, 142–5, 155, 159, 179, 184, 187–8, 193–4
transition, or transitional forces, x–xi, 5, 7, 9, 29–30, 31, 55, 61–3, 69, 75–6, 130, 155, 182, 195

uncanny, the, or *unheimlich*, 81, 97, 127, 149–50, 169, 172–5, 178, 179, 180–6, 188–90
urban life, and urban communities, x–xi, 5, 75–81, 84–5, 86–93

Vincent, Sally, 'Death and the Optimist', 1, 2, 5–6, 82

Wesker, Arnold, 9
Whitechapel Gallery, the, 9
Whitman, Walt, 8, 11
Wild, Peter, 'Interview', 22, 30, 31
Williams, Raymond, *The Country and the City*, 75–6
Wilson, Elizabeth, *The Sphinx in the City: Urban Life, the Control of Disorder*, 90, 91
Wilson, Robert, 'History on the Rocks', 94, 100
Wroe, Nicolas, 'The Reluctant Storyteller,' 5, 12, 16–17, 20

EU authorised representative for GPSR:
Easy Access System Europe, Mustamäe tee 50,
10621 Tallinn, Estonia
gpsr.requests@easproject.com

www.ingramcontent.com/pod-product-compliance
Lightning Source LLC
Chambersburg PA
CBHW070941230426
43666CB00011B/2515